Trading Chaos

A MARKETPLACE BOOK

Trading Chaos

Maximize Profits with Proven Technical Techniques

SECOND EDITION

JUSTINE GREGORY-WILLIAMS

and

BILL M. WILLIAMS

WILEY

John Wiley & Sons, Inc.

Published by John Wiley & Sons, Inc., Hoboken, New Jersey
Published simultaneously in Canada

Bill M. Williams, Ph.D., C.T.A., is a registered Commodity Trading Advisor (CTA) with the Commodity Futures Trading Commission and is a member of the National Futures Association. As such he is required by law to include the following statement with any publication:

"Hypothetical or simulated performance results have certain inherent limitations unlike an actual performance record; simulated results do not represent actual trading. Also, since the trades have not actually been executed, the results may have under- or overcompensated of the impact, if any, of certain market factors, such as lack of liquidity. Simulated trading programs in general are also subject to the fact that they are designed with the benefit of hindsight. No representation is being made that any account will or is likely to achieve profits or losses similar to those shown."

Please note that the above statement refers primarily to simulated trading programs that are designed with the benefit of hindsight. Profitunity Trading Group (PTG) and Bill M. Williams, Ph.D. trade selection processes are made *before the fact* and have never been published with the benefit of hindsight. In addition, PTG and Bill M. Williams make every possible effort to illustrate in text and performance records, any stop loss order that may have gapped due to unusual market conditions.

For general information on our other products and services, or technical support, please contact our Customer Care Department within the United States at 800-762-2974, outside the United States at 317-572-3993 or fax 317-572-4002.

Wiley also publishes its books in a variety of electronic formats. Some content that appears in print may not be available in electronic books.

For more information about Wiley products, visit our Web site at www.wiley.com.

Library of Congress Cataloging-in-Publication Data
Gregory-Williams, Justine.
   Trading chaos : maximize profits with proven technical techniques /
Justine Gregory-Williams & Bill M. Williams. — 2nd ed.
      p. cm.
Rev. ed. of: Trading chaos / Bill Williams. c1995.
Includes bibliographical references and index.
   ISBN 0-471-46308-6 (CLOTH)
1. Capital market—Mathematical models. 2. Futures market—Mathematical models.
3. Fractals. 4. Chaotic behavior in systems. I. Williams, Bill, 1932–   II. Williams, Bill, 1932–
Trading chaos. III. Title.
HG4523 .W554 2004
332.64'5—dc22

                                                                                          2003022633

Printed in the United States of America
10 9 8 7 6 5 4 3 2

This work is dedicated to the many people with whom I have shared my life and experiences. Mostly to my father, Bill Williams, for giving me the chance and knowledge to be writing this book and teaching people how to live the life they dream of. Without him, I wouldn't be living mine. I also want to thank Ellen, my mother, for standing behind me when I was not sure where to go next and for always knowing I could do it.

Thanks also to all the traders and friends that I have shared these experiences with. They have made me who I am and without you I would still be light years behind. What traders have to share amazes me every day and keeps me on the teaching path. Being a part of changing people's lives for the better is the most incredible gift anyone could receive.

To my best friend Julie who, without her infinite wisdom and friendship for all these years, I would still be trying to figure out where to live and how to get there. The bookmarks that you have given me will last forever. I look forward to sharing our meals-on-wheels one day.

My most profound thanks and love to Marcus, my partner. Without you and your love and support, this project might not have been possible; now everything is possible. Thank you for sharing your love.

J. G.-W.

This book is dedicated to the love of my life—Ellen. Late at night when I sometimes think about what my life would be like without you, I literally shudder. None of all this good stuff that has happened to me would have been feasible or even possible without your love and support. You will always have and deserve my eternal love and thanks.

B. M. W.

Contents

Preface

I began trading in 1959 while teaching at the University of South Florida in the School of Business. My ideas for trading came from a professor of accounting whose office was down the hall from mine. I would go by each day and find out what he was doing and basically I would copy that in my own account. Each of us was making more from the trading than from our teaching salaries. Jim (the accounting professor) knew what he was doing. I, however, "assumed" that I knew what I was doing.

In 1980 I decided to become a full-time trader after trading for 21 years without having lost a quarter. However, things quickly changed. I began losing and was unable to stop the decline in my account. I had spent more than $6,000 on newsletters during the first month of full-time trading and none of them were profitable for me. After a couple of years spending days each week just reading the newsletters, I decided to throw them all in the trash. They were destroying my account balance. That's when things began to fall in line. It was just me and my charts. I had decided that if my financial plane crashed, I wanted to be the pilot. I never wanted to say that I had gone broke following other people's advice. I was going to live or die in the market because of *my* thinking rather than blaming others.

In 1987 I started sharing what I had learned with a few other individual traders. By 1989 I had been invited to do workshops on our approach to trading the markets in 16 different countries. I also started private tutorials and we named this business the Profitunity Trading Group. The name *Profitunity* signified turning opportunities into profits. PTG is still flourishing and we have personally trained more than 2,000 individuals who are now financially independent traders and investors.

Fortunately, my youngest daughter was attracted to this business and now runs the day-to-day operations of the Profitunity Trading Group with headquarters in San Diego, California. She is the coauthor of this book. Both of us are active in the markets every day and our lifestyle and security is much better than we could have dreamed a few years ago.

There is an old saying that if you teach, you learn twice. That, certainly, has been our experience. As we learned, we spent our time trading, researching the markets, and taught others how to trade better. From this came two books: *Trading Chaos* in 1995, which was awarded first place as the most popular trading book in this area by Amazon.com. In 1998 our second book, *New Trading Dimensions* was published, with even greater acceptance. Now with the changing markets and further research, we feel the need for updating and sharing our most profitable methods. The older methods still work and are profitable but not as profitable as what we are currently using. The earlier books have been translated into several different languages including Chinese, Russian, Italian, German, Japanese, and French.

Our students come from around the world and include the vice president of the largest commodity exchange in the world, the vice president of the Central Bank in Moscow and a 17-year-old from New Hampshire who waited tables at $7.00 per hour to save up the tuition costs for a private tutorial. We are mentioning these facts to illustrate that there is a background of success stemming from our work over the past 45+ years in the markets.

And now is the time to distribute our latest research findings along with all the things that have always worked in taking profits from the markets.

BILL M. WILLIAMS, PH.D., C.T.A.

*   *   *

If you had asked me 15 years ago what I thought I would be doing today, the answer would not have been writing a book or teaching and trading for a living. Today I can't imagine doing anything else.

Growing up around trading my whole life did not inspire me to become a trader. I never liked math. I was scared of it actually, so I decided to go to barber school and work my way through a "real college." I chose this path because trading was all about math, or so I thought.

I worked as a hair dresser and went to school for 7 years, changing majors often, not knowing what I wanted to do with the rest of my life. A few years later, I decided to go to nursing school. I knew I wanted to work in a field that allowed me to help others. Once I received my nursing degree, I realized that I was not able to give the help that I thought I was capable of giving. The medical field was very limited in its practices and I did not necessarily agree with many tasks I was supposed to do. Between HMOs and hospital rules, I thought that I needed a higher degree in nursing to do a better job.

After a few personal traumatic experiences, I decided to move home at age 28 and go back to school. This time I started working part-time in my father's trading office. By the end of the semester, I was trading the markets, teaching classes with him and did not re-enroll for the next school term. Surprised?

It's now 10 years later and unlike the band U-2 I *have* found what I was looking for, the ability to create my own wealth and happiness. The biggest bonus is I am also able to share this incredible knowledge, first passed on to me by my father, with anyone who wants the same ability to achieve their life's goals. I hope as you read this book you will understand the power of "freedom" and just letting go. May all that you wish for be the least that you receive. The markets will give it to you if you really want it.

JUSTINE GREGORY-WILLIAMS

Acknowledgments

There are so many people who have helped us through the years. Without them we would still be charting by hand and wondering what e-mail is. A few of these people are:

Doug Forman for supporting our clients and us by keeping our software and computers running. Doug is the caretaker and programmer for our Investor's Dream software and created most of the charts in this book. Because he is also a long-time successful trader, his understanding and ideas are invaluable.

Melody Baker at CQG for her support through the years from supplying our data at meetings to giving the best customer support around.

Georgina Perez our "other mother" who always had faith in us. Without your love, prayers, and faith, our family would not be who we are today. We all thank and love you! You have no idea how much you have influenced all our lives.

Chris Myers, Jaye Abbate, and all the staff at Trader's Library for their support and encouragement. Without them this book would not have been born.

Pamela Van Giessen for her faith and support in our approach to the markets. She believed in our ideas and guided our efforts through all three books. Without her you would not be reading this.

Finally and most importantly to Ellen, our wife and mother. Although her contributions are not obvious in the text, she is a part of every sentence in this book. Ellen, you are a wonderful person and we both love you so much.

Introduction

Unless we change our direction, we are most likely
to end up where we are headed.
                                            —Chinese Proverb

I f the purpose of our trading is to acquire financial wealth, perhaps it is
appropriate to ponder exactly what money is. The first step in acquiring
wealth is to understand what it really is, in and of itself. What causes
wealth? We can begin with money and then move deeper.

First of all, money is not real. It is a form of exchange—legal tender.
Supposedly it represents value. It is the physical representation of energy
or value that rises and falls within ourselves. It does not change value because of what happens to material objects "out there" but rather changes
because of what happens "in here," inside our brains. We are the ones who
place different values on objects. I have a cane that is one of my most valued possessions and is probably worth less than two dollars on the open
market. But to me it has enormous value because it belonged to a blind
uncle who was the primary male figure in my young life. In a garage sale it
certainly would not bring more than a couple of bucks but I would not part
with it for $10,000. Its value to me is in my relationship to it rather than
what it would bring on the open market.

So money in and of itself has little or no inherent value other than what
we place on it. Material things have no money value in themselves—we
give that to them. That is why a house or a block of shares valued at
$1,000,000 today can fall to a half-million dollars tomorrow when fear of the
future is introduced into the hearts of those involved.

When you really examine it, physical money does not even represent
money in full. It cannot do that. By some estimates, as little as 4 percent of
the money in banks exists as paper cash. This is a space saver because a
stack of one million one-dollar bills would weigh a ton and if stacked would
be 361 feet high. Remember when Saddam looted the central bank in

Baghdad of approximately five billion dollars and it took three tractor-trailer trucks to haul off the loot? And those were hundred-dollar bills. Money no longer represents gold reserves either: We ran out of the ability to keep a gold standard in the 1970s.

Money—what really is this thing that we keep spending our lives trying to get more of it? Again, it is one massive illusion. It is just numbers on a piece of paper or on computer storage devices and assigned to people and entities such as companies and investments and other records. Viewing from another perspective, for every $100 or its equivalent in other currencies, only about $4 exists as printed-paper notes or coins. The rest of the $96 exists as numbers on paper and computers in banks and businesses. What keeps all of this illusion afloat? The fact that we have agreed to believe in it. Just before the Great Depression people stopped believing in it when they could not get their money from the banks. This run on the banks did not cause the depression, but it sure accelerated it by creating fear in the minds of the public.

If money is not real, then what is? Money is only the shadow of something else. Concentrating on this shadow (the physical dollar bills) is very unwise and not healthy for your bank or trading/investment accounts. A much more profitable strategy is to look at the value inside yourself and others. Watch the flow or exchange of this value between people. It is only our internal values that create money. If we can somehow learn to observe the changes in internal values in others and ourselves, we can hone in on opportunities that others miss.

Let us hasten to add that while money does represent a part of a person's internal value, it does not represent a person's entire internal value. Money represents only one aspect of a person's internal value. Otherwise the richest person would have the most elevated values and we know that just is not true. A rich person is not necessarily better than a poor person. However, it is true that in matters that pertain to money, the wealthy people have a higher internal value or they choose to exercise a higher proportion of this internal value. This ability to exercise higher evaluation is available to everyone and, just like air, is free to all. You are free to choose to develop it or not and to exercise it or not. You can choose and no one or nothing can stop you once you really make that choice.

Everything you need to be successful in the markets is already inside you. You may have forgotten it but it is still there. It is important to remember that money is not real; it is the shadow of something else. You are already a successful trader. Otherwise you could not dress properly, express yourself effectively, or even understand what is going on at this moment. You are already wealthy, but you have been taught not to express it in your daily living. Once you understand this in the deepest parts of your being, all sorts of opportunities for converting this consciousness into cash will present themselves. Fortunate coincidences present themselves every day. Why are you reading this book at this very moment?

By the way, it is not only paper money that is not real. A lot of other things that we cherish so dearly are not real either. You are about to embark on a beautiful, empowering, and liberating journey that will unveil your trading and investing world in a way that will open your eyes and free your wings. We will look under the hood of your trading and investing life. You will learn how to customize the market to your liking. Once you do, avoiding winning will become more and more difficult. This will give you freedom to experience other aspects of your life that you may not have even dreamed of before. The same goes for happiness; you will find that here as well. So welcome to an exciting and profitable journey as you incorporate these learnings into your life. The train is here, ready to go; we invite you to climb aboard.

What could this book be worth to you? Maybe $10,000 per week, $40,000 per month, or perhaps $500,000 per year? Using the exact techniques described in this book has made the members of our family multi-millionaires. There is no reason you cannot do the same.

The truth begins with know-how. Knowledge is potential power. What you do with what you learn here determines how successful you will be. The right knowledge and understanding is priceless. This book is designed so that you can become financially powerful by applying these techniques.

The first portion of this book is devoted to understanding how what is happening inside of us determines the rewards we acquire in trading and investing. If you truly understand what makes a car go, you will have fewer problems in going cross-country. And if a disaster starts to form, you will recognize it and be able to fix it before it becomes truly detrimental to your health and welfare. Then we examine what the markets really are and how they operate. We also spend time getting our various trading and investing heads on straight. We look at how you use your mind and the several different trading personalities that you possess and how your choice of which to use affects your profit picture.

WELCOME TO THE FIRST DAY OF YOUR NEW TRADING LIFE!

You can break the cycle of failure by recognizing the things that cause failure. This book not only shows you *why* most traders lose money, but it also introduces you to the latest findings in physics and psychology as they apply to the various markets. As we all know, the markets today are very different from what they were even a few years ago. In the bull market of the 1990s, trading and investing were relatively easy. However, we are now looking at very different circumstances in the markets and in the world in general. Trading in the 21st century with 20th century tactics almost guarantees eventual failure.

A person can no longer feel safe in buying a stock and holding it for years or until retirement. Millions of Americans have seen their retirement funds evaporate because stock in one or more of the companies they had invested in lost most of its value. People now want to have a more hands-on approach to managing their own investments. Long-term investments have become much less dependable and secure. Interest rates being low, many investors are feeling they need to take a more proactive part in their future and retirement. Large numbers of people (many of them baby boomers) have lost their jobs and have only a severance package to fund their future. Others have pension funds, IRAs, or 401(k)s and want more discretion over these funds. Baby boomers are now beginning their retirement and are searching for ways to protect and even increase their retirement investments. They need the proper education and understanding of how the markets really work. People now want to learn how to manage their investments on a much shorter time horizon and to build a better safety net for their losses. Our targeted audiences are both these "newbies" as well as the more experienced and professional traders. Our goals in this new book are:

- To make this material applicable in all of today's markets (stocks, bonds, options, futures, indexes, etc.).
- To teach new and experienced traders how to anticipate, recognize, and react to impending bull and bear market conditions using our techniques.
- To empower traders to be able respond to and profit from shorter term trading as well as longer term investing when appropriate. We call these techniques *trade/vesting*, which signifies using trading techniques for good entries and exits and, when the opportunity presents itself, for hanging in there as an investment.
- To explore deeper into the psyche of the trade/vestor and how to handle both winning and losing without upsetting the grace of living.
- To condense and simplify techniques in our previous books, which proved that trend traders can often more than double their profits by also including countertrend trades.
- To explore why our techniques have proved to be even more profitable in the current markets than they were when the first edition of this book was printed (Wiley, 1994).

All in all, we feel that this book will be much more applicable and easier to understand, and will deliver considerably more profitable techniques in this new 21st-century trading environment. Our own personal trading has proved this. For example, 2002, which most traders do not consider to have been a good year (the market was down big time), was the most profitable year for us in the past 45+ years of active trading. Basically, 2002 was a down market and, as an experiment, we never sold a single stock or shorted a single commodity during the entire year. It was still our most profitable year. We are very excited about these new modifications. The results of sharing these new techniques in recent workshops have been more enthusiastically received than ever before.

Now, expel the stale air from your lungs and gasp a breath or two of fresh air as you prepare for the material we are sharing here. It is different from any other book on trading and investing in that it is based on nonlinear dynamics and the science of chaos. In the *I Ching*, Hexagram 3 is titled "Chaos—Where Great Dreams Begin." In the reading it states:

Before a great vision can become a reality there may be difficulty. Before a person begins a great endeavor, they may encounter chaos. As a new plant breaks the ground with great difficulty, foreshadowing the huge tree, so must we sometime push against difficulty in bringing forth our dreams.

This *I Ching* hexagram also illustrates the so-called butterfly effect, which is a concept of chaos theory that states a very small change in initial conditions makes a great difference in what happens next and all the way down the line. Putting it into our trade/vesting approach means that we only need to change a few basic ideas to make our total results grow exponentially. Our important first change is:

Do Not Listen to the Experts!

This advice may appear a bit far-fetched at first, but it will make more and more sense as you progress through this material. Remember that trading does not work for the vast majority of those in the markets. There must be something better, and there is. Remember that financial writers know as little and probably less than you do about how the market functions. They are paid for the number of their words and not the truth or accuracy of their analysis. If they really understood the markets, they could make many times more money trading than they do writing about trading.

What I have learned and still marvel at in more than 45 years of active trading is that basically none (or giving the benefit of the doubt, very few) of the popular pundits know what they are doing. And that includes

brokers. Do you believe there is any broker in the world who would be
a broker if he or she could trade well? Being a broker is a bad job. Everyone blames the broker: their clients for not making them money and their
bosses for not selling more. It is really quite simple. All brokerage houses
are in the business of selling you stocks, bonds, or futures. Their very liveli-
hood depends on you buying. And notice how many of the prominent
brokerage houses have been or are in court attempting to defend their
profit-sapping recommendations.

We (Profitunity Trading Group) believe we have produced the highest
percentage of successful graduates who are now independent trade/vestors
in the world, and they are using the exact techniques that we are sharing
with you in this book.

MORE ABOUT OUR TRADE/VESTING APPROACH

Trading is, without doubt, the very best lifestyle that anyone could imagine.
You are totally you own boss, but that carries some responsibility because
you cannot blame your failures on anyone but yourself. However, when you
win, you don't have to say "thank you" to anyone. In other words, there is
no necessity to be politically correct and what a difference that can make
in your enjoyment of living. My wife, Ellen, once wrote a magazine article
in which she described trading as "sliding down the razor blade of life." It
is exciting, invigorating, and highly profitable. And it can be a simple laid-
back way of enjoying your life and the rewards of your effort.

However, the average traders tend to be a nervous, worried, exhausted,
and confused people who sometimes wonders why they ever chose this
path at all. The average trader feels that trading the markets is a highly
stressful occupation. Here are some actual questions we have received
from active traders:

- How can I both enjoy trading and make profits trading the markets?
- Why am I so addicted to doing this when there are so many disap-
  pointments (losses)?
- How can I keep serenity inside myself and my loved ones while living
  in this turbulent world of the markets?
- How can I stop worrying so much in such a threatening atmosphere?
- Why do so many traders and investors lose money so consistently?
- How can I distinguish among all the hucksters who are hawking their
  wares as being *the* answer, when none of them seems to last even a
  couple of years?

- Why does my broker give me such bad advice?
- Why do all the newsletters I read boast of such enviable track records, but when I start trading on their advice, my trades lose money?

For many, when they are winning, there is an undercurrent of fear that the next trade will probably be a loser. They exhaust themselves as they try to control the present and the future while their minds futilely search for ways to recreate the past.

They yearn to trade while being more relaxed, calmer, in control, and excited about trading. To most traders, the possibility of that kind of life seems like a long-lost dream. The joy of trading is gone, and their life is filled with stress. They have tried all the hotlines, newsletters, psychobabble books, and private sessions. Their love of the market is wearing thin. Something is very wrong. But what is it?

Those of you who have worked with us and are familiar with our work know that what we say comes largely from our own experience. We have had much help and advice from other traders and from researchers using modern technical tools, but the actual implementation of this research is a personal matter. We are going to look closely at how we create our own internal struggle, which goes on whether we are winning or losing. Our years of research and trading experience have produced what we think is the most successful approach to trading available today. A world-class trader who is in the same category as George Soros once offered us a high seven-figure amount for the exclusive use of this material. The restrictions were that I would not show anyone this approach and that I would never trade the markets using this approach. He felt it was worth that much if he had exclusive use of the material. That money is a mere pittance compared to what is possible using these techniques.

Our approach to trade/vesting was once described by one of our students:

> *Dancing with the market*
> *Is moving with*
> *The flow of the market—*
> *Up, down, or sideways—*
> *With a feeling of harmony,*
> *Trust, gratitude,*
> *And yes, even love.*

To really dance well and enjoy the process of dancing, you must let yourself be moved by the music rather than follow any preplanned agenda. In other words, the dance floor (markets) must become a friendly place. *Friendly* here means comfort, relaxed enjoyment, and a place where *you* feel friendly. I want to assure you, based on not only personal experience but also the experience of more than 2,000 individuals whom we have privately trained to become independent speculators, the market *is* a friendly place. Any unfriendliness always comes from us, not from the market.

We have come a long way on this issue of dancing with the market and are amazed at how obvious it all becomes once a person starts experiencing the reality of this approach to trading and investing. An ancient Buddhist saying goes: "The road is smooth; why do you throw rocks before you?" We all do this in the market. All of us, at times, throw rocks before us, and it is difficult to dance on rocks and come out pain-free. So let us begin by clearing the debris and making way for a more profitable, peaceful, joyful, and abundant trading life.

Our first task is to really understand how the markets actually work and why the majority of market participants consistently lose money. Read this book very carefully and then evaluate whether this approach is suitable for your personality. The most important requirement in becoming a successful trader is your ability to give up old ideas about how the world and the markets work. We are not writers but rather traders, so we hope that these words will communicate clearly what you must *do* and *be* before becoming consistently successful in the market place.

You may want to view our Web site at www.profitunity.com for new information about trading and learning. You may also want to download our fully functioning software that incorporates our trading approach. This software contains sample data that you may use as practice to make sure you understand how we trade the markets. This approach works in all markets including bonds, stocks, futures, and options.

Over the past couple of decades our students have learned an approach that provides:

- A foundation of trust in themselves so that they can operate without fear or hesitation.
- A methodology that develops confidence and a belief in their own consistency.
- The ability to execute trades flawlessly and recognize mistakes.
- The skill not to give their money away.

We call this approach *super-natural trade/vesting*. "Super" because of the results it gets and "natural" because it deals with the true nature of the markets. This material is an operator's manual for traders, those wanting to trade, and those who have traded and lost and are ready to do it right. It is for eagles who are tired of living in chicken coops. It is for those who are ready to get a license to drive their own minds and make their own trades.

Most of you reading this material have spent a great deal of time and effort in consciously (note the word *consciously*) attempting to beat the market. Maybe we need to stop using the conscious mind and try something else. That is what this book is all about.

What is included here is excluded elsewhere. You will not find this approach in the usual material on trading. Other approaches teach you how to use stochastics, RSI, and software, but they do not teach you how to operate your mind in a trading environment. If you are willing to learn, we can teach you. And now we can get on with it. In Chapter 1 we examine chaos theory and why it is a better language for understanding market behavior and your personal behavior while in the markets. So get ready for some surprises in your thinking and in your profitability.

Following Chapter 1 we build a solid psychological foundation to allow us to use the proper tactics that will bring us steady and ample profits in any market.

> The market is a creature of chaos—A far from equilibrium soup simmering on the uneven flame of trader psychology.

The Market Is What You Think It Is

There Is No Reality, There Is Only Perception

Words are things, and a small drop of ink
Falling like dew upon a thought, produces
That which makes thousands, perhaps millions,
think.

—Lord Byron

GOAL

To understand how the markets really work and why the majority of market participants consistently lose money.

A number of years ago I attended a meeting in Boulder, Colorado, with a newly arrived swami from India. Muktananda proved to be a most interesting fellow. He gave no lectures; he only told stories and wove those stories into an instructional format. Accompanying him was an interpreter, complete with saffron-colored robes, from the University of Colorado. Muktananda maintained that not being fluent in English was a great advantage to becoming a guru in America. He started his lecture with the following story.

1

There was a student in India who wanted to become enlightened. He left his family in search of an appropriate guru to guide him further on his journey. Stopping at one guru's place of business, he inquired as to this guru's method of becoming enlightened. The guru said, "Becoming enlightened is really quite simple. All you need to do is to go home each night and sit in front of a mirror for 30 minutes asking yourself the same question over and over. That question is: Who am I? Who am I? Who am I?"

The prospective student replied, "Hey, it can't be that simple."

"Oh yes, it is just that simple," replied the guru, "but there are several other gurus on this street."

"Thank you very much," said the student, "I think I will inquire down the way."

[Today we call this action seeking a second opinion.]

So the student approached the next guru with the same question. "How do I become enlightened?"

The second guru replied, "Oh, it is quite difficult and takes much time. Actually, one must join with like-minded others in an ashram and do Sava. Sava means 'selfless service,' so you work without pay."

The student was excited; this guru's philosophy was more consistent with his own preconceived view of enlightenment. He always had heard it was difficult. The guru told the student that the only job open at the ashram was cleaning out the cow stalls. If the student were really serious about becoming enlightened, the guru would allow him to shovel all the dung and be responsible for keeping the cow stalls clean. The student accepted the job, feeling confident that he must be on the right path.

After five long years of shoveling cow dung and keeping the stalls clean, the student was becoming discouraged and impatient about enlightenment. He approached the guru and said, "Honored teacher, I have faithfully served you for five years cleaning up the dirtiest part of your ashram. I have never missed a day and have never complained once. Do you think it might be time for me to become enlightened?"

The guru answered, "Why yes, I believe you are now ready. Here is what you do. You go home each night and look at yourself in the mirror for 30 minutes, asking yourself the same question over and over again. That question is: Who am I? Who am I? Who am I?"

The very surprised student said, "Pardon me, honored one, but that is what the other guru down the street told me five years ago."

"Well, he was right," responded the guru.

"Then why have I shoveled cow dung for five years?" asked the student.

"Because you are stupid, that's why," replied the guru.

I think of that story quite often while working with traders. One of the first problems I encounter is convincing traders that making profits in trading is really quite simple—notice, I did not say *easy*. There is a world of difference between a concept's being simple and being easy to carry out.

Looking at yourself in the mirror for 30 minutes each night is a simple concept, but asking yourself the same question over and over again and seeking an honest answer is not easy. As a psychologist I have found that we humans have two innate tendencies: (1) We tend to *overcomplicate* everything we touch and, because of that, (2) we cannot see the obvious.

To most traders and investors, the market is a dangerous and undependable animal. Their mottoes are: "Don't count on it" and "Get it before it gets you." They see the market as a dog-eat-dog world where other traders/investors are the dogs. This is not an accurate picture of the markets.

THE SIMPLICITY OF *ALL* MARKETS

The markets are not mysterious and unfathomable. The primary purpose of any market is to ration, at a reasonable price, existing and future supply to those who want it the most. You trade almost every minute of your life. Profiting in the markets is much easier when you really understand the underlying structure. To keep it as simple as possible, take the Flintstones as an example. You remember Fred Flintstone, a rather rough and outdoors kind of guy, and his more domestic next-door neighbor, Barney? Fred sees himself as a macho he-man who likes to hunt dinosaurs. One day he goes out and kills a big something-a-saurus even though his freezer is already full of dinosaur burgers. Barney does not enjoy hunting and killing but he likes eating dinosaur Whoppers®. Barney prefers to sit around his backyard whittling wood and making clubs. Fred rarely takes time to make his own clubs.

Fred wanders over to Barney's backyard and gets an idea. Why not swap Barney a couple of platters of dinosaur burgers for that new club he is finishing. So he puts this proposition to Barney: "Barney, I'll give you two platters of dinosaur Whoppers for that new club. How 'bout it?" Barney says, "Okay, you got a deal."

Fred and Barney have just created a market. *It is just that simple!* Both Fred and Barney valued what they wanted more than what they had. To Barney the burgers were more important (valuable) than the club he was making, and to Fred the club was more valuable than the burgers.

All Markets are Created When Two or More People Have an Equal Disagreement on Value and an Agreement on Price

When you bought your last car, the car was worth more to you than the money used to pay for it. However, to the person who sold you the car, your money was more valuable than the car. You created a miniature market when you made your deal. We buy bonds when we would rather own the bonds than the money we are paying for the bonds. Our fantasy (trading is a fantasy game; more about this later in the introduction) is that the value of the bonds will go up relative to the dollar. We bought them from some unknown trader who was just as confident that their value was going to go down. We have a real disagreement on current and future value, but we agree on price.

Every market in the world is designed to ration or distribute a limited amount of something (whether it be stocks, agricultural products, currencies, dinosaur clubs, or whatever) to those who want it most. The market does this by finding and defining the *exact price* where, at that moment, there is an *absolute balance between the power of those who want to buy and those who want to sell.*

The stock, commodity, bond, currency, and option markets all find that place of balance very quickly whether they are using open outcry or computer balancing. The markets find this place before you and I can detect any imbalance and before even the traders on the floor become aware of any imbalance. If the preceding scenario is true—and it is—then we can come to some very simple and very important conclusions about information that is distributed through the market and accepted without question.

WE PROMISE YOU THE TRUTH AND SOMETIMES IT IS NOT PRETTY!

You can break the cycle of failure by recognizing the things that cause failure. This book not only shows you *why* most traders lose money; it also introduces you to the latest findings in physics and psychology as they apply to the various markets and to your thinking patterns.

You probably dream about what every other investor/traders desires, which is success in the markets. However, when you trade, you come away with fewer goodies than you had counted on.

Profitunity is here to change all of that. Perhaps the Profitunity approach is the cure that you had dreamed of and prayed for, and wondered why someone has not figured it out. The approach taught here is all you will need to stop forever the endless cycle of trading and losing. This approach can completely change your trading future in a way that may seem extreme. It will do it by eliminating errors in thinking from your game plan and replacing these errors with something that works. Here are some basic fundamental truths that you must understand to become a consistent winner. We call them the five sacred Cows Terminators.

Trading becomes perplexing when you think about all the different stocks and commodities, the electronic retrieval systems, the fast execution of your orders, and the second-by-second monitoring of the markets and still, fewer than 10 traders out of 100 are consistently successful over time. That is simply unacceptable. This 90+ percent failure rate represents the concrete boots that keep you anchored at the bottom of the ocean of money promised by trading gurus. You, most likely, are drowning in a sea of broker or advisor promises.

Now let us clear our minds and expel the old ideas about life and trading as you begin to use your Five Sacred-Cow Terminators. These may appear to be strange at first but will make more sense as you progress. Remember trading does not work for most of those who trade. There must be something better and there is! So we get rid of five common ideas that are promoted as truth but simply do not work and will drag you under in your search for profits. Our first job is to eliminate these Five Sacred Cows from our minds and our trading.

Sacred-Cow Terminator #1: Don't Listen to the Popular Experts

Remember that financial writers know as little as and perhaps even less than you do about the markets. They are paid by the word and not by truth. As stated earlier, if they really understood the markets, they could make many times more money trading than they do writing about trading.

Ask yourself a question: Why do none of these analysts and commentators ever show their personal trading track records? Could it be because they are not personally able to make profits in the markets? If they were good at trading, they probably would be eager to tell you how much profit they are making.

Crazy, huh? If years of platitudes from dead traders who buried their secrets with them, other catch phrases, and hype have led 90+ percent of you to fail, then what you have listened to has aided in your failure. You must decide to do something different or continue to make it worse.

Sacred-Cow Terminator #2: There Is No Such Thing as Bullish/Bearish Consensus

Oh, yes, they tout that on TV and in every financial newspaper and even your broker may share this misinformation with you. However, let us examine if there could be such a thing as bullish and bearish consensus. If the markets are doing their job (and they do it well), their primary job is to make sure there is *no* bearish or bullishness in the markets. Those who tout the bull-bear information get it by surveying a group of traders and asking their opinions about the market. They survey those who are *not* in the market at the moment because those who are in have voted their preference and their vote is already in the markets. If, for example, they report a 75 percent bullish consensus in bonds, all that means is they have not surveyed all the bears. The markets cannot endure even 50.01 percent bullishness before the price rises. Remember that the market's primary job is *to instantly find that exact place where there is an equal disagreement on value and an agreement on price.*

Sacred-Cow Terminator #3: There Is No Such Thing as Oversold/Overbought

If there is no such thing as bullish or bearish consensus, then it logically follows that there cannot be any such thing as an oversold or overbought condition, even though analysts talk about it all day on CNBC-FNN and have an oscillator that supposedly measures it. How can it be measured when the markets are specifically designed to destroy any oversold or overbought situations in microseconds, well before the traders see it on their screens and days before they start talking about it?

Sacred-Cow Terminator #4: Most Money Management Suggestions Are Ineffective

You do not read much about money management without running into someone's ineffective ideas such as "Whenever you buy a bond, immediately put in a $500 stop." Sometimes they say things like "Always use a 25 percent trailing stop" to maximize your profits. Think about this concept for a moment. When you follow that advice, you are trading only your bank account or your wallet, neither of which has one iota to do with the actual market movements. Most of us have had the experience of using a wallet stop, only to see the market turn around and leave us with a much smaller equity than we would have had if we had traded market movement. That kind of protective thinking comes directly from fear, and in the markets, fear never wins in the overall picture. Our only hope for consistent profits is to get in synch with the market and attune our own personal strategy and energy to that of the market.

Sacred-Cow Terminator #5: Common Formulas for Profitable Trading Do Not Work

Let us examine another common misconception among traders. Two often-repeated formulas for successful trading are (1) buy low and sell high and

(2) to make profits you must trade with the trend. Those two statements are absolutely incompatible. If you buy low or sell high, you are standing in the way of the trend, not following it. And if you follow the trend, you are not buying low or selling high. The Profitunity strategy is to know when to use either one of the two approaches. There are times when it is best to trade against the trend and other times when you want to go with the trend. The choice of which strategy to use is determined by the market itself. Mother Market always tells us exactly what we should do. And when we do not, the market will tell us where we went wrong and what we have to do to correct the error and get back into the profit-making mode.

UNDERSTANDING, ATTITUDE, SCIENCE, AND CHAOS

Making use of the Five Sacred-Cow Terminators lets us agree with Mark Twain who supposedly said, "I am less and less interested in what's so and more and more interested in not believing what's not so." As we start eliminating these misconceptions, we can begin to see the market as it really is. Trading becomes a more profitable occupation when it is based on reality rather than on someone else's imagination.

This necessity of understanding what the markets really are and how they work was expressed very eloquently by Warren Buffet, probably the best trader on the planet, when comparing trading the markets to a poker game: "If you are in a poker game for 20 minutes and you don't know who the patsy is—you are the patsy." In our words, if you are in a trade for 20 minutes and you do not know who the paymaster is, you are the paymaster. One purpose of this book is to make you patsyproof and keep you from being a paymaster in the markets you trade.

There *is* risk in the markets. There is risk in day-to-day living. There is enormous risk whenever you drive your car. On some highways, only inches separate your car from the cars speeding in the opposite direction. A swerve of only a few feet could bring a death-dealing head-on collision. Every time you take a short drive, you are literally risking your life. Yet you drive almost daily and remain suave about the danger. The reasons: you have gained *understanding* and *experience*.

As you gain understanding and experience in trading, the markets need be no more dangerous than the route of your Sunday drive. For safe driving, you must have a vehicle you are familiar with, the right tools in case repairs are needed, and the right attitude. This book is all about having the right understanding and the right attitude for using the right tools. We refer to it as "Attitools."

Science is concerned with producing the right understanding and tools for civilizations to prosper and advance in knowledge. Traditional science, which created automobiles, factories, air and space travel, computers, and many other advances, turns out to be impotent in two vital areas: (1) living systems and (2) turbulence. Classical physics can describe every nanosecond since the (assumed) big bang, but it cannot approach any explanation of blood running through the left ventricle of the heart, the turbulence in a white-water river, or the tasseling of corn. If the market is anything, it is living systems (humans) working in turbulence (the markets).

Physics in the 20th century will be remembered for three revolutionary developments: (1) relativity, (2) quantum mechanics, and (3) the science of chaos. Einstein left us with one constant—the speed of light. Quantum mechanics took that away. Now, the science of chaos is changing our entire worldview.

We developed a whole set of mathematics under the crippled logic of our evolving, developing brain. This logic leaves immense areas of our world undiscoverable and indescribable.

Recently a new look at the world, the science of chaos and nonlinear dynamics, has been emerging. Chaos is a particularly unfortunate name because chaos actually refers to a higher and different degree of order. To learn more about the science of chaos and its effect on our actions in the market see Chapter 3 in our first book, the previous edition of *Trading Chaos* (Wiley, 1994), and Chapter 2 in our second book, *New Trading Dimensions* (Wiley, 1998).

In summary we can say the current educational approach to trading is not effective in producing consistent profits for over 9 out of 10 traders. The old approach is simply not producing results in today's market. Throughout this book we will present the latest findings in the science of chaos and nonlinear dynamics and show how they can be used in defining and managing your trading and investing account. The result will be easier trading, less hassle, and more profitable outcomes.

MARKET IDEAS: FACTS OR OPINIONS

Ideas rule the market. However, two kinds of ideas affect the market: *facts* and *opinions*. And each one produces different kinds of effects.

A fact, as defined here, is something that affects every trader/investor on earth, regardless of what they are trading (stocks, commodities, options, bonds, etc.). Actually, there are relatively few facts. It is a fact that you are alive. Other facts include birth, death, gravity, electromagnetism, the earth, or the markets. Facts are things that *are*. They affect everyone whether in the market or not. For all practical purposes, they cannot be changed. You can eliminate facts (like destroying a building) and you can manipulate them (like making cars and airplanes) but you cannot change the facts themselves.

As an example, the dodo bird is no longer here. It is no longer a fact. The record that it was here is a fact, the bird is not. So a fact can be manipulated or eliminated but it cannot be changed.

However, the largest category that affects you and the markets are *opinions*, which is really the same as *beliefs*. Opinions are ideas about facts, and unlike facts they only affect some of the people some of the time. They are, however, very potent, because your opinions about the markets and their movements affect how you trade, what you do, and how you feel about your performance. Opinions are very different from facts in that they can be changed. As your opinions change, so do your experiences and results in the market.

What gets most traders in trouble is that they tend to confuse opinions with facts. They tend to treat their opinions as facts of the markets, instead of ideas about the facts. Typical opinions that some traders call facts are:

- Trading is a struggle.
- Winning is due to luck.
- I am powerless against the floor brokers.
- No one wins consistently.
- The markets are always scheming against me.
- It is a dog-eat-dog market.
- My broker hates me.

Let us extract the facts from these opinions.

- Trading is
- Winning is
- I am
- No one
- The markets are
- It is
- My broker

Those items are facts. Anything you add to them is an opinion. Opinions can be either positive or negative. Whatever they are will govern your experience in the markets. An opinion is like a set of filtered glasses through which you view the markets and trading. They only allow you to see things in a certain way. These glasses block out any incoming information (chaos) that does not agree with your opinions. Instead of reacting to the incoming information, your opinions guide and limit your responses and understanding. If opinions are working for you, that is great. However, if you are not happy with your results and your trading, it means that your glasses need adjusting. There is hope because opinions are not facts. You chose (at some level) the opinions you have and you do not have to keep them if you do not want to.

Where Did Your Opinions Originate?

It all starts at the beginning, your birth. From the first moment out of the womb you started experiencing life and you began to try to understand what was going on around you. You were not just a hunk of squirming flesh. You were much more aware than most people thought. Studies have shown that newborn infants only 60 seconds old were able to make imitations and responses to facial gestures of an adult. As you grow, you continue to try to make sense of this new world so you make choices or decisions about what your experience means. Once you make a tentative decision, you automatically look for confirmation that your decision makes sense, that it is "correct."

Your parents are most helpful in this regard. You watch them, their responses, hear their words, and use that data for making and confirming your decisions. You accept some of their responses and reject others. Some very interesting psychological studies concern children who are called "invulnerables." These are children raised in chaotic, schizophrenic, neurotic environments by psychopathic parents and siblings, and who seem not to be affected by the ideas and behavior of the rest of the family. They are not genetically or otherwise superior to those children who do succumb. They have just made different decisions about life and about themselves. As you grow, you continue to listen to relatives, playmates, and authoritative adults, and continue to make decisions.

Once you have made the decision that your particular interpretation of an experience is correct, you have given birth to an opinion. From that point on, you tend to channel any new incoming information (chaos) into that assumed format. You massage or distort the incoming information in amazingly creative ways so as not to see the actual facts themselves. Most of the decisions you make today about the markets are actually outgrowths of decisions you made about life as a child. They tend to be permanent throughout your life unless you change them.

Let us assume two traders buy the same stock or commodity and it moves drastically against them. One chooses to focus on the idea that it is a tragedy and he always makes the wrong decision and will probably go broke if he continues to trade. He confirms earlier decisions that the world is unpredictable and you have to be very, very careful because it truly is a dog-eat-dog world (market). The second trader tends to review the reasons for getting into the trade and reassesses the facts and indicators, realizing that he is capable of dealing with the markets and plans how not to get caught in the same situation again. The same raw experiences processed through two different sets of filters produce two completely individual sets of guidelines.

You are the source of your experience in the markets because your decisions about life color your thoughts, your imagination, your emotions, and your actions. Your attitude toward the markets is like a magnet for attracting good or bad trades. There is lots of profit in the market and the part that you experience is a result of your opinions about it.

Your Results Reflect Your Opinions about the Markets

For some, it is quite difficult to understand that you are the source of your success in the markets, especially in a society that tends to promote the idea that life is something that happens to you. But successful people are those who have the willingness to accept that they happen to the markets (life), not the other way around.

There is no other way around it. If you are failing in the markets, you are holding opinions that keep you from winning. If you have poor health, you are holding opinions that are keeping you from becoming well. What is in your life reflects what is in your mind. For a full scientific verification of this idea see Lynne McTaggart's new book *The Field—The Quest for the Secret Force of the Universe* (HarperCollins, 2002).

Here is a part of a belief system that was taken from a person we trained who realized that money was an aspect of her life that was just not working. By a process of questioning we found that her basic opinion about money was that

> *Money is time.*

Then, of course the next step was to discover her basic opinion about time, which was

> *Time is limited.*

These two opinions produced the following logical sequence in her bio-computer: Time is limited, and money is time, therefore, money is limited, therefore, no matter how hard I try or how much I learn, I will never have enough money.

Since we only act in accordance with our basic opinions about the markets (life), this lady was continually making choices in the market that would make a profit and follow that with other decisions that created losses. There was no system or approach in the world through which this person would come out a winner. There simply was no winning alternative in her databank. This story does have a happy ending because she was able to change her opinions about time and money, and she became a winner using the same entry and exit strategy that she had used all along that created consistent losing trades.

To show how different opinions can produce the same effect, here is another example. In this case it was a man who held the following three basic assumptions about life:

> *You always get what you deserve.*
> *I am a good person.*
> *Money is bad.*

which led to: I deserve what is good, and therefore, I do not deserve money.

This situation could have been humorous except it was ruining not only his life but also the lives of his wife and children. The same effects would probably have been produced if the second two beliefs were "I am a bad person" and "Money is good."

Remember that apples grow from apple seeds but the seeds do not *cause* the apples. What causes apples is the continuing urge toward fulfillment. And that continuing urge for fulfillment produces successful traders and investors.

 SUMMARY

The markets are really quite simple. Quickly and efficiently, they find that point where there is *equal disagreement on value and agreement on price*. We illustrated that concept with the Flintstone market and the trade between Barney and Fred.

Two large problems still face any new trader. First, most traders (90 percent) are using the wrong logic maps. Second, there are no consistent, effective, currently available techniques for precisely aligning one's energy with that of the markets.

In Chapter 2 we examine the new science of chaos and nonlinear dynamics as it applies to trading and investing. We will see how we can use the insights from this newest of all sciences to improve our trading and investing prowess.

Chaos Theory

A New Paradigm for Trading

> *It's well known that the heart has to be largely regular or you die. But the brain has to be largely irregular; if not, you have epilepsy. This shows that irregularity, chaos, leads to complex systems. It's not all disorder. On the contrary, I would say* chaos is what makes life and intelligence possible. *The brain has been selected to become so unstable that the smallest effect can lead to the formation of order.*
>
> —Ilya Prigogine

GOAL

To gain a better understanding of chaos and Fractal geometry.

The word *paradigm* comes from the Greek root *paradeigma*, which means "model or pattern." Adam Smith, in his book, *Powers of the Mind* (Random House, 1975), defines a paradigm as "a shared set of assumptions." Smith (p. 20) continues, "The paradigm is the way we perceive the world; it is water to the fish. The paradigm explains the world to us and helps us to predict its behavior."

Social paradigms determine our behavior and values. Medical paradigms determine how we think about our bodies. Our paradigms about the market both determine and limit our interaction with the market.

A paradigm is the filter through which we view the world. It is our view of reality. And because it determines our reality, we rarely notice it and even more rarely question it. Our personal paradigms determine our personal reality and our assumptions about our world. We do not think about these assumptions, we think *from* them.

We never see the world directly; we always see it through these paradigm filters. We never see the world in its entirety; we see only pieces. The same is true with the market. We never see it all; we see only pieces of it. And our mental frameworks naturally bias us toward seeing only those parts of the world (market) that support our paradigms.

Paradigms also filter incoming information, which tends to reinforce comfortable preexisting paradigms (belief systems and mental programs). That is why the market is like the Grand Canyon and reflects whatever you shout into it. The world is an echo of your own personal paradigms.

This viewpoint about paradigms calls into question the notion of a fixed objective universe (market). Just as an object appears differently in infrared light, in ordinary daylight, or on an X-ray negative, how reality (the market) appears to us has less to do with what is actually there than with how we perceive it.

Adam Smith pointed out (1975, p. 20): "When we are in the middle of a paradigm it is hard to imagine any other paradigm." For example, suppose it is 1968 and you are asked to predict the world leader in watch manufacturing in the 1980s. You say the Swiss, because they have dominated the watch market for so many years. However, a paradigm shift occurs, from mechanical watches to electronic watches. The Japanese, because they recognize the new paradigm, capture most of the world's watch market. The Swiss, by clinging to the old paradigms, steadily lose their market share of more than 90 percent in 1968 and hit a low of below 10 percent during the 1980s. (Ironically, the Swiss invented the quartz watch in the first place.) Whenever there is a paradigm shift, all the rules change. In a wrong paradigm, even the right actions do not work.

Our personal paradigms control the way we process and respond to information. Your feelings or paradigms of viewing the markets are very different after you pick 10 consecutive losers as opposed to 10 consecutive winners. The following story illustrates how drastically and quickly our paradigms may change.

There is a Hollywood actor who likes to get away to his cabin in the mountains each weekend. He drives there over curvy, mountainous dirt roads. He usually drives his Porsche convertible and enjoys see-

ing how fast he can take the curves. He rarely meets anyone on these roads because there are few cabins in the area and even fewer visitors.

One Friday afternoon as he zooms through these curves, he meets an oncoming car that has careened over into his lane. There is a substantial cliff to his right, so he brakes his Porsche as hard as he can and stops just before a head-on collision.

The other car is also a convertible. The driver pulls around his stopped Porsche, she guns her engine, points, and shouts "Pig." This puzzles him. He was in his lane, it certainly was not his fault, and he was not hogging the road. As she drives off in a cloud of dust, he turns and shouts loudly, "Sow!"

Now he is fuming. He floors the accelerator, gains speed around the next curve, and collides with a large hog standing in the middle of the road.

His interpretation of the other driver's motives and behavior changes immediately. His response had come not from what she said but from his personal paradigm.

The particular paradigm through which we view the market determines our feelings and our behavior. The science of chaos gives us a new and more appropriate paradigm (map) to view the world, the markets, and our personal behavior.

Let us look at this new paradigm, try to understand it better, and begin to make the connection of how we can use it to get a more accurate picture of market behavior.

CHAOS AND OUR PERSONAL WORLD

We humans have a habit of misnaming our most important concerns and tools. For example, what we call our "conscious" mind (left hemisphere) is the only part of our brain that ever goes unconscious or sleeps. The other parts of our brain work continuously without a break. Similarly, physicists have chosen the word *chaos*, a term that is fundamentally misleading, as the name for the new science that studies complex nonlinear dynamic systems.

Chaos does not refer to randomness; just the opposite is true. Chaos is a higher form of order where randomness and stimuli become the organizing principle rather than the more traditional cause and effect in the Newtonian/Euclidean sense. Because both nature and the human brain are chaotic, the markets, as a part of nature and a reflection of human nature, are chaotic as well. It is time to recognize that our standard education gives traders the wrong impression and the wrong logic maps. No matter how elaborate linear mathematics gets, with its Fourier transforms, orthogonal functions, regression techniques, artificial intelligence, neural networks, genetic algorithms, and so on, it inevitably misleads traders about their overwhelmingly nonlinear markets. The markets are connoisseurs of chaos.

The

normal

distribution

stands out in the

experience of humankind

as one of the broadest generalizations

of natural science. It has been used as a

trading instrument in the markets, in the physical

and social sciences, and in medicine, agriculture, and

engineering. It is an indispensable tool for the analysis

and the interpretation of the basic data gathered by observation.

The structure of the previous three sentences represents the Gaussian or normal distribution curve. It makes a statement about the nature of randomness. But as a means of finding one's way through the wilderness of trading, this standard leaves much to be desired. As Nobel laureate Wassily Leontief put it, "In no field of empirical inquiry has so massive and sophisticated a statistical machinery been used with such indifferent results" (quoted in Gleick, 1987, p. 84).

Commodity and stock prices simply do not fit the bell-shaped model. They do, however, make some configurations that look amazingly like figures in other places such as shorelines and riverbeds. Benoit Mandelbrot, at the IBM research center at Yorktown Heights, New York, worked with masses of cotton price data. He was looking for some common parameters between nature and human behavior. He found that numbers producing aberrations from the point of view of normal distribution produced symmetry from the point of view of scaling. "Each particular price change was random and unpredictable. But the sequence of changes was independent of scale; curves for the daily and monthly prices changes matched perfectly. Incredibly, analyzed Mandelbrot's way, the degree of variation had remained constant over a tumultuous sixty-year period that saw two World Wars and a depression" (Gleick, 1987, p. 86).

Chaos is not new; it has been around since before time and humankind. We are the products of chaos, not the inventors of it. Chaos is what got us here and chaos will take us further into the future. Even in our brain, one part (the left hemisphere) is looking for stability and another part (right hemisphere) is looking for chaos. We (self, body, personality, and all) have developed on that tricky interface between stability and chaos.

Chaos is the meeting ground between yin/yang, black/white, here/there, now/then, or our development. In shaman terms, it is the tonal and the nagel. In markets, it is choppy versus trending. In trader's behavior, it is winning and losing. It is sleeping and waking, planting and harvesting.

Figure 2.1 shows the transformation from linear flow to nonlinear or turbulent flow. In Figure 2.1a, the stream is moving in a very stable fashion and is quite predictable. Figure 2.1b shows more water running; turbulence is beginning to build up behind the rock. Add more water (energy in the form of rain and gravity), and the turbulence increases and there is less predictability in the stream (Figure 2.1c and Figure 2.1d).

Our brain also develops different behavior, depending on the flow of energy. It is sometimes stable, like the stream in Figure 2.1a. When trading the market, it is often turbulent, like the stream in Figure 2.1d.

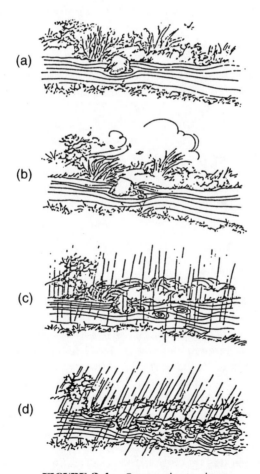

FIGURE 2.1   From order to chaos.

Since Aristotle's time, we have spent much more time educating and using the stable (linear left hemisphere) part rather than the chaos (non-linear right hemisphere) part of our brain. According to our current linear logic map, truth lies in stability or never-changing knowledge, so there is little benefit in developing a strategy for dealing with or using chaos.

Nonlinear logic makes it obvious that stability is temporary and chaos is forever. Since the early 1980s, millions of dollars have been thrown at the concept of chaos in attempts to, first, make sense of the markets and, second, profit from that knowledge. Research has made an effort to better understand chaos and the interaction between the mass of traders and the market itself. Our research finds that the chaos of our minds is reflected in the market. Both are an elaborate mixture of chaos and stability. Prigogine has written: "The brain is a creature of chaos, a far from equilibrium soup simmering on an uneven flame of daily life" (Prigogine and Stengers, 1984, p. 48).

Stability and chaos are also described as linear and nonlinear activity, whether that activity involves growing, producing, reproducing, or even just thinking. If we were to create the world from our left hemisphere perspective, we would have straight rivers, round clouds, and cone-shaped mountains. Nature, however, had other forces. Our natural world came from nonlinear sources. Products created by humans, such as language, came from the left hemisphere and consequently are digital and linear. We have created our trading systems in the same way we created language, and just as language cannot describe nature, so linear trading systems are unsuccessful in describing and capturing profits from the market. Remember, chaos got us here and chaos will take us where we want to go.

FRACTAL GEOMETRY

The science of chaos represents considerably more than a new trading technique. It is a new way of viewing our world. This worldview is actually older than recorded history but, until the mid-1980s, we lacked the powerful computers or other equipment needed to deal with this worldview on a mathematical and functional basis. Chaos theory is the first approach that successfully models complex forms (living and nonliving) and turbulent flows with rigorous mathematical methodology.

Fractal geometry, one of the tools of the science of chaos, is used to study phenomena that are chaotic only from the perspective of Euclidean geometry and linear mathematics.

Fractal analysis has revolutionized research in a myriad of different fields such as meteorology, geology, medicine, markets, and metaphysics.

This startlingly new perspective will profoundly affect all of us for the rest of our lives. Fractal analysis is a powerful new paradigm that, together with quantum mechanics and relativity theory, completes the scientific world first glimpsed by Galileo.

Although classical physics can model the creation of the universe from the first one-thousandth of a second of the big bang to the present time, it cannot model the blood flow through the left ventricle of a human heart for one second. Classical physics can model the structure of matter from subatomic quarks to galaxy clusters, but cannot model the shape of a cloud, the structure of a plant, the flow of a river, or the machinations of the stock market.

Science is very comfortable with its ability to create models using linear mathematics and Euclidean geometry. It is not, however, impressive in dealing with nonlinear turbulence and living systems. Simply stated, a nonlinear effect occurs when the power of an effect is a multiple of the power of the cause. There is an absolute chain between cause and effect in the Newtonian world, and all shapes are smooth and regular in Euclidean geometry. Neither of these approaches can begin to explain market behavior.

The smooth and frictionless surfaces, the empty space, the perfect spheres, cones, and right angles of Euclidean geometry are aesthetically appealing, even soothing. They are not, however, descriptive of the rough, jagged world in which we live and trade.

From this Euclidean/Newtonian world, we develop our linear mathematics, including parametric statistics most often symbolized by the normal or bell-shaped curve. This approach facilitates understanding by simplifying and abstracting out elements we think are unessential to the system. The key word here is *unessential*. In the real world, these discarded unessentials do not represent unimportant deviation from the Euclidean norm; rather, they represent the essential character of these systems. By abstracting out these unessential deviations (now known as *Fractals*) from the norm, we are able to glimpse the real underlying structure of energy and behavior.

As Benoit Mandelbrot, who first coined the term *Fractal*, so aptly put it:

Why is geometry often described as cold and dry? One reason lies in its inability to describe the shape of a cloud, a mountain, a coastline, a tree. Clouds are not spheres, mountains are not cones, coastlines are not circles, and bark is not smooth, nor does the lightning travel in a straight line . . . Nature exhibits not simply a higher degree but an altogether different level of complexity. The number of distinct scales of length of patterns is for all purposes infinite. The existence of these patterns challenges us to study these forms that Euclid leaves aside as being formless, to investigate the morphology of the morphous.

Mathematicians have disdained this challenge, however, and have increasingly chosen to flee from nature by devising theories unrelated to anything we can see or feel. (Quoted in Gleick, 1987, p. 98.)

Mandelbrot and other scientists such as Prigogine, Feigenbaum, Barnsley, Smale, and Henon found incredible revelations in this new approach to studying both inanimate and living behavior. They discovered that at the boundary line between conflicting forces is not the birth of chaos, as previously thought, but the spontaneous emergence of self-organization on a higher scale. Moreover, this self-organization is not structured along the Euclidean/Newtonian pathways but is a new kind of organization. It is not static but rather is imbedded in the fabric of motion and growth. It seems to be relevant to everything from lightning bolts to markets.

This new internal structure is found in the exact spots that earlier researchers had labeled random (nonessential) and discarded. The stages marking the onset of turbulence—and their timing and intensity—can now be predicted with more exact mathematical precision.

The themes that emerge are that order exists within chaos and chaos gives birth to order. To get a better fundamental grasp of this change in perspective, we look at a typical problem with linear analysis. Then we can begin to apply this new approach to trading.

How Can We Measure the Length of a Coastline?

Lewis F. Richardson, an English scientist, first addressed the problem of calculating the length of a coastline or any national border. The problem was solved later by Mandelbrot. At first glance, this seems a silly problem but it actually raises very serious issues concerning the viability of Euclidean measurement for certain classes of objects and for the markets.

Imagine that you are assigned the task of measuring the coastline of Florida. Your boss wants an accurate measurement and gives you a 10-foot-long rod. You walk the perimeter of the peninsula. You finish your work and calculate your answer. Then your boss decides that the 10-foot-rod missed too much detail. You are given a yardstick and instructed to repeat the process. You redo your work and come up with a much larger measurement. Using a one-foot ruler would yield an even longer measurement for the coastline, and if you use a one-inch ruler and still keep your sanity, your answer would rise toward infinity. The shorter the measuring device, the more detail is captured. A coastline is representative of a class of objects having an infinite length in a finite space.

The length of a coastline is not a measurable quantity in the Euclidean approach to measurement. If Florida had a smooth Euclidean shape, there would be a fixed answer to the question of its length. But virtually all natural shapes are irregular. They defy absolute values of traditional measurement.

Mandelbrot invented a new way of measuring such irregular natural objects or natural systems. He named it the Fractal or, more properly, the fractional dimension. The fractional dimension is the degree of roughness or irregularity of a structure or system. Mandelbrot found that the fractional dimension remains constant over different degrees of magnification of an irregular object. In other words, there is regularity in all irregularity. When we normally refer to an occurrence as random, we indicate that we do not understand the structure of that randomness. In market terms, this means that the same pattern formation should exist in different time frames. A one-minute chart will contain the same Fractal pattern as a monthly chart. This self-similarity found in commodity and stock charts gives further indication that market action is more closely attuned to the paradigm of natural behavior rather than economic, fundamental, mechanical, or technical behavior.

Mandelbrot also found a close similarity between the Fractal number of the Mississippi River and cotton prices over all the time periods he studied, which included world wars, floods, droughts, and similar disasters. The profoundness of this observation cannot be overstated. It means that the markets are a natural nonlinear function and not a classical physics linear function, and it explains, at least partially, why 90 percent of traders using technical analysis lose consistently. Not only is technical analysis based on the false assumption that the future will be like the past, but it uses inappropriate linear techniques for analysis.

Just as Euclidian analysis cannot accurately measure the coastline of Florida, neither can it accurately measure the behavior of a market. The electrical activity of the heart is a Fractal process. So is the activity of the immune system. The bronchial tubes, lungs, liver, kidneys, and circulatory system are all Fractal structures. The entire physical structure of humans seems to be Fractal in nature; perhaps most importantly, the human brain is Fractal in structure. It is theorized that to work at all, humans' memory, thinking process, and self-awareness must all be Fractal in structure and functioning.

Given the foregoing, it would be reasonable to theorize that any pattern that was the result of human interaction (e.g., the markets) should also be Fractal in structure. This means that the market is generated by turbulent collective activity and is a nonlinear phenomenon.

Any trader with a bit of experience has learned that the markets are not a simple, mechanical result of supply and demand. If humans were machines, price action would be a simple two-basin attractor system of supply and demand forces. A pendulum hung between two magnets is a simple two-basin attractor system (see Figure 2.2). Two-basin attractors

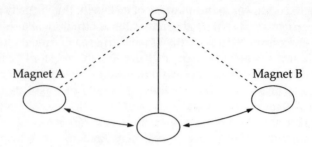

FIGURE 2.2   A two-basin attractor.

are simple, linear, and boring. A two-basin market would have no complexity, nonlinearity, turbulence, or volatility.

If a third attractor is placed near the pendulum, chaos or Fractal structure is introduced to the system. In our own modeling, we have delineated five different magnetic attractors that affect the price movement from one basin to another. The system is nonlinear, dynamic, and chaotic. And it works.

Because the markets are a nonlinear, turbulent system produced by the interaction of human beings, price and time actions are the perfect places to seek Fractal structures. Time and again, turbulent processes in nature produce magnificent structures of complexity, without randomness, in which self-similarity can be observed. Finding the Fractal structure of the market produces a way to understand the behavior of the system—that is, the price movement of a particular commodity or stock. It is a way to see pattern, order, and, most important, predictability where others see only chaos.

The primary purpose of this book is to show you how to trade using Fractal geometry. Twenty-three years of intensive research have been dedicated to the Fractal geometry of the markets. Without boring you with the details of this research, here is just one example of how Fractal analysis contributes to the better understanding of the trading tools for the market.

Fractals are produced on computer screens by using a process called *iteration*. Accretion is a nonsystematic iteration. Something is added to something else, and that bigger thing is added to something, else, and so on. The simplest model of iteration is the summation sequence known as Fibonacci numbers. The sequence starts with 0, and the first two terms are 1 and 1. Add 1 to the starting 0, and the answer is 1. Add the second 1 and the answer is 2. From that point, the two immediately preceding numbers are added together to get the next number in the sequence. So, add 1 and 2, and the answer is 3. Add 2 and 3, and the answer is 5. Add 3 and 5, and the answer is 8. Add 5 and 8, and the answer is 13. The sequence continues to infinity. The curious property of this iteration process is that each number in the sequence is exactly .618 of the next number, no matter what two numbers in the sequence one examines. The .618 ratio is the invariant product of systematic accretion.

The world is awash with .618 relationships. Seed patterns on flowers are Fibonacci numbers. The heart muscle contracts to exactly .618 of it resting length. The perfect .618 structure is exemplified by the nautilus shell. A more personal example is the human navel, located at .618 of a person's height. Volumes have been written, simply listing and categorizing incidences in nature of this .618 phenomenon.

The Rosetta stone of Fractal geometry is the Mandelbrot set, shown in Figure 2.3. The Mandelbrot set, the master Fractal and the building blocks of Fractal geometry, is produced by graphing the numbers resulting from the iteration of a second-degree polynomial on the complex plane.

The Mandelbrot set is structured in Fibonacci .618 relationships. It is composed almost exclusively of spiral and helixes. If you stand a nautilus shell on end, and butterfly it as you would a steak, you will get a figure very similar to the Mandelbrot set. This set may very well be the keystone that connects Fibonacci numbers, the Elliott wave, (see Chapter 7 in *Trading Chaos* for a full discussion of the Elliott Wave) and Fractals into one coherent paradigm.

In our own original research, the Profitunity Trading Group has discovered several repeating patterns that allow a degree of predictability about

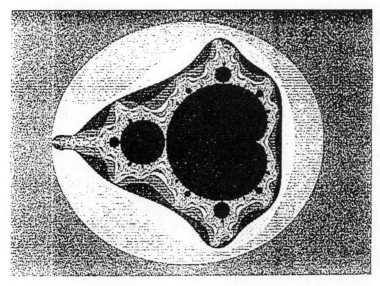

FIGURE 2.3   The Mandelbrot set.

future market movements that are quantum leaps ahead of the accepted current technical analysis. These are discussed in Chapters 8 through 12.

FRACTAL GEOMETRY AND THE MARKETS

Wherever chaos, turbulence, living systems, and disorder are found, Fractal geometry is at work. As noted previously, Fractal actually means a fractional dimension. Imagine you are looking at a three-inch ball of twine from 200 yards away. It will look like a dot, and a dot has zero dimensions. Now imagine you are walking toward the ball of twine. You notice that it is, indeed, a ball of twine and thus has three dimensions. As you approach more closely, you see it is in reality made up of one long string that has only one dimension. By using a magnifying glass and looking even closer, you will see that the string itself is actually three-dimensional. So, depending on your perspective, you have seen zero dimension, then three dimensions, then one, and then back to three. What you see in the market depends just as much on your perspective or your current paradigm. Actually, your current perspective *is* your paradigm. If you are coming from a linear perspective, you will never see the real market and will be at a disadvantage when it comes to trading and making profits.

The Fractal is also a measure of irregularity. The more irregular and choppy a market is, the larger will be its Fractal number. The Fractal number of a portion of a move will always peak at the turnaround point. Therefore, all market trend changes are accompanied by a higher Fractal number than the bars leading up to the change in trend.

Figure 2.4 shows British scientist Michael Batty's generation of a Fractal tree by a computer. Each branch splits into two to create a Fractal

FIGURE 2.4   Computer-generated Fractal tree.

canopy. The illustration on the left has six iterations or bifurcations. By the thirteenth iteration (the illustration on the right), the tree begins to look more realistic. Fractal modelers can produce different species of trees by changing the Fractal number. Fractal trees illustrate the point that Fractal geometry is a measure of change. Each branching of a tree, each bend in a river, each change of direction in a market is a decision point. This notion became a crucial factor in discovering the "Fractal" of the Elliott wave.

 SUMMARY

The science of chaos supplies us with a new and provocative paradigm to view the markets and provides a more accurate and predictable way to analyze the current and future action of a commodity or stock. It gives us a better map with which to trade. It does not depend on constructing a template from the past and applying it to the future. The science of chaos concentrates on the current market behavior, which is simply a composite of (and is quite similar to) the individual Fractal behavior of the mass of traders. For a more in-depth look at the science of chaos from an academic and research point of view, I suggest the following readings listed in the Bibliography: Peters (1991a, 1994), Deboeck (1994), and Chorafas (1994). Most of the current research techniques are found in physics and mathematics journals.

The Fractal is the underlying structure of both the market and individual traders. In Chapter 3 we examine the two basic types of underlying structures and how they add to our market paradigm.

Defining Your Underlying Structure—and How That Affects Winning and Losing

I change not by trying to be
something other than I am.
I change by becoming
fully aware of who I am.
    —Zen theory of existential change

GOAL

To comprehend the market's energy,
the structure of structure, and the
two types of underlying structure.

One of the primary contributions of the new science of chaos is that it examines natural phenomena. One of Mandelbrot's pregnant findings was that the Fractal dimensions of rivers are similar to those of commodity markets—an indication that the markets are more a function of nature than a process designed by the left hemisphere of the human brain. Our view is that economics, fundamentals, and mechanical and technical analysis do not accurately reflect the market's behavior. If the markets were linear, there would be fewer losers—particularly in view of the high intelligence of the average trader. If traditional logic worked, there would be less complaining and more narratives of success.

The science of chaos provides three primary principles for study of the markets. Collectively these principles govern the behavior of energy; from a physics standpoint, everything in the universe is energy. These principles are discussed fully in Robert Fritz's book, *The Path of Least Resistance* (Ballantine Books, 1989). Their key meanings are summarized here.

PRINCIPLES FOR STUDY OF THE MARKET'S ENERGY

1. Energy Always Follows the Path of Least Resistance

While a river runs downstream, its behavior is determined by the path of least resistance. Gravity energizes it as it flows around rocks and along curves in the riverbed. A commodity or stock market is like a river. As it moves through each trading minute, it takes the path of least resistance. We all do that—not only in the market, but you, me, and everything in nature. It is part of the inherent design of nature. You are reading this sentence at this time because this was the path of least resistance when all your time management factors were examined. You are sitting wherever you are because that location was on your path of least resistance. In a market, you will exit from a losing trade when the pain of losing one more dollar becomes stronger than the pain of saying that you were wrong in taking the trade. The path of least resistance wins again.

2. The Path of Least Resistance Is Determined by the Always Underlying and Usually Unseen Structure

The behavior of a river, whether it is calmly flowing downhill or creating rapids, depends on the underlying structure of the riverbed. If the riverbed is deep and wide, the river will flow calmly downhill. If the riverbed is shallow and narrow, the riverbed will create rapids. The behavior of the river can be accurately predicted by examining the underlying riverbed.

Suppose you needed to get up and go to the bathroom now. You would most likely walk through one or more rooms or doorways. Why not just take a straight-line course through the walls to the bathroom? Because you learned long ago that you injure yourself when you walk into walls. As you walk toward the bathroom, you probably are *unaware* of how your behavior has been determined by the architect who designed the locations of the openings and by the builder who mounted the doors in their present position. The architect and the builder gave your rooms their underlying structure.

Similarly, the underlying structure of your life determines your approach to trading. Whether you are aware of the structure or not, it determines your behavior and your reaction to any movement in the market.

Many traders who keep repeating their trading behavior produce losses. They often feel powerless and frustrated. They attend seminars, read books and underline appropriate passages, study NLP (neurolinguistic programming), have private sessions with market psychologists, and then find themselves back in the same old losing rut. If that has happened to you, you simply have not changed your underlying structure.

If you make only superficial changes, nothing has really changed. Permanent change happens only when the underlying structure is changed. When your personal underlying structure is aligned with that of the market, winning becomes the path of least resistance.

As a trader/investor, you will always know when you are going against the path of least resistance. Tension immediately builds up in your body and mind. If you are tense about trading, you are not floating down the river. Once you learn to determine the underlying structure of a market, you can make peace with the behavior of the market and simply "float like a butterfly, sting like a bee."

3. The Always Underlying and Usually Unseen Structure Can Be Discovered and Can Be Altered

Most traders and investors seem to be trying to change the course of the market/river by using bailing buckets. That task is impossible. However, if they were to hike up the river to its source, they might be able to change the entire course of the river by simply moving a few rocks so that the water flows in a different direction. Sometimes a slight change in cause can produce mammoth changes in behavior. This possibility is not addressed by linear Newtonian/Euclidian physics.

You can change the flow of your life and your trading. To do this easily and permanently, you must work with the underlying structure rather than the behavior produced by that underlying structure.

Once a new and different structure is in place in your trading, the overall thrust of your trading, like the current of a river, builds momentum and aids you in getting the results you want.

The basic concept derived from these three principles is this: you can learn to recognize the underlying structure that is driving your trading and then change it so that you can create what you really want from the market.

To be able to recognize the underlying structure, we need to examine more closely the structure of structure, the keystone to all our results in trading and in life.

WHAT IS STRUCTURE?

Any structure has four elements: (1) parts (components), (2) plan, (3) power source, and (4) purpose. All structures contain movement and an inclination toward movement; this means they have a tendency to change from one state to another state. Some structures have more tendency toward movement than others do. In a more stationary structure, the parts tend to hold each other in check; in a less stationary structure, the parts have a tendency to permit easier movement. A wheelchair has a greater tendency toward movement than a rocking chair does, and a rocking chair has a greater tendency toward movement than a couch does. A couch has a greater tendency toward movement than a building does. In each case, the underlying structure determines the tendency toward movement.

This underlying, usually unseen structure is everywhere in our life and is especially potent in our ever-changing reaction to a changing market.

Edmondson (1986) described the concepts of R. Buckminster Fuller's synergetic geometry:

According to Fuller thinking isolates events; "understanding" then interconnects them. "Understanding is structure," for it means establishing the relationship between events.

Structure determines behavior. Structure determines the way anything behaves—a bullet, a hurricane, a cab driver, a spouse, a market. The way the pits are structured determines the behavior of the traders in the pits.

The structures that have the most influence on your trading results are composed of desires, beliefs, assumptions, aspirations, and, most of all, your understanding of the underlying structure of the market and yourself.

The study of structure is independent of and quite different from the study of psychology. However, there is a potent relationship. As you apply structural understanding and principles to your trading, two insights emerge.

First, most of us, probably more because of ignorance than arrogance, have a tendency to ignore nature and simply use it as a backdrop for our more important activities. Traders act according to the underlying structures that rule their entire lives. Since both the markets and the traders are part of nature, it should not be surprising that both act according to natural underlying structure. Chaos and Fractals are new concepts for most traders. Most see their lives as a struggle against nature or the market rather than as being intimately connected with nature and the market. As the composer Hector Berlioz commented, "Time is the great teacher, but unfortunately it kills all its students."

The second insight from the study of structures is that some structures produce more and different types of results than others. Structure is impersonal. Some structures lead to pain, no matter who is within the structures. Most traders attempt to change their behavior rather than the structure of their life. They believe that changing their behavior will change the structure. Just the opposite is true. As Robert Fritz notes in *The Path of Least Resistance*, "You can't fool Mother Structure."

Some structures lead to final destinations; other structures simply oscillate. Next we examine both types and later, in Chapters 8 through 12 we will note the difference each makes when used in the markets.

Type One Structure

A Type One structure produces an action-reaction, back-and-forth, figure-eight type of behavior: one type of desired behavior leads into an opposite undesired behavior. A simple example is the pendulum. At the top of its arc, gravity changes its behavior to a downward direction. As it progresses, it builds up momentum. The momentum pushes it downward past dead center and toward the opposite side of its arc. Then gravity begins to slow it down. The pendulum loses all the built-up momentum, reaches the top, and begins movement in the opposite direction (Figure 3.1).

Most traders are captured by and operating in Type One structures. To repeat a frequent example, suppose you put on a trade and decide to be very conservative with a tight stop. You tell yourself you need the tight stop so that if you are wrong it will not hurt too much. The market has a normal retracement that stops you out; then the market zooms in the direction you thought it would. You analyze your loss and decide that your stops are too close. You must give the market "room to move."

On the next trade, you place your stop unusually far away from your entry, to give the market plenty of room. The market retreats and gives you a very large loss. You simply cannot withstand this big a loss. Again, in your analysis, you decided to tighten up your stops.

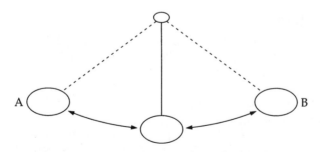

FIGURE 3.1   Pendulum as Type One structure.

Most losing traders are trapped into this back-and-forth strategy of trading their last mistake. In a Type One structure, change is experienced from time to time but it does not last. Any progress turns out to be temporary. A Type One underlying structure makes us vacillate back and forth just like a pendulum. Any time you seem to be getting the same results over and over, you are enmeshed in this Type One structure. Someone once defined insanity as "doing the same thing over and over and expecting different results." If you are trying to diet but find your weight yo-yoing or are trying to quit smoking or you want to win and you keep losing, you are in a Type One underlying structure.

If you seek the typical psychotherapist (remember, I have been one) at this point, you will hear words like "self-sabotage," "failure complex," "afraid of succeeding," and so on. The assumption is that inner states of being—emotions, inhibitions, fears—generate your dysfunctional behavior. All of these typical approaches insist that something is wrong with you. The underlying structure here is also Aristotelian and Newtonian: One looks for a cause, finds a solution, and brings about a different effect.

If your underlying structure is one of oscillation, no solution will help because psychological solutions do not address the underlying structure that causes behavior. At times, some of these approaches appear to work, but their effects are temporary. Check out for yourself traders who have used this type of approach; evaluate what percentage of their change has been permanent. Our research clearly shows that the vast majority of traders fall back into their old losing habits. The only permanent change we have found is in those who have altered their underlying structure.

If you are in a pattern of oscillation (remember, all oscillators move around and always come back to zero), do not consider it a problem that you have to overcome. This structure is not adequate to get you to be a consistently winning trader. Fortunately, there is an alternative to this oscillating underlying structure: the Type Two structure.

Type Two Structure

> Notice the natural order of things. Work with it
> rather than against it for to try to change what is
> so will only set up resistance.
>   —Zen proverb

We have identified Type One structure as being based in the left hemisphere of the brain. Type Two structure is located in the creative part of the brain. Type One structure attempts to solve problems (quit losing); Type Two structure is geared for action that brings something new into being.

Rather than solving problems, it creates results. The contrast is not unlike the difference between classical physics and quantum physics. Classical physics postulates that you have to have something to make something else. Quantum physics maintains that something can be created from nothing. Classical physics says that stuff comes from other stuff; quantum physics says that stuff comes from "nonstuff."

When you are successful in solving a problem, all you have is the absence of a problem. You still may not have the result you desire (to be consistently profitable). Our Aristotelian problem-solving mentality has become a way of life. Most of us never consider an alternative approach.

On the national political scene, discussion centers on the problem of the deficit, the problem of inflation, the problem of the homeless, the problem of taxes, the problem of AIDS, the problem of education—ad infinitum. The greatest leaders in history were not problem solvers, they were builders and creators. Franklin Roosevelt and Winston Churchill were not trying to solve the problem of the Axis in World War II; they were building a foundation for the future they wanted for the entire world.

Problem solving certainly has its place, but it has not proved effective in creating winning trading attitudes. Most often, it changes nothing. Here is the key. The path of least resistance in problem solving leads to moving from worse to better and then to worse again. You take action to lessen the intensity of the problem. As the intensity lessens, you exert less effort and less motivation to take further action. This sets up the typical figure-eight pattern where there may be much action but no real progress.

To state this another way, in a problem-solving mode, as soon as you become successful you tend to quit doing the very thing that made you successful in the first place. This sequence is taking place in most businesses today. A new restaurant opens and offers excellent food to attract patrons, but then slips to more ordinary cuisine and loses customers. In a romantic relationship, we court each other, put on our best face, are constantly considerate, and make a commitment to marriage. As soon as we are married, we tend to quit doing all those nice little things that made the relationship attractive in the first place. For traders who are trading to solve problems rather than to create profits, the pattern is similar.

Medicine is interested in solving problems rather than creating an extraordinarily healthful existence. Medical science is not a method for creating health. Law is interested in solving the problem of crime rather than rehabilitating those who perform criminal acts. Law is not a method for creating sane civilizations. Psychotherapy, likewise, is not a method of creating peak experiences and personal effectiveness.

Carl Jung (1975), after spending years of dedicated work in this area, concluded that most often the problems themselves were irrelevant. He made this astute observation:

*All the greatest and most important problems of life are fundamen-
tally insoluble . . . They can never be solved, but only outgrown. This
"outgrowth" proved on further investigation to require a new level of
consciousness. Some higher or wider interest appeared on the patient's horizon, and through this broadening of his or her outlook the
insoluble problem lost its urgency. It was not solved logically in its
own terms but faded when confronted with a new and stronger life
urge. (p. 29)*

Problem solving does not enable you to create what you want (profits);
often, it perpetuates exactly what you do not want (losses). You do not
need to transform your trading, you need to transcend it.

Type Two structure is a whole other world where everything is "au-
tomagically" working for your progress in attaining your goals. There is little wasted motion or backtracking. You are at the control of a rocket ship
where all the energy is channeled in the most appropriate direction, and
everything you do seems to contribute to your progress with very little
digression.

With Type Two underlying structure, rather than simply solving problems, you are now on the road to creating. Creating is a technique you did
not learn in school, at home, or on the job. It is probably the most important
skill you can master in order to trade well. It is very different from reacting
or responding to circumstances. One happy note is that your present circumstances do not in any way limit your creativity in making profits in
trading. The creative process has a different structure from your reactions
or responses to present circumstances.

A trader responding to present circumstances is imprisoned by them.
Circumstances are the walls of your cell. When you are creating, you are
free and your freedom is not threatening to you. All your life you have been
told what, when, and how to do things. Be at work by 9:00, take only an
hour for lunch, and do not leave before 5:00. PTA meeting is Wednesday
night. Get eight hours of sleep. I must accomplish three projects before I
will be considered for that promotion. Quarterly taxes must be in by Friday.
Rules and demands come from everywhere.

Now you enter trading, where there are basically no rules. You trade
when you want to, how much you want. You determine your risk. You *create* your profits. The average person has no education or experience to
produce this type of result. Traders subscribe to newsletters and hotlines or
camp out with CNBC in search of guidance. The real guidance can only
come from inside, and the results will always be in line with your underlying structure.

SUMMARY

In this chapter, we looked at how the world works, both inside and outside your body. We examined the three principles that are in tune with nature and natural functioning:

1. Everything follows the path of least resistance.
2. The path of least resistance is determined by the always underlying and usually unseen structure.
3. The underlying structure can be discovered and it can be changed.

We then looked deeper into the *structure* of structure and distinguished between the almost universal approach to problem solving versus the more effective and profitable creating type of structure.

In Chapter 4 we examine what has to happen in your mind to ensure winning ways. This is equally as important as your entry/exit techniques, if not more so. There are two personality roads; one leads to losses and possibly catatonic states and the other to highly conscious and successful living and trading. We are now at the point of "gearing up for trading." Have a go at it and have a good time while experiencing some new ideas.

CHAPTER 4

Gearing Up for Trading

Nature's way is simple and easy, but men prefer the intricate and artificial.

—Lao Tzu

GOAL

To understand what has to happen before you analyze the market— How to get prepared internally.

Diogenes was a famous and very wise man. He found that owning things impaired his enjoyment of life. He narrowed his possessions down to only the clothes on his back and a bowl. Then one day he saw a dog drinking in the river and decided he really did not need a bowl. He became famous throughout the land. So famous that the most powerful man in the world at that time heard of him. Alexander the Great went to the river where Diogenes spent much time to meet him. They struck up a conversation and Alexander was extremely impressed. Toward the end of this conversation Alexander said to Diogenes. "I admire you more than any man on the face of this earth. One day I would like to be like you. To really relax and know myself."

Diogenes asked, "Why not do it now?"

Alexander said, "No, I can't. First I must conquer the world and then I will come back here and we will spend much time together."

Diogenes replied, "I never conquered the world, why don't you stay now?"

Alexander answered, "No, first I conquer the world, then I will come back."

Diogenes said, "You will never come back, you will die first."

Alexander did finish conquering the known world. His last conquest was India and sure enough he died on the way back from India.

If we understand these two personalities, we will understand the difference between winners and losers in the market. Alexander the Great would be the losing trader and Diogenes would be the winner. Why? Because of their understanding of the world and themselves.

Some of these differences are worth examining. Alexander was in the process of "becoming" while Diogenes was just "being." This behavior reflects the functioning of the two different parts of the mind. Our conscious mind is Alexander the Great. Always moving, always conquering some new field, new technique, new buzz words (e.g., Fractals, candlesticks, macd, adx, neural networks, fuzzy logic, strange attractors, artificial intelligence).

We can approach the subject of winning trading by finding out more about our minds. We each have a minimum of three minds (superconscious, conscious and subconscious) and they work differently and even speak different languages. It is as if you live in a three-room house where English is spoken in the living room, Spanish is spoken in the kitchen, and German is spoken in the bedroom. And each occupant of the house can speak only one language.

One part of your mind uses scientific techniques for discovering what is *true*. And let me quickly add here that I am not all that interested in what is *true*, because *truth* changes. It was truth that Zeus ruled the world. It was truth that the world was flat. It was truth that Nixon was not a crook. It was truth that Ollie North was a patriot. It was truth that heaven has streets paved with gold. It is academic truth that the markets are a random walk. No, I am not interested in the truth; I am much more interested in *lies that work*. The main element of the scientific approach to finding the truth is to eliminate the things that are not true. This is known as creating a null hypothesis. Let's take the unfolding understanding of the mind.

An early field of study, phrenology said that each part of the brain (remember that the brain is an organ and we are trying to find out what the *mind* is) had a different function. You have probably seen the phrenology charts that plot where the bumps are and what they mean because of their geographic location on the head. Then came scientology and Ron Hubbard, who maintained that the mind was full of engrams. Next came Wilder Penfield, a brilliant brain surgeon in Canada who found that by electrically stimulating various parts of the brain you could re-create certain memories.

Some religions consider the mind the devil's workshop. And in many respects I think they may have their hand on the real thing. The Eastern religions believe that at the core, the mind is an illusion.

Carl Pribram in California believes that the mind is a hologram. Actually he makes a case that everything is a hologram—you, me, the world, everything. This is certainly the best explanation of memory, since memories are stored as holograms.

Alfred Adler said there is only movement. Watch the movement, everything else is illusion and camouflage.

Of all the things that we think are problems, there is good news. We only have one problem and that is the mind. The primary disease of the mind is constant occupation. The mind is like a shark in that it must constantly move or it dies. If the mind stops moving, it dies also. Happens every night when you go to sleep. The mind is like a dance of thoughts. The dance is only movement and when thoughts stop moving, there is no dance. The market is also only movement. There is a market dance and just as you have no destination when you dance (you are not trying to go straight across the floor), the market has no destination. It does not really matter whether the market is at 10,000 or 1,700. It is only alive while it is moving. When it stops, there is no market.

THE MARKET REFLECTS THE MIND

At a very deep level there simply is no such thing as your mind. There are only thoughts parading through and telling you that you are conscious and awake. As a sort of parallel, there is no such thing as a crowd, there are only groups of individual people. In a room we may be labeled as a crowd, but where is the crowd when the people leave? And just as a crowd is nothing but individuals who happen to meet at a certain place on a time line, the mind is really nothing but a group of thoughts that happen to meet on a time line.

It appears there are many hindrances to making profits in the markets but actually there is only one: the mind. In life, we think we have numerous problems but again, there is really only one and that is our mind. If we can solve that problem, then all the rest of the problems are solved automatically. They simply vanish. Actually, they never existed in the first place apart from the problem of the mind itself. Our mind creates all our problems in the market and in our life. And no matter how many problems we solve in the market (or our life), more will appear because we have not solved the basic problem of the mind itself.

The problem of the mind is like a tree where you keep cutting off the leaves and more keep appearing. Every gardener knows that the way to thicken a tree is to prune it. The process never ends until you get at the root cause. And that root cause of our problems is our mind. Our trading problems are not going to be solved by learning more about the rsi, macd, Williams %R, the Market Facilitation Index, or astrology. This learning process will never end; new leaves are always growing and next year there will be someone with a brand new gimmick, whether it is candlesticks or chaos promising you riches galore. Let me tell you a classified top secret and you must swear never to reveal it to anyone else. These gimmicks will not work! Nothing old, new, or different will ever work as long as the problem is the mind. The gardener must get to the roots of the tree and we must get to the root that we call our mind.

THE STRUCTURE AND NATURE OF THE MIND

We divide the mind into three parts: the left hemisphere or our conscious mind; the core, which we usually refer to as our unconscious mind; and the right hemisphere, which we prefer to label the paraconscious mind. Let us examine the conscious mind.

The conscious mind is a goal-seeking servo feedback mechanism. Since it is always trying to get somewhere (which is why you are reading this book), it can never be "here." This mind wears a sweatshirt that says "More Is Never Enough." Alexander the Great was going to relax and meditate as soon as he conquered the world, but he died trying to get home. And so you and I will die trying to conquer problems unless we get to the roots. This is the real reason 90+ percent of all traders lose money consistently. Remember that any time the market is open and moves, 50 percent of all contracts are making money, while 90 percent of all traders are losing money.

The purpose of the conscious mind is to solve problems. That is its job. "I don't have a quarter for the telephone, what can I do?" When the conscious mind is confronted with a problem, it consults with its memory banks and tries to find a similar situation from the past that was solved successfully and applies the *exact same techniques* to the current problem. Remember that the primary programming of the left hemisphere is survival. It does not evaluate the success in any long-term effects. Its primary role is the preservation of the status quo.

Preserving the status quo is the number one problem in trade/vesting. Realize that the conscious mind is not a good judge of what is most profitable in trading the markets. There are four major functions of the conscious mind, and each of the four can be detriments to being successful in the markets.

1. Judgment. Assessing what is proper and what is not. Evaluating whether one technique or another is the best in the present situation.

2. Awareness of time. The left hemisphere is the only part of the mind that conceives of time as proceeding from the past to the present and then on into the future. All the other parts of the mind simply delineate between now and not now. Time does not flow smoothly the way we sense or feel that it does.

3. Understanding of spoken and written language exists only in the left hemisphere. The rest of the mind communicates in other ways, such as vibration, feelings, emotions, or scenarios. And since dreaming comes from the core, you almost never dream about reading a book. You may dream about how you felt reading a book but you don't read in your dreams, because the part of you that is dreaming cannot read. If you are aware of reading in your dreams, it is classified as a lucid dream, which is quite rare.

4. Struggle. Efforting and trying hard only happen in the left hemisphere. Whenever you catch yourself efforting or trying hard, you may rest assured that you are trapped in the idiot part of your mind. The epitome of noneffective trading is the trader who is trying hard to get in some winning trades today before the market closes so he can tell his buddies or mate about his trading prowess.

The left hemisphere can only process information at about 16 bits per second and it processes linearly and digitally. It is woefully inadequate to comprehend even the slightest complexity and is always attempting to make concepts ridiculously simple and abstract (all women are weak, lawyers are dishonest, doctors only want all your money, brokers can never be trusted, the locals always skim my orders, etc.). Other simplified concepts include it must go down because the RSI is over 90 and the stochastics are +80. RSI and stochastics have zero effect on the market. They are simply a historical description of the market. In fact, all technical and cyclical systems are based on the assumptions that the future will be like the past. And that is a terribly ignorant and erroneous assumption on which to base anything.

However, these assumptions make sense at the level of the left hemisphere. A man marries a woman who turns out to be a lush, a drunkard. After several miserable years, the man splits to look for a more suitable partner. What does he do? He looks around, finds someone he thinks is very different. She is not a lush; she simply likes having a good time, like me. They marry, she turns out to be a lush just like the first. There are people who go through this torture four or five times. What they do not see is that they are using their left hemisphere programming to solve the problem of how to pick a life partner based on left hemisphere survival mode. That first wife may have been a lush, but I survived. Remember that the number one program in the left hemisphere is survival. I may not be all that happy but I am not dead yet.

Ever wonder why in trading that you keep getting yourself into the same types of bad situations, such as not getting out of a losing trade at the end of the day, over and over again? You will not solve this problem by learning a newer and better technique. There is nothing in the study of Fractals or chaos or cycles or indicators or astrology or the *I Ching* to solve this problem. What you must have is a program transplant. Actually what you really need is a "trance-formation." You need to get out of the conscious-mind survival trance that is holding you back.

Your current trance holds you back by filtering the incoming information to your decision-making machine. The last time I bought bonds, I had my stops too tight. The market went down and got me out by two ticks and then took off in the direction I knew it was going to go. So this time I am going to do what? I'm going to place my stop three times as far away as I usually do. What happens? It gets me; this time my loss is three times what it usually is. I cannot take that kind of loss—back to close stops for me, no matter what. You know what happens next—same as time before last. Most traders spend their trading lives trading their last mistake just as most generals spend their lives fighting the last war, which more than likely is not appropriate to today's skirmishes.

Trading successfully (assuming one knows the very basic terminology of the market and placing orders) is not a matter of adding to your arsenal, getting more equipment, more indicators, more newsletters, or more books. This will not make you a better trader. In fact, there is nothing you will get by reading this book that will change you from a losing trader into a winning trader, except the admonition that change must come from you.

TRADING IS AN INSIDE JOB

You may be sitting there thinking there is something in computers, in charts, in the brains of the advisors that you are going to suck up and use and then be successful. If you believe that, I have some underwater lots in Florida I would like to show you.

You see, all traders share two instinctual traits: (1) We overcomplicate everything we touch and because of that (2) we cannot see the obvious. And the obvious is that nobody trades the markets. We all trade our belief systems. When some of you think about this, it begins to produce a crisis.

A crisis is simply a close encounter of the truthful kind. To be successful in the market, you must understand the truth of the market and what you trade is the first truth.

Let me be clear, I am not putting down any indicator, any approach, any system, mechanical or otherwise. I am not a missionary trying to get you to heaven. I really am not trying to convince you of anything. What I am telling you is the truth, it is yours and it is free; you can do whatever you wish with it. It will not affect me or my success one way or the other. Sure, if we meet sometime and you were to say, "Bill, you were right on!" I would be very pleased. That would be great psychic income and I would enjoy some very fine ego stuffing. I would love it, but I have no investment in you confirming that my approach is truth. I don't even care whether it is true or not—it works! And as I said in the beginning I am much more interested in lies that work than truth. And I surely am not interested in your doubts. As the comic Dave Gardner used to say, "Don't tell me about your doubts, I've got enough of them. Tell me something you believe in!"

Here is the *big* point! If you can let go of the trader you think you are, you will discover what trading would be like if you had wings. Letting go of the trader you think you are will produce a crisis, and a crisis, again, is simply a close encounter of the truthful kind. Permitting the truth in the market to do what it is intended to do will permit you to trade the way you want to.

A crisis occurs when some inner lie we have been unconsciously telling ourselves is about to surface and be seen as a lie. Seeing this is very powerful. In fact it is so powerful that we call it TNT—truth 'n trading. Any time you have pain in trading, it is directly caused by your resistance to the truth of the market.

One of the wonderful things about life and the market is that whenever we have a crisis or a problem of any kind, we do not need to search for an answer anywhere except where the problem is. You know the story of the drunk who lost his car keys in the dark grass but decided to look for them under a street light because he could see better there.

So when you have a crisis or a bad time in the market, realize that the very best solution is exactly where the problem is. If you are not trading well, look at your problem. Do not look for another system, technique, or indicator because that new solution will always, always, always create an equal or bigger problem. That is the nature of life and that is the nature of the market.

If we just give up on the left hemisphere for answers, we will realize from this new elevated level of consciousness that there never was a problem in the first place. What we think of as a problem was created by our deceiving survival programs of this idiot mind whose job it is to solve problems. This idiot knows that if there are no problems, it is out of work. Since the primary program is survival and you survive by solving problems, how do you get tenure? How do you create job security? Of course, by creating bigger and better problems to solve.

Suppose you have been working very hard and developed a constant frown on your face. You feel inside that everything is not quite all right, and you spend much time and effort in trying to figure out what is the best thing to do. Then someone shows you a mirror and you see the frown for what it really is. Very naturally you simply let go of the effort of frowning. You relax and the frown goes away. Successful trading is exactly the same way. There is a bumper sticker that says "If sex is a pain in the ass, you're doing it all wrong." Our version of that is "If you are not having fun trading, you are doing it all wrong." If you want to take away the worry and the frown of trading, get a mirror. And the very best mirror of all is the market. Tell me what your real, deep down attitude is and I will be able to accurately predict your results in the market. Tell me your results in the marketplace and I will tell you what your attitude was while you traded.

When you trade the markets, there is nothing to hide behind. At the end of the day you either have more money, the same, or less. If you lose, there is simply no one to blame. The converse of this statement is that if you win, you do not have to say "thank you" to anyone. That, my trading friend, is the truth.

The market will always be a reflection of you. It is like the Grand Canyon. When you holler, "Help," what you hear is "Help." When you holler "God," what you hear is "God." When you holler "Astrology is the answer," you hear "Astrology is the answer." When you holler "This is a crappy market," those words will echo. Life and the markets are both self-fulfilling events.

Just the awareness of this phenomenon can improve your trading drastically. What you really need to see through is your choice of belief systems. You can choose. As a matter of fact the most important choice in the whole world is "either to choose to choose or not to choose." If you choose to follow a mechanical system you have not really chosen to trade the market. And all mechanical systems will fail. You need to see through your need to be dependent on others. Your true nature is all you need. Let it show you what you do not need.

Every trader and investor wonders if there is a great secret to successful trading, and there is, but it is not really a secret. It has been right in front of us all the time. Listen quietly for a moment. Everything can change right now. Learning to hear this supreme secret is no more difficult than choosing whether to swim against the current or to let it carry you safely downstream. Let this secret speak to that secret part inside of you. Listen to it now. It is showing you *THE HOLY GRAIL*, which is . . .

WANT WHAT THE MARKET WANTS

Locked inside of those five simple words is the secret for uncompromising power and effortless trading. Want what the market wants. This will give you a new kind of power in the market. It will put you on the same side of the desk as the market rather than being an opponent of the market behavior. It will give you a new kind of power that never fails to put you on the winning side of any trade.

It is not what the market has brought you that you do not like; it is your reaction that turns that gift into resentment. Each moment the market is open it is offering you a taste of reality and allowing you complete freedom to react to each new reality presented.

Your unhappy feelings come from the market failing to conform to your ideals of what *should* be happening. The market is not denying you success and happiness; it is your ideas about the market that have failed you. So give up on these wrong ideas instead of giving up on the market. Your ideas are nothing but a constant source of conflict. What happens when you do not *want what the market wants*?

- You are often nervous and anxious because the market may not cooperate with your plans.
- You are usually scheming in some way to outsmart the market.
- You are either in a battle or recovering from one (usually a loss).
- You are easily angered when interrupted or distracted by something.
- You are driven to trade more, risk more, to go temporarily catatonic.
- You are jealous of other traders who are making profits.
- You feel that what you have is what you are and not making profits means you are nothing.

Now let's look at the other side. How is life when you *want what the market wants*?

- You are never disappointed with what happens.
- You are in the right place at the right time.
- You are quietly confident no matter what the circumstances.
- You are out of reach of anger and anxiety.
- You are awake and sensitive to the market movements.
- You are free of that feeling that you may have missed out.
- You are in command of events.
- You are mentally quiet.
- You are eternally grateful.

How do you tell when you *want what the market wants*? Easy. If anything you do is the source of anxiety or sorrow, that *want* is yours and not the market's. To paraphrase Johnny Cochran "If your want has pain, it is in vain." In trading, never accept any emotional or mental suffering as necessary.

In trading you must be in the right place at the right time and the same thing is true with your mind. You must be coming from the right place at the right time. Mind location is much more important than trade location.

Let us experiment with how the mind works. Think of a lemon. Now we know that this thought is not the lemon itself. Yet really think about a lemon. Picture the yellow color and pretend you just sliced it in half. Feel the pressure of the knife going through first the skin and then the meat of the lemon. Can you smell the aroma of this freshly cut lemon? In fact, your mouth has probably begun watering. Maybe it has even begun to pucker. And remember the thought of the lemon is still not the lemon itself. What has happened? The thought of the lemon triggered a series of unconscious accumulated memories that rushed to our awareness, producing all the different sensations connected with things that are lemonlike. Your thought lemon produced temporary but definite feelings. This concept is easy when it concerns lemons but less obvious when it comes to the markets.

Think about the word "I." The thought is not the thing, just as our lemon example. The difference between the examples is there are millions of times more unconscious accumulated memories involved with the concept of *I* than are involved with the concept of lemon. When we think of *I* we include all our history, our past trading results, how scared we have been in the market, and many other things. No matter how many times or how strongly you feel it, this sensation of *I* is not you. We are not our past-accumulated memories. We have only unconsciously identified with them at that moment. Next time you get upset at all in trading the markets, *do not go crazy or catatonic—go really conscious*!

The next time you are in a losing position, do not get angry or anxious. These feelings are borne out of memories that are identified with fear of losing, fear you are wrong, or whatever. You are thinking, another loss and another hurt, when will I ever get it right? Then you start defending your position. It was the durable goods announcement that did me in, or my Elliott wave count was off, or that damned hotline steered me wrong and I knew it all the time. However, the next time, instead of defending your position and its old habits, you now understand that the feeling of being threatened or attacked is not who you really are. Your true nature never needs to defend any psychological or emotional position. So you can simply drop your reaction and be in a good position for the next unbiased decision based on wanting what the market wants.

By starting your life over each time you look at a chart, you are not borrowing your life (trading) from an overheated reaction. You simply let that negative feeling live and die. When you allow yourself to let go of what was old, you are being true to what is new. You do not have to go on trading with anxious, angry, and fearful feelings that always accompany any trader who is trying to make the market do what he or she wants it to. *Independence is confidence.*

Letting go of the unconscious memories is like one day happily realizing that hitting yourself over the head was the cause and not the cure for your daily headaches. The inner poundings that you wished would go away did go away when *you* stopped pounding.

Remember that trading should be fun. When you grow lighter in spirit you quit dragging around more and more old thoughts and habits. That lightness, then, lets you see the obvious about the market. You are trading as if you had wings. Your savior is your awareness of your fears, not running away from one scary scene in the market right into the arms of another. To discover the wonderful world of reality outside the reality of your memory banks and the left hemisphere, let these thoughts go by realizing that they are not you. In the past you have only identified with them, which put you under their control.

The secret of doing this is to *walk away from trading the "How" into trading the "Now."* This passageway leads to the right hemisphere wherein lies your intuition, your insight, and your inspiration. Thinking and trying will never get you there because that is where you have been all the time and you did not know it. Simply remove the blindfold and look into the mirror. The blindfold is your habits and the mirror is the market.

DIFFERENCES BETWEEN TRADING IN THE HOW AND TRADING IN THE NOW

When trading from the how, we often *fear* what we can't understand. Trading from the now, we understand that fear is a mental mistake. Trading from the how we seek systems to overcome tormenting losses, while trading from the now we understand that there are no magic systems, so we simply drop the question of how and get on with it.

Trading from the how we look to the past to guide us to a successful future, while trading from the now there is freedom from the past trading with no thought about tomorrow's trading because you are trading in the painless present.

Trading from the how we are reluctant to admit when we are wrong, while trading from the now we are free from the punishing need to pretend that we are always right. To be really truthful here I would have to say that I have never been right once in all my life on any trade. That's right, I have never been right on any trade of the tens of thousands I have made . . . not even once!! Every time I was in a winning position I had too few contracts or shares on and every time I was in a losing position, I had too many contracts or shares in the trade. So I honestly have never been right even once. Thankfully you do not have to be right to make a lot of money in the markets.

Trading from the how, we spend valuable time looking back in regret over past losses, while trading in the now, the past losses only exist for practical purposes and never as a source of pain or problems.

As Diogenes said: Remember that real success is not measured by what you are driven to achieve, but what you quietly understand." *When you understand that no one really knows who they are and what the market is about, you will stop looking for them to tell you who you are and what the market is.* Charles Kettering once said, "The task is not to master the problem but to make it give birth to the solution. Illumination is superior to domination." In trading, your choice is to continue dealing with the same problems and frustrations over and over again or let go of that unhappy condition altogether by seeing through to the actual cause.

In conclusion, here are some hints for taking charge of your trading:

- Before you turn to other people for help, honestly see if they have ever really helped themselves. Look at their wings, not their words.
- When you understand that no one really knows the market, you can stop looking for someone to tell you what it is.
- People always want you to be what they want you to be to please them. Be yourself and please yourself.
- Why do you want approval from those who do not even approve of themselves?
- When you know where you are going, you are free from the concern of where anyone else is going.
- If you do not leap, you will never know what it is to fly.
- If you are headed for the mountaintop, what do you care what the people in the valleys are doing?
- You can have a relationship with something you do not understand, but that relationship will always be on its terms (e.g., the market).
- Struggle trading is exhausting; inner trading is inexhaustible.
- If you allow others to tell you where you are going, then you must also depend on them to tell you what you will need for your journey.
- Let go and grow in the market.
- The only thing you lose when you let go of something you are afraid to live without is the fear itself.

SUMMARY

At this point we trust that you are giving at least as much attention to your various minds as you are trading strategies. Strategies may change over time with the markets but your relationship with your minds will always create winners. We strongly suggest that you reread this chapter from time to time. Our experience in working with traders in one-on-one situations tell us that most traders need to read and reread this material before it really makes sense at the deepest levels. Once it does reach these depths, you will wonder why successful trading is so simple and why you did not see how this arrangement runs your entire life both in and out of the markets.

We have attempted in this chapter to point out the importance of preparation before you start to trade. We saw how your different minds influence your behavior in the arena of the markets. And since the market is constructed by millions of other minds it becomes a great advantage to understand what is going on below the surface of price changes. We individual traders are unable to move the market and therefore must give up our individual preferences and realize that the 'Holy Grail' is simply wanting what the market wants.

In Chapter 5 we view winning personalities from another perspective. We examine three different personality types and how their personality affects their success in the markets.

What Type of Trader Are You?

An Exploration into Your Trading Consciousness

*If you see in any given situation only what
everybody else can see,
you can be said to be so much a representative of
your culture that you are a victim of it.*
                                        —S. I. Hayakawa

In 1492, Christopher Columbus and his small fleet consisting of the *Niña*, the *Pinta*, and the *Santa Maria* left the port of Palos, Spain, and headed for the Canary Islands. Six weeks later, they left the Canary Islands and three months after that they bumped into America. Columbus accidentally discovered America when he was seeking a westward route to India. To his dying day, Columbus believed he had achieved only what he had originally set out to do and denied discovering a new continent.

While Columbus was not the first European to encounter America, he did achieve what no known previous explorer had achieved: Without staying in sight of land he sailed directly across the uncharted sea by navigating by the stars. The significance of the achievement of this 1492 expedition cannot be taken lightly. Without the voyages of Columbus, there would have been no conclusion that a "new continent" had been discovered. The Americas would not have been opened to European incursion—for good or for ill—at that time in history. The development of American civilization, and perhaps even world civilization, could have proceeded along entirely different lines. (We know that many different people and groups came to this continent before Columbus. Columbus, however, gets the credit because that was the belief at that time.)

Life has changed significantly since Columbus discovered America more than 500 years ago, but human nature has changed very little. Columbus was a true speculator by ignoring popular opinions and risking everything on his analysis of the geographical situations at that time. His willingness to take risks led him to the discovery of the New World although that was not his original intention.

CHRISTOPHER COLUMBUS: AN ANALOGY FOR TODAY'S TRADERS

A theory about Columbus and his era, which was pointed out to me by Jerry Stockings, a former stockbroker, certainly can be applied to today's investors and traders. Today, as in Columbus's day, there are three types of people with regard to risk taking: the leaders who are willing to look beyond the accepted standard and reach for something greater; those who are willing to follow those leaders and embrace new ideas and take risks; and those who are unwilling to take risks or accept change and will only recognize the known and proven.

In this example, Columbus represents the leader and risk taker; his crew represents those individuals who are willing to embrace new ideas and take risks in order to reap the benefits of those risks; and the men and women who were unwilling to take risks were the landlubbers who remained safely at home with their lives unchanged.

What category do you think you fall into? The one you choose can be an indication of what type of trader you are or what type of trader you can become. In the markets, we have individuals who feel more comfortable in the role of Columbus (the traders). Other individuals feel more comfortable in the role of the crewmember (the investors). We also have the individuals who feel more comfortable assuming the role of the landlubbers (the savers).

If you are an independent thinker and enjoy making decisions, even if you are acting against the majority opinion, you are most likely a person who feels comfortable in the Columbus role. It should be noted that the risk-taking adventurer is usually the most successful aggressive trader.

Those who fall into the crew member category are at a slight disadvantage because their success or failure depends on the success or failure of their leader. It is not uncommon to hear complaints from crew members about people, circumstances, or things that happen to them as if they have no control over those circumstances. The crewmember feels that any outcome really depends on outside circumstances. Crew members do what they are told by others who supposedly have more knowledge. Trader A will use a black box trading system that has been proven over time, but will eventually start to fail. Investors will most likely then turn to a broker or some type of financial advisor, thinking since they do this for a living surely they will know how best to proceed in the markets. Until the market crash of the tech stocks in 2000, most traders/investors could not have gone wrong with either choice. They are now finding out it is not that easy.

Then, finally, there are those who feel more comfortable in the role of the landlubber. They feel more secure because they do not worry about taking risks; but they also do not take the steps necessary to make a possible fortune or dare to dream about going on new adventures. They tend to be content or willing to put up with their level of discontent. Landlubbers tend to be procrastinators. Their thinking is that it is safer to put off making a decision than being held responsible for making one. These people will place their money in CDs, savings accounts, and 401(k)s if they have that capability through their job. What they do not realize is that they are not making money. If inflation occurs, they barely will be breaking even. Today's interest rates have significantly changed the future of these types of savers/investors. By the time they retire, the money they thought they would have saved enough to live on comfortably most likely will not be enough.

These same personality characteristics can apply to our financial choices, which can be divided into three similar categories. Your quality of life, including success in your trading life, is more dependent on your belief systems than on your knowledge about trading.

Like Columbus, you can approach life and trading as an adventure, an opportunity, a learning experience, and an exploration with an endless number of possible outcomes.

If you approach trading like a crewmember, you see trading as a series of problems, burdens, or activities that you must carry out based on the opinions of others who may or may not know what they are doing. This makes you an investor who is depending on others to give you knowledge and to point out the best plan of action for your financial activities.

If you are a landlubber, you approach life and your financial situation as a boring routine that each day flows by just like all other days with nothing lost but nothing gained. By putting your faith in saving your money, you are actually losing money every year if inflation is higher than the interest you are earning on your saved money.

Uncertainty is a part of all life. We never really know what life will present to us tomorrow. The opportunities the markets bring us vary from day to day, but our approach to the market is usually constant in that *how* we trade is based on *our belief system*.

Just as uncertainty is part of life, it is part of trading. You can be one of the adventurous traders who marches ahead fearlessly based on your belief system. You can be the investor who tags along with someone else's analysis and recommendations by watching Louis Ruykeyser and reading the *Wall Street Journal*; or you can be the landlubber and stay where you are focused on the possibility that something can be lost instead of the possibility that everything can be gained.

It is easy to fantasize that you are a Columbus in retrospect, but it is much more difficult to be like him in the present. Who are you right *now*? Which category best describes you in the present moment? Who had the better life in the fifteenth century—Columbus, the crew, or the landlubbers? Who is to say? One thing is for sure, the only one you remember is Columbus.

Problems arise when you think you are of the mindset of one of these personality type groups, and you actually are in the mindset of another. For example, if you think you are a crewmember but you are really a Columbus personality type deep down inside; or if you think you are a landlubber but *you want* to be a crew member on a ship with a great leader.

If you want to be an explorer and are a landlubber, you are probably dissatisfied and unhappy. If you are an explorer and think you are a landlubber, you will most likely become tense and stressed out as new challenges continually show up in your life and in the markets.

Our years of experience working individually with traders—more than 2,000 on a daily basis—tells us that the Columbus theory stands true. Not everyone is cut out to be an S&P 500 trader. Many start out trading on a position basis (end-of-day) and do well. Then they decide that they want to trade intraday, and everything changes.

Constantly through the years, traders have come to us thinking they were day traders and actually found out they were not. They tend to lose a great deal of money before facing the facts. When they did, they found that these markets did not fit their belief system, therefore, their efforts did not result in success.

In trading, a captain (Columbus) will always do better over time than the crewmember or the landlubber. A crewmember who thinks she is a captain will create needless tension about whether she should or should not have taken a trade. Typically, as soon as they get in the market, the anxiety starts; if the market goes against them a few ticks, it creates fear in those who are not sure-footed leaders. Based on this fear, they will place a stop, and it becomes the bottom tick. They wind up getting out of the market just as the market heads back in the direction they thought it was going in the first place. A crewmember can sometimes make a profit, but it takes a lot of difficult work, and the profits are usually small. Such a trader needs a captain who will settle for nothing less than success.

A landlubber (saver) who thinks he is a captain will blow out fast and then become furious at the market and his methodology. Landlubbers usually are so far out of touch with the markets that their trading is short-lived. They are seduced by "jack'em up and glaze'em over" programs and infomercials that promise great results with little or no delivery.

TRADERS REAL-LIFE EXAMPLES

Of course, there are different variations and degrees, but the basic belief systems of these personality types are the same. Following are a few examples of each. All names have been changed.

When Ryan, a 28-year-old millionaire and founder of his own Internet company called me, he was looking for consistency in entering and exiting his trades. Since founding his own company, he also started investing in other Internet stocks and trading the Nasdaq. He did very well in the beginning, up over 68 percent in the first 3 months. Then he began losing money and quickly realized that he needed the proper ship and navigation tools for his journey to be a success. This realization started him on the process of finding a system or indicators that fit his belief systems. He knew that he was not risk averse, because he enjoyed trading and the volatility of the Nasdaq and S&P 500.

Ryan was not afraid to lose money. In fact, he enjoyed the challenge of each new trading day and what the markets had to give him; and he knew with the right tools that the markets could be the greatest lotto in the world!

That is where our company, PTG, came in. Once we discovered his belief system, we started on the journey. Ryan was not afraid of loss and taking large risks. He told me that there were days that he lost more than $30,000 in the markets. There were also days he made $40,000, but he was not consistent. He would try to out-think the markets. He was not able just to follow them, which is one of the keys to success in trading. What he most needed was consistency and discipline in his trading.

Since his risk/reward ratio was so high and he was not a very patient person, we knew Ryan was not going to take baby steps in approaching the markets (like paper trading for practice). He jumped in headfirst with his new indicators and the market knowledge he had learned from us. His trading improved almost overnight. Because he had the tools he needed and liked, he was able to steer his own ship and to take responsibility for his wins and losses. He did not lose sight of the horizon. His ship set sail for new lands each day, and he could not wait to see where it went!

This year he was up over six figures in his trading account and is looking at doubling that next year.

Let's look at another example.

Jack, a 38-year-old lawyer with two children and a flourishing trial law practice called us one afternoon with some questions about the stock markets. He read one of our ads with a testimonial from a client that he found interesting. He had most of his money with Charles Schwab in an investment account. He did not have much input and wanted to be in the tech sector due to some advice from a fellow lawyer.

In addition, CNN, FNN, and his newsletters all agreed; they all said the tech sector was the place to be, so 50 percent of Jack's portfolio went into mutual funds and the rest went into tech stocks. Jack had been very pleased with the returns over the last 5 years. His account was up and he did nothing. So when the train wreck came and the Nasdaq fell 38 percent in 5 weeks, Jack felt he was part of the carnage.

Was there something he could have done to prevent this from happening to him? His goal with this money was to put his two children through college, and he knew if the markets continued to fall this would not be possible.

He wanted to know if we could help him learn how to handle his own money or to at least be able to look at the stock markets and have an understanding about its future direction. He wanted to know when to exit a stock and when to consider a longer term investment.

As a successful lawyer, Jack did not like the feeling of no control and was ready to take some responsibility for his money. His stockbroker gave him little comfort after the fact and never advised Jack to get out. Jack thought that was the reason he was paying him—to be vigilant and advise him when it was best to get out of the market when the loss would be as small as possible. He was paying him quite well for this false peace of mind.

The stockbroker offered him no advice for the future. He told Jack it was part of the game and the markets would come back up. The one thing he could count on was that his broker would push certain stocks that he was told to push each day and would make his commission, no matter what the outcome of the trade.

He was now in search of a black box system or something to help him better understand the markets. All of the financial newsletters and experts had great explanations after the fact, and while they were quoting "the S&P 500 had gone 10 years without a decline of more than 20 percent," they were also telling seasoned investors "that some sort of major decline was overdue."

Jack was not a seasoned investor, so the train wreck was totally unexpected and was not something he was willing to endure again. It was clear that Jack did not want to be a day trader, but he was ready to take on the responsibility of learning how to interpret charts. We could tell that Jack was not aggressive, so we concentrated on markets that were not very volatile but that gave him the possible returns that he wanted. He did not need to take all signals or invest more than 20 percent of his portfolio in one sector. He used very conservative stops and took profits when the indicators told him to.

With his new knowledge and skills, he was able to watch his mutual funds and know when to switch them or exit his positions. This method of trading was profitable, great and stress-free for him. By focusing for 20 minutes each evening, he is able to go through his portfolio and notify his broker if any orders need to be placed. Then he is ready for a pleasant dinner with his family. All Jack needed was some feeling of understanding of the markets and the ability to use the knowledge that fit into his belief systems . . . not someone else's.

Here is a final example.

Andrew is a 52-year-old financial officer for a large company. He does not particularly like his job, but he has been there for 20 years and he only has 10 more years until full retirement benefits will kick in. Most of his money is in his 401(k), and the rest is in his local bank making less than inflation. His brother-in-law has made a large amount of money in the markets, which piqued his interests; but Andrew's belief systems did not allow him to take risks. Andrew's wife thinks the way her brother-in-law jeopardizes his future savings is crazy.

Andrew was pulled in two directions: On one hand, he was thinking about the possibility of making more money and retiring earlier or possibly retiring with the ability to have a better quality of life; on the other hand, he was thinking that taking a risk would cause him to lose all he has. His biggest fear was that he would not be able to cover the cost of inflation by the time his retirement kicks in. He really wanted to increase his return on investment (ROI), but he is doomed to failure. Having been an analyst all of his life, he is not comfortable with taking risks. In fact, he makes sure that his company does not take risks.

Andrew, the saver type, was difficult to work with in the beginning. It was hard to find out exactly what he expected from the markets or if he even should be in the market at all.

We first had to identify his goals and see how realistic they were in relationship to the amount of risk he was willing to take. In Andrews's case, he decided that he wanted to put some of his savings in a mutual fund that paid a little higher interest rate than the bank. The rest of his money remained in his 401(k) so that he could trade it, but he decided that he would paper trade for a year before risking any real money. After all, he was an analyst and he felt the need to prove to himself that what he was pursuing would work, as was our claim. Then depending on his results, we would assist him in making a plan for how much he wanted to trade and what type of stocks he would be involved in.

Since he was going to trade his 401(k), he was only able to go long on stocks. He wanted long-term investments like blue chip stocks that he felt would outlive him. For Andrew this was comfortable. He could be as conservative as he wanted yet still have an understanding of what his money was doing. He was beating inflation and he could sleep at night.

Knowing who you are and what group you are in can make your trading life easier and more fun. It will also make you more perceptive about people and about trading. Applying this information can make all aspects of your trading life flow more smoothly. The key to success is being able to trade your belief systems and have fun. If you are able to achieve that, the money just seems to follow.

 ## SUMMARY

You must begin your journey to find out where it will lead. It may have a much greater impact on your life and the lives of others than you ever expected. For example, Columbus never knew he had such a great impact on America.

As a trader the most important thing you can do for your future success is find out what category you fit in to and trade accordingly. In this chapter we have discussed the three types of traders, each with his/her own belief system and expectations from the markets. If we do not know what it is we want then it is almost impossible to have it. I think it is crucial that we define what we want from the markets, and what we are willing to give up to get it. If you are trading in the correct "forum" for you then you will see the results that you deserve.

Columbus did not know what he would find when he left Europe but he knew there was something greater out there and was willing to risk his life for it. The markets offer the same wonderful journey with an unknown outcome until we are there. It does not matter if you are the Columbus, a Landlubber or Crew Member type as long as you are able to follow your goals and dreams. You too may end up discovering new land in your trading journey that you never knew was there. The possibilities are endless, so make sure you enjoy your journey and share your knowledge with others along the way.

In Chapter 6 we delve even deeper into what really creates winning market strategies, followed with the actual trading techniques that we use every day in various markets.

CHAPTER 6

Super-Natural
Trade/Vesting

*The more I study physics, the more I am drawn
to metaphysics.*

—Albert Einstein

What an arrogant way to title a chapter. What do we mean by "super-natural" trade/vesting? We call it "super" because of the results we get and we call it "natural" because it deals with the true nature of both the markets and our thinking processes. The purpose of this approach is so that you can trust your own mind while trading, and so that you can rediscover those natural impulses from your childhood that will allow you to trade better and have confidence in your own experience. This approach not only teaches you *how* to trade well but more importantly how *you* trade well.

This approach is an operator's manual for traders, for those wanting to trade, and for those who have traded and lost and are ready to learn how to do it "right." It is an approach for trade/vestors who are ready to get a license to drive their own minds and make their own trades.

Most of you reading this have spent a great deal of time and effort in *consciously*—note the word "consciously"—attempting to beat the market. And in an average trading group, about 90 percent of you have failed. Perhaps we need to stop using the conscious mind and try something else. And that is what this chapter is about. What is included in this chapter is excluded elsewhere. You will not find this material in the usual books on trading and investing. Other approaches teach you how to use stochastics, rsi, and software, but do not teach the important stuff such as how to operate your mind in a market environment.

Think of each of your brains (minds) as a different musical instrument. Knowing which one you are playing allows you to create music by putting your lips to the woodwinds, a bow to the strings, or a stick to the drums. Most failures in the markets are caused by not knowing how a particular part of your mind works. When we lose, it never occurs to us that we might simply be using the wrong instrument. It is as if we are trying to blow on a drum or pluck a flute. We just think we have to blow harder or pluck faster.

Using the appropriate instrument is a learned skill and can be taught. You can use this chapter to explore the possibilities waiting to be clarified within your mind. It is meant to give you direction and shape, to bring to light the art that lies dormant in your life.

As an illustration, how do you stand on your own two feet? Standing is a global skill (everyone does it). Trading is a global skill (everyone does it—just now you traded whatever else you might have been doing for reading this) and so is speculation (investing). In learning any global skill, one must first master the component skills involved, such as tensing this muscle, contracting that one, and so on. Once the component skills have been achieved, the global skill becomes automatic and is placed in the memory banks of the core mind.

> Practice is the bridge between
> your *intellect* and your *intuition*.

Our purpose here is to acquire the skill of thinking *with* the market, not thinking *about* the market.

YOUR UNDERLYING PSYCHOLOGICAL STRUCTURE

For best results and most insight, it is important that you do the following exercise before reading any further. You most likely will be somewhat amazed at the insights you have without being consciously aware of them. So, ideally have someone read you these instructions aloud and you take plenty of time to fill in the details. *The more details you provide, the clearer and more important the following insights will be.* If you do not have someone to read these to you, then read only one paragraph at a time and either record your impressions or write notes about each one of them. It is most important that you do not skip paragraphs or read ahead.

A Journey to the Inner You

Sit or lie down as comfortably as possible and close your eyes. Imagine all the possible or impossible situations that your mind likes to draw. Do not say anything. Give yourself plenty of time and do not rush. Open your eyes as little as possible and remember as many details of your experience as you can. Remember what you saw, did, and thought. Write your details on a blank sheet of paper.

> For the most insight and benefits,
> do not read ahead before
> doing this experiment.
> Spend at least 60 seconds
> with each paragraph,
> filling in details.

Now, imagine you are standing on a path in the forest. Look around. How does the forest look? What time of the year is it? How does the path look? Is the path straight or winding? Are there rocks in the path? Try to include as many details as you are conscious of.

(Write in details before reading further.)

Now let's take a stroll along the path and see what we might discover. You see a key lying on the ground. What does the key look like? Describe it in detail. What is its purpose? What does the key open or lock? Take plenty of time—there is no hurry. What do you do with the key?

(Write in details before reading further.)

As you continue down this path you come to an old draw well. On the draw well there is a bucket and a cup. Describe the well. Is there water in it? If yes, how is the water? What do you do?

(Write in details before reading further.)

You continue on the path as it leads you deep into the woods. You see a bear is coming and seems to cross your path. What will happen? What do you do? Do not forget details.

(Write in details before reading further.)

After encountering the bear, you go on and arrive at a little clearing. You see a house in the woods. How does the house look? What do you do? What happens?

(Write in details before reading further.)

You go on with your journey and come to a lake. How does the lake look? What do you do?

(Write in details before reading further.)

After you leave the lake, you continue your walk through the forest and come to a big white, long and high wall. The wall is higher than you, you cannot see over the wall and you cannot see the end of the wall. Imagine what you do.

(Write in details before reading further.)

Now come back, take a few deep breaths and think about what you have imagined. Refer to your notes and recall as many details about your walk as possible and we will examine what was going on in your brain and what it really means.

Evaluating Your Walk in the Woods

The *forest* represents your present position in your trading life. Spring represents feeling that your life is before you; summer, you are in the highest part of your life; fall, your life seems settled and you do not expect so much; winter, you are feeling in the depth of your life.

The *path* is how you feel your trading life is going; smooth or over hurdles, straight or soft winding, or dense and overgrown.

The *key* represents your relationship to the markets; for example, an old but nice key that you are take with you, or an old rusty key that you throw away.

The *well* symbolizes the joy of living and trading. Did you drink from it?

The *bear* represents your feelings, how you handle anxiety and fear, and how you handle trades that are going against you. Did you go away or close your eyes, or did you meet and deal with your feelings about losing?

The *house* represents your mind or soul. Is somebody in your house? Did you go inside to look around? What did you find?

The *lake* represents your sexuality and some of your deepest feelings about yourself. Did you enjoy your sexuality and swim or do you see a deep, black, muddy lake?

Finally, the *wall* represents the end: death and how you deal with feelings about death. Some jump over the wall, some try going around the wall, some turn around and walk back, and some do whatever to be able to see what is on the other side of the wall.

All of our years of actively trading the markets have taught us one undeniable fact. No one trades the market; we all trade our individual *belief systems*. In our personal tutorials we go much deeper than is possible in a book to determine just how and why your personal belief system is aiding or hindering you in profitable trade/vesting.

HOW YOUR BELIEF SYSTEMS AFFECT YOUR RESULTS IN THE MARKETS

> The market is a creature of chaos—
> A far from equilibrium soup simmering on
> the uneven flame of trader psychology.

Paraphrasing this statement, *trading is always an inside job*. It has been said that in life there is only one disease—constipation (congestions), and in the market the same is true. Therefore to consistently win we must:

> *Go with the flow,*
> *Ride the tide, and*
> *Bend with the trend.*

The market is the library that has all the answers. Our job is to learn to ask the right questions. What you learn is to "speed read" the market. After you have mastered these rather simple techniques (found in the following chapters), you should be able to look at any market on any time frame and know exactly where you should get in, which direction, and how to protect your position—all in 10 seconds or less. You should be able to do this because the market is a three-dimensional happening:

> *Time + Price + Your Psychology*

That is it, very simple when you really understand what is happening. And if you understand, you also know that the market never beats you, it merely gives you a chance to beat yourself. Beating the market means that you know something the market does not, and that is what is known as a fat chance.

You do not want objective systems because the market is not objective. The markets are an ever-changing social process. Being reasonable does not work either. Economists are reasonable and they are almost never right. Astroeconomics talks about aligning ourselves with the forces of nature; the Profitunity approach is about aligning ourselves with the forces of the market. Both the universe and humankind are a part of that force.

And learning more is rarely the answer. There is the old story about a very intelligent man who read all there was about philosophy and became a philosopher. Then he read all there was about mathematics and became a mathematician. Then he read all there was about swimming and he drowned. Trading the markets is much more like swimming than philosophy or mathematics. There are some things that you just have to do more than read about. And in the library of answers that we call the market, you are your own library card.

What we want to discover and know is the essence of the market. Think of it as water. Water can manifest itself in many ways—snow, ice, hail, sleet, fog, or steam—but the essence is still water. We want to deal with the essence of the market as it changes form.

The universal mind is like water. Individual minds and individual markets are the various forms of this universal intelligence. Instead of tapping into this universal intelligence, most of us become somnambulistic traders in that we are asleep while trading. The real trader in you is yet to be discovered and experienced. The question is, do you want a cookbook or a map? Do you want a recipe or do you want to understand the chemistry of cooking? The Profitunity approach is for traders who want a license to drive their own brain.

Let us make our assumptions clear. One of your authors traded for years as a fundamentalist and made no serious money. Then he spent two decades trading as a technician including those years when technical analysis was a dirty word spoken only by gypsies and other brainless traders. Now he has come to the conclusion that the market is behavioral. Basically it is nothing more or less than millions of traders just like you and he who go through all the gut-wrenching behavior that you and he do when putting on a trade.

Remember our description of the market in Chapter 1 where we used the Flintstones to illustrate what any market is about? We saw that what creates and moves a market is the value that we carry in our heads and actually has nothing to do with objective value or with reality except indirectly. There was simply an agreement on price and a disagreement on value.

> Remember, there is no reality
> there is only perception.

Therefore we all trade values, and the markets are run by our composite values, not by economics, governments, fundamentals, or technicals. And it is *not* a random walk; it only seems like a random walk when we look at the wrong indicators. When we see clearly what is really happening, the frustration of trading turns into the fascination of human behavior.

Most of you reading this are still in the process of becoming; otherwise you would not be reading this. You would be out playing golf, sailing, swimming, or watching sports. You are reading this to get better. Getting better is the worst game you can play because it puts you into a *have-do-be* world. For example, suppose you wanted to be a tap dancer. First you would have to *have* certain equipment such as clothes and special shoes with taps. Next you would have to *do* something like taking tap lessons or watching tapes. Then after years of practice you might *be* a tap dancer.

That is our most common approach to change of any sort. However, both the markets and the world work on a *be-do-have* approach. First, in your heart of hearts you choose (decide) to *be* a trader. Then you go out into the trading world and *do* the trading so that some day in the future (remember this is a left-hemisphere function) you will *have* all those things that you think you want today. We are like Alexander the Great in that we first must conquer the world before we can relax and just be happy. And just as Diogenes told Alexander, I am here to tell you that you will die first.

So what is the answer? The answer is to align yourself with reality and move from there.

The key to this situation is to understand the function of the left hemisphere, which is survival. As discussed in Chapter 3, the master program in this computer is survival of death. The second-level program is to make sure you have tenure, which means always having problems that need solving. Think about it, if your main job is to solve problems and suddenly there are no problems to solve, you start worrying about your job security. So what is the logical thing to do at this point? Create some new problems, and that is what every trader does. The most common trading behavior today is found in the person who can win, win, and win and then lose it all on some stupid decision. We all do it to one degree or another. A little closer look at this mechanism, which both (1) keeps the dance alive and (2) keeps us from being consistent winners, is in order.

HOW OUR BRAINS ARE WIRED

A Brain and A House: An Analogy

Think of a two-story house with a basement. The conscious mind (left hemisphere) lives on the first floor and can see out the windows. The conscious mind's view, however, is somewhat limited by the trees and shrubs outside the house. Its only way of communicating with the outside world is by telephone (we are arbitrarily ruling out such mechanisms as astral travel). Your telephone is connected with the core brain that lives in the basement. All of your incoming and outgoing information must go through this channel in the basement. The core, or the basement, also contains all the memory banks. The core has no decision-making power in the sense of answering the question "What?" Its primary purpose is to furnish memory information when requested by the conscious mind. For example, you walk out of this building and decide to go to town. The memory banks in the basement pull up appropriate information about going to town. You remember where the train station is and you remember how to call a cab and how much it cost the last time you took a cab into town. All of this type of information is stored in your memory banks in your core or basement of this structure.

What are the limits on the information that is pulled from the memory banks? Your former experiences in life, of course. You are limited in solving your problems by your past experience with the same type of problem.

Here is another subtle but vital key to this whole operation. When these problem-solving techniques are being stored, they are stored globally. Everything that happens is stored with impressions of all the senses. That means that everything that happened when you were going through this or a similar problem earlier is recorded in the memory files. If you were once in a fire and saved yourself by crawling on the floor and someone yells "Fire," you automatically will start to crawl on the floor. Why? Because it worked the last time. It must have worked because you are here. In other words, you survived and survival is the purpose of the conscious mind.

Application to Trading

Suppose you were in a tight spot in the market. We generally fail to see two things. First, we all have a tendency to trade our last mistake and, second, the conscious mind is really succeeding because once again we have survived and the conscious mind still has its job security and may just expand by considering going into other endeavors so that there can be some new problems to solve.

We do this every day in trading. We think when we lose that we need other techniques, more information, a new indicator, or an entirely new approach. What we really need is a new mind. All our trading problems could be solved by a change in the mind. The conscious mind is committed to the course of solving the problem by keeping the status quo. If you are a losing trader, you most likely are going to stay a losing trader until you change your mind. Now that you are convinced you need a new mind, let us see how our core works.

Your Core Brain (Mind)

The core brain is the storehouse of memory and is the connection with the paraconscious or the right hemisphere. The core is hundreds of thousands of times more powerful than the conscious mind in handling information. What you ate for lunch is now being taken care of by the core. Your rate of breathing, the chemical makeup of your blood, your thermostat, and all your memory banks are being handled at this moment by the core without any conscious thought on our part. The immediate question that should pop into your head at this point is how can we harness this enormous power to help us in our trading? Believe me there are ways, and when you do engage this mind, it will transform your trading on the spot. Not another day, not after three months of paper trading, but right then.

Remember that the functions of the conscious mind are language, judgment, time consciousness, and the need for struggle. None of these functions happen in the core, so to use the core we have to take these functions *out* of our trading decision process. An example of core functioning is happening right now as you look at this page. You are focusing your consciousness to a very narrow degree by reading these words. Your eye, meanwhile is taking in hundreds of thousands of times more information than you are consciously aware of. You are in the process of map making. You are abstracting from all the stimuli that impinge upon your retina and sorting out only a minute few by your conscious focusing. This process is necessary, otherwise we simply could not respond to any part of our environment.

Repeating for emphasis, the purpose of our core is to be a repository of information in the form of memory banks and the filter for incoming information through our five-plus senses. The core also has the responsibility for maintenance of our body and mind. It is a highly intelligent, extremely well-functioning apparatus that most traders make very little use of in trading. Its primary limitation is that it is not creative and cannot act inductively. It believes everything that is programmed into it. If you have very early programming about failing or accumulating a lot of money, it is going to affect your trading quite adversely. The other main function is to be a direct contact with the right hemisphere paraconscious part of your brain and mind.

Putting this into computer terminology, the conscious mind is the programmer and the software, the unconscious (core) is the actual central processing unit (CPU) and the paraconscious is the modem that connects this computer to every other computer in the universe.

Right Hemisphere—the Paraconscious (The Modem Connecting You to the Market and All the Other Traders)

The paraconscious part of the mind is the part that *knows without knowing how it knows*. We often call this part of the mind the source of intuition, and it is probably the most important part in causing either profit or loss in trading. When one is dominant in the paraconscious part, everything works out effortlessly. The key word here is "effortless." You can always tell from which part you are dominant because the market and the world are a mirror of your mind functioning. If you feel the world (market) is supporting you and that life itself is a support system just for you, you are operating from the paraconscious or the right hemisphere. If trading or life is a struggle, then you are coming from the idiot part of your mind, the conscious "drunken monkey" part. If life seems to be a roller coaster with some very good and some very bad times, you are operating from your core.

When you operate from all three parts of your mind, using them as they were biologically designed to be used, then you are at your happiest and operating with the most efficiency.

The right hemisphere is the source of your three big I's: insight, intuition, and inspiration. It has the creative function. It is the part that most closely resembles the behavior of the market.

PUTTING THESE IDEAS INTO A TRADING FRAMEWORK

Back to our story of Alexander the Great. He represents the left hemisphere. We learn to use this part of our mind in our present educational system. We are not taught how to use the other parts of our mind, not even in college or graduate school. The most important subjects in life are simply not addressed in our educational system today. You are reading this for the same reasons that Alexander the Great had to go to India. If you want to be really successful at trading, you must become more like Diogenes and learn to relax and study the river. And this is a job that you must do on yourself. No one in the entire world can do it for you. It is a process of distraction subtraction. We do not need to learn more and more of what is not so. We need to use more of what we already know but sometimes do not know that we know.

Alexander was in the process of *becoming*, and we need to be in the place of *being*. Let us look at what life is about for most people and make it as generic as possible. To look at our life and the results we get, we must also look at reality. Keeping this generic, we define reality as what is. In other words, the reality at this moment is that you are reading these words. By definition, everything else is nonreality or what is not. We can diagram this concept by calling our present reality Space 1 and everything else as Space 2.

Space 1 ———▶ Space 2

The primary reason we invent this S1 → S2 viewpoint is to find out who we are. And the only way to find out who we are is to realize *that "what was" (S1) before you invented (made up) S2 was totally okay*. Most of us build up some sort of resistance or unhappiness to Space 1 (the current reality is not okay) and that traps us in the left hemisphere mind, which is always looking for bigger problems—not a consistent winning strategy. This function is the basic operating procedure for Western culture.

Here is an important fact: Space 1, or reality, is not very motivating. The reason you are studying this approach is because you have a fantasy (Space 2) that if you spend the time and effort to read this, you may go back to trading and create a better record—that something might happen while you are studying this book that will make you a better trader. In fact, every time you place an order you do so because you have a fantasy that the market is going to move one way or the other. A market that does not move (in other words, it does not support our fantasy) will have no traders. We could define the market, then, as two people getting together with opposite fantasies—one thinks the market will go up and buys from another person who is equally convinced that the market is going down and thus is selling. The exception here is brokers. They are *selling* to you at the same time they are telling you the market is going up. Why? Because their primary job is to sell, which is more important to their company than your being profitable.

The Western Trader's Worldview

When subscribing to the Western worldview, we see ourselves primarily as a body, a few cubic feet of skin-enwrapped flesh, with a specialized chunk at the top end called a brain. Complex chemical interactions in this brain chunk somehow give rise to instincts, emotions, thoughts, and self-awareness.

We believe that anything inside the skin is "me," and anything outside is "not me." This not-me part includes everybody else and everything else, including other traders and the market itself.

The Other View—We Are All One

There is more than one way to think of ourselves in relationship to the rest of the universe and in particular to the market. For thousands of years, people of other ideological persuasions have maintained an alternate opinion, which we call the paraconscious or the right-hemisphere view. This other persuasion in modern times includes such diverse peoples as Orientals, Zen Buddhists, quantum physicists, theoretical mathematicians, professional musicians, artists, and others.

In this worldview, the universe and the market are, to paraphrase theoretical physicist Sir James Jeans, more like an "enormous mind" than an "enormous machine." And each of us is more like an integrated thought in a great big mind than like an isolated little cog functioning almost independently in a great big machine (as in the Western view). The important element in this view is that we are each much more than a tiny, isolated mind/body. We are instead a tiny but important part of a collective consciousness, which includes all that has ever existed. We have just momentarily lost sight of this fact when we, by chance, were born into this culture with its prevailing Western view.

Invisible Connections

A mushroom growing in your front yard appears to be an individual plant. Yet the thumb-size piece we call the mushroom is actually only a tiny, temporary part of a fungal network (known as a *mycelium*) that exists underground, year-round, and which may be as large as a football field. Those thousands of mushrooms spread around a meadow, seemingly separate, are all organs or parts of a single organism. That knowledge brings up an interesting question and a possible alternative worldview. The question is, does that tiny little mushroom believe that it is an independent operating organism or does it realize that it is just a part of a much much bigger organism? That thought brings up an even more provocative thought that, even though we think we are independent human beings, could we be a part of a much larger organism and could part of that organism be the market?

The Cosmic or Market Ocean

A wave in the ocean seems to have an individual identity of its own. It appears and exists for a while. You can watch it move rather steadily in a specific direction. You can listen to it, and if you are walking the beach, you can guess how far it will go. We call this wave a trend in the market. Then it disappears back into the ocean (we call the ocean a *bracketed market*) of which it is composed. Try thinking of yourself as a wave that just appeared from the ocean and will go back to where you came from. Then you begin to get a real feel and kinship with the market. Thus we are a recycled piece of the universal consciousness just the same as the market.

How Our Concept of God Keeps Us from Understanding the Markets

In the Western worldview, God tends to be seen as above and separate from the world. God is the creator of the universe, almost as a person might create and then run a business. In the alternative worldview, God is not separate from the world, but is the consciousness out of which everything is formed. So God is the entire universe, which includes you, me, Mother Teresa, and Al Capone. From the Western point of view, when someone says "I am God," it probably means that they are crazy, and they expect everyone else to bow down to them. From the alternate point of view, when someone says "I am God," it may mean that they understand that everybody and everything is God also, because God is the "stuff" out of which everything and everybody is made.

CAUSE AND EFFECT IN THE MARKET: THE ASSUMPTION ON WHICH ALL SYSTEMS ARE BUILT

In the Western world, each individual performs specific actions that have particular effects on the world. In the alternate worldview (chaos theory), everything you do is connected to and dependent on everything else. Think about your neighbor's cat. Its movements in the neighborhood, in the Western view, seem random, and completely independent of anything else. Yet, in the alternate worldview, the cat is drawn to one yard because of a honeysuckle bush that was planted by a family who left the Old Country after an earthquake in the 1920s. The next occupants bought a watchdog after thieves broke into a neighbor's house. In a very real way, the cat's movements today are connected to an earthquake in the past and the fear of a potential crime in the future. This same interconnected viewpoint applies to your trading in the market. Actually this viewpoint is probably the main reason why technicals do not work for technicians, and two people can trade the same technical approach whereby one will profit and the other will lose.

So we live and trade in two worlds. Just as a physicist knows that his kitchen table is composed largely of empty space between electrons, he still confidently uses it to support his lunch. You can live and trade in the world using a Westerner's view. At the same time you can begin to open your mind to the possibility that the alternate worldview has a validity of its own.

Steps to Understanding the Alternate Worldview

First of all, putting things in discrete steps is purely a Western worldview. The steps actually blend, melt, and overlap into each other. However, for most traders the first step is Clearing the mind.

> *It ain't what you don't know*
> *that gets you into trouble.*
> *It's what you know*
> *that ain't so.*

Our minds are just chock full of thoughts and, as we have pointed out previously, the conscious mind is nothing more than a series of thoughts, nothing else. As soon as a moment of boredom, restlessness, doubt, desire, or fear creeps in, your thoughts are off and running. At this very moment your mind is trying to wander off in all kinds of directions. (When will he get to something real that will make me money, I wonder how my football team is doing, I wonder. . . , oh I might learn something so I better pay some attention.) This very procedure (inconsistency) is why we make mostly wrong decisions in the market. Your conscious mind is like the proverbial "drunken monkey" that leaps aimlessly from branch to branch.

Our conscious mind is full of thoughts that plan for the future or analyze the past. We constantly make judgments about everything. (Right now you are most likely judging me and what I am saying—he is full of B.S., he may have something, this strikes a real chord in me, or whatever.) Some of these thoughts may last a lifetime as we spend years being obsessed by the same strong desire or beating ourselves endlessly with the same seemingly unmanageable fears.

ON WATCHING THE MIND

One of the best ways of working with thoughts is by noticing them, counting them, labeling them. After a while you will notice familiar patterns and sequences of thoughts that affect your trading performance. The key is to pay *less* attention to the *content* of each thought and more attention to the process by which they arise and pass away. As we become more adept at watching the mind, we are able to choose how to deal with each thought that arises. We can pay attention to the ones we choose and gently withdraw attention from those that we do not want to pay attention to. Eventually, we will be controlling our thoughts, rather than being controlled by them.

And our thoughts will control us, if we allow them. As Epictetus said more than 2,000 years ago, "Men are not worried by the things that happen, but by their thoughts about those things." No one can control the markets. We are at the mercy of the market movements, but we can control our mental reactions to whatever happens, if we just learn to understand how our thought process works.

When you go to a movie you have a choice. You can focus all your attention on the screen and watch just the *content* of the movie. When you watch this way, if sad events occur on the screen, you will feel sad. If happy events occur on the screen, you will feel happy. If the filmmakers are skillful, it will be a simple thing to manipulate our beliefs and feelings.

However, we can choose to focus our conscious (left hemisphere) attention more widely, on the entire *process* of "being at the movies." Then we will be aware not only of the action on the screen, but also the fact that it is just a movie. As we watch the film, we will also be conscious of many other aspects of the situation. Is the theater crowded or empty? Are the other patrons engrossed or bored? What special effects or techniques are used to produce the scene that is playing right now? What feelings does each scene or character evoke for us? Do we like or dislike those feelings? What are the goals for the director and how do we think it will end? If we were the director how would we have it end? We can relate to the market with the same choices about using our consciousness. Repeating an earlier statement, when the market is confusing or bringing up pictures of disaster we have three choices, easily remembered by the three C's. We can go *crazy*, *catatonic*, or *conscious*. In other words, we can . . .

Relate to Our Mind Rather Than React to Our Thoughts

It is really important to realize that everybody has a wild and crazy mind, filled with the same type of untamed, tangled thoughts that run through your own mind. Imagine thinking that you were the only person in the world that had to urinate every day. You would be acutely aware that you must continually perform this seemingly unnatural act, but you might never see anyone else do it. Einstein pee? Robert Redford take a leak? Impossible.

It is just as painful, if slightly less ridiculous, not to realize that everybody has the same kind of drunken-monkey mind as you do. Few people are open enough to talk to you about the fears, phobias, and fantasies in their minds.

Listening in the Now

One of the biggest problems caused by this drunken monkey is its constant attempt to flit to the future or languish in the past. Staying in the now is nearly impossible because there are a lot more problems in the past and future than in the now. When we think about the past or the future, we put the actual reality of living, the now, out of our mind.

When we are thinking of how much work we have to do while the market is going against us or thinking of what we will say next during a conversation with a friend, we cannot be present to listen and to respond meaningfully right now. Just as when we are busy filling our fork for the next bite while chewing the present mouthful, or pondering dessert during the entrée, we are simply not present to enjoy our eating right now. Same with trading.

I made my living in college playing in a Dixieland jazz band and we often improvised, especially playing the blues. Worrying about the note I had just played, or planning ahead for the next sequence that I wanted to play, impaired my ability to create improvisations freely. I had to learn to let go of a note as soon as I had played it, without thinking about the note to come. Then my music began to improve. The exact same thing happens to us while trading. We get so caught up in the next opportunity or the next trade that we miss the tune the market is playing right now.

So the first step in super-natural trading is to stop, look, and listen to what is going on in the process of your thought patterns without getting all involved in the content of those thoughts. Remember that the left–hemisphere conscious mind feels the compulsive need to keep you occupied all the time with problems to solve. Otherwise it thinks it might not survive and go out of business.

TECHNIQUES FOR TRADING

Relaxation

Relaxation is to the body what meditation is to the mind: a process of turning the attention inward while letting go of the physical tensions that normally inhabit our bodies. We can learn to use visualization to help us relax and relaxing to help us meditate and meditation to help us trade better.

Then we learn to investigate our behavior as an anthropologist studies a foreign culture. Alert curiosity replaces disdain or denial. Stepping away from a place of critical judgment, we can seek to find out what is true, even if it is not flattering. It is easy to love our finer points and nobler qualities, but the unflattering aspects of ourselves—our fears, greed, and stupidities—are exactly the parts that we most need to be compassionate toward.

In trading we often first feel frustrated, then threatened by our own lack of control of the market. Almost instantaneously the feelings of frustration and fear turn into anger, as our mind attempts to cover up these insecure and painful feelings with more aggressive ones. Acting on these aggressive feelings, we may then lash out at ourselves, our broker, or our loved ones, without even knowing why.

Importance of "Don't Know"

Most of us do not like a know-it-all, and yet we are often hesitant to admit that we do not know. The left-hemisphere conscious mind thinks that if we do not know what is going on, we better darn well find out. However there is a wonderful and profitable openness and satisfaction to the don't-know state. There is room for anything in the openness of "don't know"—it leaves us space for every possibility. "Don't know" is at the heart of Zen Buddhism's beginner's mind, the Jain's doctrine of maybe, and the Christian injunction to "be as a little child."

So much of what happens in the market is impossible to predict or control. Learning to cultivate a sense of "don't know," learning to let this uncertainty be okay, helps us to recognize and accept the painful truth—that we are often unable to control what happens in our lives, to ourselves, to our loved ones. Once we accept this fact, we no longer have to waste energy denying it.

Once we understand that we cannot move the market, trading becomes an inside job. While you may learn valuable things studying material like this, it all boils down to you, your chart, and your call to the broker. Basically, trading is the art of mental self-control. Trading is not anything occult, or esoteric, or outside of normal, daily life. You are trading every minute you are alive. You decided to read this instead of something else. You decide to stop and get a cup of coffee. All of these are trade-offs, and you know what? If you learn to handle your trading in the market properly, the rest of your life will improve also. We have found an extremely high correlation between traders who understand the market and their participation in it to happiness in other parts of their lives. It is interesting to note that the former professions of successful traders today are mostly psychology, engineering, and doctoring. Good trading calls for a high degree of mindfulness. It is the most powerful tool you can possess, a mental spotlight that can illuminate any action or thought.

There is more about the "Don't-know" attitude later in this chapter.

What to Do with Feelings of Doubt, Fear, and Resistance

Minds being what they are, at some point you are going to say, is this effort worth it? Whenever you find yourself asking this question, remember that you are not observing or watching the mind or the market. Take advantage of this opportunity and use these thoughts to focus on the fact that they are thoughts and not you. Just as smelly old manure can be turned into valuable fertilizer, you can use even thoughts of doubt, fear, and resistance to hone your observational skills, merely by watching them. *They then will become your teachers and not your tormentors.*

Again, think of the market as a dance rather than a race. In a race, the goal is to reach the end faster than anyone else, or faster than you have ever done it before. In a dance, the goal is to enjoy what you are doing *while* you are doing it. So give a lot less effort in worrying about taking full advantage of every opportunity and just do it. Even in a race, excessive concern over how you are doing (looking back over your shoulder too much) will actually decrease your performance.

We often tell our traders, "You have tried in every way to consciously solve your problems with no real effect. You have tried this and you have tried that and have failed utterly. Now it is time to close your eyes and get in touch with another part of your mind. The part that keeps you balanced in your chair, that pumps your heart and a thousand other things this part of your mind does for you every day of your life including dancing. Your conscious mind should decide where you want to go but without the unconscious mind's cooperation, you will not get there."

Actually Try This Example

Begin by thinking about a time in the market or elsewhere in your life when you disappointed yourself, a time when you did not feel good about things. Warning—this is not the time to deal with Heartbreak Hotel, Indiana Jones, or the career crash and burn. Push those to one side now. This time simply think about one of those times when a few things went wrong. Take a particular and real day from your past. As you think about this event, notice what images and sounds come to mind. Mentally, go through the entire experience, taking whatever time needed to really replay the experience in detail. What happened and when, and then what happened next, and so on. To make this exercise more real for you, here is some space for a few answers.

What happened? _____

_____

_____

When did it occur? _____

How did you feel then? _____

_____

_____

What happened next? _____

_____

_____

Once you have gone through the experience from beginning to end, pause for a few seconds. Now go to the beginning of this same experience, only as you watch and think about it this time, listen to "fun" music. Maybe circus, rock and roll, top 40s, pop, or Dixieland music—play it loud and clear and have it play all the way through as you rewatch that experience.

Now rewind that experience back to the beginning and this time play it without the music. And notice your response to it this time. Has it changed? For some, the incident becomes ludicrous or humorous. For most, the previous disappointed feelings have become neutralized or at least greatly reduced.

What happened? The code in your brain for that experience is now different. We have all had disappointments in the market that change or lose their negative effect over time. Why wait? We now have the technology to change them in an instant.

Now to enlarge on this experiment, think of another disappointment. If your experience of the last disappointment has not changed as much as you would like, use it. Quickly go through the movie of this instance and pick out one frame that symbolizes for you the whole experience. See if you are in the picture, like looking at a snapshot at an event you attended. If not, and that is usually the case, begin to zoom out so that you can see more and more of the scene until you can see yourself and watch it all as an observer. Then consider what kind of picture frame you might want to put around the picture—a modern steel frame or an old-fashioned gold one? When you have picked out a frame, add a museum light. You might even want to make it in a style of a famous painter as if it were a Renoir or a Gauguin or a famous photographer. Take a moment to clear your mind. Breathe.

Now think of that instant that used to disappoint you. Yes, the feelings have changed, and they will stay changed because you have used the way the mind codes information to make the change. Check it again now. Check it in an hour. Make a note in your appointment book to check it next week. You will find that it stays changed. Notice that you did not force the change. Again, it is like looking in the mirror and noticing that you have a frown on your face. It is more a letting go. Remember that trying hard is a left-hemisphere conscious function. You do not need to repeat an affirmation for weeks without results. You are beginning to learn the code. What you did is change how you are thinking using only the brain's coding principles. Obviously it was only a small incident but now it is changed, and you have a rapid technique for changing negative memories so they no longer bother you. (If you would like more information about the possibilities and specifically how you can use the newest and most productive techniques ever outlined in psychology, go to our Web site www.profitunity.com or contact our office.)

Think what this recoding can do for your perspective when you are trading and the market goes against you. You can quickly change that frustration-to-anger syndrome to one of a winning syndrome. Welcome to the world of super-natural trading.

A good exercise to do outside the market and one you can try today is a mind-clearing exercise. Watch the clouds in the sky, or the flames in a fire, or the foaming waves at the beach. Do not try to make sense of what you see. Do not try to look for patterns. Do not judge what you are seeing. Do nothing but see. Just see. As soon as you notice a thought creeping into your mind go back to just seeing.

Try the same exercise on a one-minute or a tick chart and experience if you can just see without imposing your judgment needs onto the market.

You can also practice listening the same way. No thought, no judging, no attempts to make sense. Just listening. If thoughts intrude, notice that you are thinking, and then focus your attention back on listening. Instrumental music is usually the easiest type of meditative listening to begin with, as any music that contains words tends to inspire thought when you hear the lyrics. When you get the hang of it, everywhere you go and everything that you do can become the basis for a mind-clearing meditation. This is a rather advanced stage of living in the now. This state is also the best place from which to trade.

FOCUSING ON THINKING

The Thought-Counting Meditation

This exercise will help you start withdrawing your attention from the *content* of your thoughts and begin looking more closely at the process of your thinking. First, set a timer for one minute. Now close your eyes, and begin to count your thoughts. As soon as a thought appears in your mind, count it, but do not get into the content of that thought. If you do, you may only end up with a count of one thought for your entire minute.

Compare this with a bird-watching competition. Competitive bird watchers go out with binoculars to try to identify as many species of birds as they can in one day. They do not study each bird. As soon as they see one, that is it—on to look for the next one. You, in a similar way, are a thought watcher for the next 60 seconds. If no thoughts come up, say to yourself "no thoughts," which is perfectly valid thought and should be counted, or else just relax and enjoy a moment of spontaneous mind clearing.

Keep a count of your thoughts, including thoughts such as "Gee, I haven't had many thoughts yet" or "uh-oh, was that thought number seven or eight?" If you get a thought that you just cannot let go of, try to remember what thought it is. That information will be useful later. Fear thoughts and desire thoughts seem to be the hardest to let go of, for most people. But remember, it is not the fear or the desire thought that is the problem—*it is the inability to control your reaction to that thought that may create a problem in trading.*

Although this exercise is not easy, there is no way to do it wrong. Its sole purpose is to learn to look, for this moment, at your thoughts as objects, like birds, or rocks, or other people. Nothing to take personally, just thoughts.

The next time you do this exercise make a brief mental or written list of the types or categories of thoughts commonly featured in the movie of your mind. Some of mine are planning thoughts, in which I try to decide specifically what to do. Desire thoughts include wishes for anything from sex to profitable trades to world peace. Fear thoughts include any type of worry: money, work, retirement, you name it. Happy, thankful, or appreciative thoughts are the sun on my face, the smell of potatoes cooking. Judging thoughts are those in which I approve or more likely criticize anything or anyone. Righteous thoughts are those in which I am right and someone else is wrong. Angry thoughts could be those directed to myself, in which case I consider them as falling into the specialized subcategory of self-hating thoughts, or at anybody else.

Now sit comfortably and observe each thought as it swims into awareness. Observe it long enough to decide which one of your categories it fits into, then go on to look for the next. If no thoughts seem to be coming forth, then just relax and enjoy a few seconds of effortless mind clearing. If a thought does not fit any of your other categories, then make up a new one. After this experience, see if you can tell which thoughts occurred most often. Which thoughts were easy to let go of? Which ones were hard to let go of?

Feeling Your Thoughts

Just as we meditated on the feeling of standing and walking, we can also meditate on the feelings of thoughts. Begin with a moment of your favorite meditation, just relax and clear your mind a bit. Then call on one of your "grabby" thoughts, perhaps a fear, or a desire, or an anger into your mind. Observe the thought and ask yourself: "What does anger (or whatever) feel like?" Is it a hot feeling or a cool feeling? Does my body feel tighter or looser? Is there an enjoyable element to this feeling, or is it only painful?"

Just watch the thought—step back and turn it around in your mind like an object that you are investigating. Does looking at your thoughts in this way change your reaction to the thought? In what way? If you find yourself getting caught up in the content of the thought, watch the caught-up-ness. How does it feel to be caught up in a thought like that?

Living in the Now

We traders (as well as all others) tend to live most of the time in the past or the future. Only rarely is our attention focused on what is happening in the right now. Are you living in the right now? You think so? Then, quick, without thinking about it—are you inhaling or exhaling? You probably had to refocus your attention on the breath before you could answer that question. Where had your attention been?

Thoughts about what we just did or did not do and thoughts about what we should or should not do continually clutter our minds. How often we use past thoughts in a self-hating way. "I should have done differently." "I should have taken that Fractal." "I sure messed this one up." How often we use future thought to upset ourselves, such as "What if that happens?" or "It probably won't be profitable."

Virtually all of our thoughts are either based in the past or future, and absolutely all of our fears and desires come from the past or anticipation of the future. Desires are usually remembrances of past pleasures that we plan and hope to recreate in the future. Fears are usually memories of past pain that we plan and hope to avoid in the future.

Living in the now exercises such as thought counting or slow walking just does not leave much time to think of the past or future.

The Zen of "Don't Know"

The heart of Zen is the koan, a question with no rational answer, such as why does ice cream have no bones? Observe your mind as you focus on such a question. Does it strive for an answer or does it reject it as ridiculous? A feeling of "don't know" is generally uncomfortable for most Westerners. But just let it be okay to "don't know." Look for that open spacious feeling of the don't-know mind. The don't-know mind has room for absolutely anything and everything.

Choose a situation in your trading whose outcome cannot be predicted. Focus your attention on the question, while trying to maintain a sense of "don't know" in your mind. Notice the attempts to make rational predictions. Is it in a fifth wave? Is there a conjunction of Jupiter and Mars? Watch your mind as it vacillates between answer seeking and "don't know." Try incorporating more of "don't know" into your daily life. Will I catch that plane? Don't know. Will the bus be on time? Don't know. Will the bonds go up tomorrow? Don't know.

One last question. Will you use these techniques in your trading? Don't know? That's okay too.

Remember that how we respond to whatever happens is more important, in the long run, than what happens. This approach teaches us that *how* we respond to our thoughts is more important than the thoughts themselves. We are learning to watch the process of the mind, instead of getting caught up in the content of each thought that passes through. And we know that the process of learning to deal skillfully with whatever occurs is far more important than attempting to control the outcome or content of each particular incident in our lives.

If we practice living in the now, with awareness of and compassion for our daily fears and desires, we can deal powerfully and effectively with whatever happens in our lives. Painful thoughts, even unpleasant events, can be used to remind us of the meditative work that is our most real and important job on this Earth. In this way we can turn all that happens, painful or pleasant, into grist for our meditative mill. We will be building our bridges from the very boulders that seem to block our path.

All of this ranting and these exercises may seem a long way from "how to make profits in the markets this week," but if I (B. W.) have learned any one thing in almost a half-century of actively and successfully trading the markets, this is the key: *Your thoughts are your life!*

STOP! PLEASE

Stopping is the most exciting activity in the universe. Somewhere on your path you will stop. Someone once said that death is God's way of saying "Slow down." An old Sioux wise man said, "Man is the only animal that thinks he thinks." What do you think thinks? Thinking is a brain (body organ) process. It is analogous to digestion, the process of the intestines. The brain is an organ of the body. We "watch" the brain operate and listen internally to the brain's thoughts. We are not the body, the brain, or our thoughts.

In trading, we tend to keep learning more and more about what is not going on and that keeps us from seeing what is really happening. Most market education simply removes us from our natural ability to know.

You can *not think*. You can understand that it is not you that is thinking, but it is you that is observing your thinking. You can disassociate your
real self from the thinking principles by careful observation. You can control the operation of your body's brain, the digestive system for your mental food. In order to experience the real you, it is necessary not to think
about anything. The real self does not think, it knows.

> The only difference between a Buddha and a non-Buddha is that the
> non-Budda does not know he is a Buddha.
> —Guatama Buddha, circa 600 B.C.

I (B. W.) was once asked at the end of a presentation to hundreds of active traders in Chicago, "If you had to sum up everything you have learned
in your decades of trading in one statement, what would that be?" At that
moment I was stumped to pick out just one sentence and I have thought
about that question many times during the years, but now I think I have it.
Here is the pearl of the greatest advice I could possibly share with you:

With the wand of science,
We explain, decide, and discuss.
But only in the silence
Will the market speak to us.

In meditation, the gross vibrations of the left-hemisphere conscious
mind are stilled so that the far finer perceptions of the right-hemisphere
paraconscious mind become apparent. At one level we have only one sense
and that is the sense of touch. Sound waves touch our ear parts. The mol-
ecules making up odors touch receptors in our nasal apparatus, light
touches the eye, and so on. To use these sense outlets, our attention is focused in these organs. The "attention" is all we are. The mechanism recording the impressions of the attention is not the self. Therein is the bind.

In becoming still, we exist in our pure state. Primitive humans had less
information and much less to think about—fewer distracting ideas to keep
them from mental peace and quiet. The sophisticated trader with a head full
of all sorts of ideas, could have a harder time finding stillness than his un-
complicated brothers and sisters.

THE MIND MISTAKE

We do not have any such thing as a mind anywhere in our bodies. Point to
your mind. It cannot be fingered, operated on, or gone out of. And there is

no such thing as giving someone a piece of something you do not have. Just inside the walls of our skull is an organ, the brain. As already pointed out, there are three basic parts of this brain organ: left, right, and middle. We must operate from a centering point to be most effective in the markets.

The way most of us trade is analogous to having a U.S. highway map and planning a trip to California from Florida by using every route on the map. A more direct route to silence, stillness, and cessation of thought is available in your own school of common sense. Just stop. If you are always thinking about it, you will never stop to experience what it actually is. Becoming still is the greatest accomplishment that you can ever achieve: to become what we already are. It is a lot easier to become more of yourself when you actually know what your real self is.

By stilling the body and disconnecting from our incessant thoughts through meditation, we contact our true self in the finer vibrational fields of what might be termed the "spirit side of life." By returning to our inner self frequently, the very best that is in us begins pervading every department of our life. We begin the process of being as good as we really are.

All of life's experiences, no matter how seemingly distorted, are directing you to stillness. There comes the time when nothing outside will answer your question. Genuine progress in your trading will begin once you have experienced your inner nature. This experiencing your inner nature should obviously take precedence over everything.

There is, quite factually, what could be called another world that interpenetrates ours. It is a phenomenal world of finer forces. We are all in it; some are of it. The highest levels of consciousness are available at all times, everywhere. Only by stopping can we be there now, right now!

No amount of thinking can accomplish what a small amount of not *thinking can.* Nothing you can do will make you more of what you can become than by seriously doing nothing. It is a topsy-turvy truth; we get more by doing less and less.

RESONANCE

If you place two guitars tuned to the same frequencies across the room from each other and you pluck one of them, if the other guitar is quiet, the same string on that one will start vibrating. The same is true with the market. If your mind is quiet and receptive (it cannot be one without the other), you can sense the vibration of the market real time and hear and resonate with the tune the market is currently playing. However, as soon as you start thinking and evaluating (a left-hemisphere function), it goes out of tune and you are singing the wrong song. That is why the markets are so confusing to most people. The secret is being quiet, passive, and receptive without the mind's judgmental interpretation of the present.

A trader's mind operates constantly from early morning until the exhausted trader collapses in bed at night. This rut of an energy drain can go on unabated for years, like a constantly fast-idling car engine that sometimes races but never has the key turned off. The vast majority of thinking is detrimental to personal peace and profits in the market. Thoughts of the past are a waste. Most thoughts of the future are the same. Many traders spend countless hours rethinking past actions and thus contaminate themselves in the present, usually with negative or guilt-filled vibrations. Other traders cannot see what is happening in present tense (all they really have) because they are constantly thinking into the future when "we will trade well."

If you are at inner odds, tired of struggling with the market, get back together with your *self*. This will create resonance between your brains and the markets. Make it a daily habit and you will trade better. Remind yourself that you are in a big show and the center ring is inside yourself. The market is you. *Just be and you will see.*

What we have been discussing in this section is on the periphery of a subject for which our language has no adequate words.

> We do not need more *ex-perience* in trading,
> we need more *in-sperience*. When you are inside,
> you can hear the heart of the market beating.

 ## SUMMARY

In this chapter we examined how we use various parts of our minds and how some parts are much more compatible to profitable trading in the market than others.

We have spent more pages in this chapter than any other because of the importance of the concepts contained here. Creating resonance between your intellect and your intuition is key to continuing profits. This is somewhat difficult at times because we have no previous training in how to acquire this inter-brain resonance. In our journey through the woods we found that casual imaginations can point to deeper causes of our behavior. While deep psychotherapy is not indicated, learning more about how each of our brains work and interconnect with other parts of our brain/body continuum will transform our profitability. While it is not a common word found in trading manuals we are approaching that misty concept we label spirituality. In the context we are exploring there is no direct connection between spirituality and religion.

If you have read and understood the chapters so far, you are now ready to get on with it and learn exactly how we trade in all markets. In Chapter 7 we discuss the five universal levels in going from a novice to an expert in any field. Using this material, we can locate precisely where we are on the road to excellence in trading and investing. Chapters 8 through 11 are then devoted to recognizing what is really happening in the markets and how to be consistently profitable in your trading. We hope you now agree with us that the cornerstone to this profitability is how you see the markets and how you engage your various minds.

CHAPTER 7

Navigating the Markets

The Need for Good Maps

*The biggest risk you will ever take
Is not betting on yourself.*

GOAL

To study the universal steps from novice to expert and apply them to becoming a successful trade/vestor.

So far, we have discussed the present condition of most traders, looked at how really simple the market is, examined chaos as a more effective trading paradigm, and delved into the two different structures of *structure*. In this chapter, we construct an interactive map that will guide us through the rest of this book. We want explicit directions and feedback that will tell us where we have been, where we are now as trade/vestors, and what must happen for us to improve our trading ability.

THE STAIRWAY TO PROFITS

One of the problems of learning to trade is that there is no regular progression that takes a beginning trader from ignorance to knowledge or from losing to consistent winning. The programs currently available either teach the vocabulary of trading or simply provide a series of favorite indicators. Neither of these approaches produces good consistent winners.

There is, however, a universal five-step progression from first interest or novice to becoming an expert in any field of endeavor. This progression was examined by two brothers, Hubert L. and Stuart E. Dreyfuss (1986), in a book about computers, and by James F. Dalton, Eric T. Jones, and Robert B. Dalton (1990), in a book about the markets. This progression will provide us with a framework for creating our map as we move from one level to another and for studying the historical and scientific differences at each level.

Imagine that you have just attended a piano concert featuring Mozart sonatas. During and after the concert, you have become so uplifted and inspired that you decide, "Whatever it takes, I am going to learn to play the piano. No matter my background, lack of musical talent, age, or whatever—I am going to play the piano!" To parallel this scenario, assume that you have been persuaded—by potential profits, challenge, enjoyment, lifestyle, and so on—that you are going to learn the Profitunity approach to trading commodities and stocks.

For your music goal, you would most likely buy or rent a piano, buy an instruction manual, and hire a teacher. For your trading goal, you would most likely buy or lease some quote equipment and begin tuning in to CNBC and other market-oriented stations. You might subscribe to some newsletter, and hire "teachers" in the form of workshops, books, and/or tutorials. In each case, at this level, you are a *novice*.

You are exposed to all sorts of material that will create either good (effective) or bad (losing) habits and concepts. You are very excited and are living on what psychology calls "germination" energy. You feel as though you are entering a new romance. You have an abundance of energy and almost every thought is, "Let's get on with it."

In music, you are learning the basics—the value of a whole note, a half note, a rest, and so on. You learn where middle C is and the correct fingering for playing a scale on the keyboard. You are dealing with individual notes and octaves as opposed to tunes and compositions. In the Profitunity approach, you are learning to trade so that you do not lose money while gaining experience in the markets. Let us examine this Level One or novice level.

LEVEL ONE: THE NOVICE

The objectives in music at the novice level are: to learn the rudiments of music notation and to begin to understand the vocabulary and abbreviations on the sheet music. In science, the characteristics of this level are numbers. In music, they are the written notes. In computers, they are the binary digits. In physiology, the key is the left hemisphere of the human brain.

In history, it is the Middle Ages. In math, it is the level of arithmetic. The assumptions are Aristotelian in that everything is discrete and you can count and/or classify everything in the universe.

Trading is no different. At Level One of trading, we are learning the basics of the market: vocabulary, how to put on a trade, what margin requirements mean, and so on. We begin to see the enormous amount of information contained in the tools at this level. These tools are the price bar or OHLC (open, high, low, and close) and volume. We are looking at the market on a bar-by-bar process. We are focusing on only two bars, the present bar and the one immediately preceding it. Our primary interest is to understand the evolving behavior of the market rather than to attempt to fit some pattern or template from the past onto the current market behavior.

This understanding is the first step on the way to becoming an expert trader. As a novice, you learn how to determine who is running the show and what is currently being done. You begin to identify trends of various lengths. Most novice traders search for a mechanical system that will make them rich and successful if they can just put the pieces of the market puzzle together. Forget this idea; it will not happen. If you are trading from this perspective, you are doomed as soon as your luck runs out. There simply are no good mechanical maps to follow at this level. In our opinion, there never has been a consistently successful mechanical system. There is not now and there most likely never will be, even with artificial intelligence, analog processors, genetic algorithms, orthogonal regression, and neural networks. As you understand how the market really works (remember the Flintstones), you will understand that the market is designed to destroy any successful mechanical system. *All mechanical systems die!* They are linear tools and cannot accurately or adequately describe a nonlinear market. If there *were* a consistently successful mechanical system, it would not be worth $3,000 but could be sold in hours for $30 million. Note that we are talking about a mechanical system that will work consistently and profitably over time.

The maps used by novice traders are generally price comparisons, which all fall short of being adequate because price is an effect and not a cause. They are comparing effect with effect. This technique generally does not lead to profitable trading. Every now and then, it will send out a good signal, but using these tools does not produce consistent profits. I have laid down this challenge around the world: For every instance where some typical trading signals—divergence, above or below 80 percent, and so on—produced a profit, I can show you five signals of the same type that would have produced losses, including stochastics, RSI, momentum, channels, and some other old reliables.

The function of the novice level is to enable you to trade in the market and not lose money while you gain experience. In the typical scenario, most novices, whether in music, romance, or trading, tend to generate an enormous amount of germination energy. What follows this elation is usually depression.

"I didn't realize that, to really play the piano well, I need to spend four hours practicing each day for years."

"That girl (boy) didn't look quite so good after I learned more about her (his) personality."

"Trading is really a much trickier business than I anticipated. Each time I take a step forward, that seems to be followed by a step backward."

At this point, most novice traders leave trading. Past statistics indicate that the majority of new traders last just over 3 months in the market. For those souls who can weather this depression by continuing to practice music or to learn more about trading, there are great rewards in store.

As you practice this microscopic study (we only look at two adjacent bars) of market behavior, you begin to get insights into how the market really works. You begin to realize that it is a product of nature and not of economics, fundamentals, or technicals. Just as skill in bicycle riding comes only after enough falls to teach you the internal principles of balance, so the novice level teaches you about the balance of the markets. This knowledge then opens the doors of opportunity to enter the next level of understanding, perception, and performance.

LEVEL TWO: THE ADVANCED BEGINNER

At Level Two, we expand our horizons timewise to include more bars than we examined at Level One. We are now moving from novice to advanced beginner. The advanced beginner in music has learned the basic notes and chords, has started to put together music that is pleasing to both the player and listeners, and is enjoying the newly acquired skills. Let us look at some of the differences between Level One and Level Two.

Whereas Level One in math is arithmetic and numbers, Level Two is *space* (geometry). In music at Level One we are concerned with tones; at Level Two, we become concerned with tunes. In computers, Level Two is the analog computer. In history, it is the Renaissance. It is looking at the shadows as well as the leaves. It is moving from one dimension to a higher dimension. Information is available that is not obvious at Level One. In the market, some examples of Level Two maps are the Fractal and the Elliott wave. The time frame has now changed from comparing two adjacent price bars to a more panoramic view of 140 bars or more.

At this point, all traders reach a crucial impasse. Is the motivation for trading strong enough to overcome the temporary frustrations of the market's learning experiences? Just as gravity provides frustrations that help you learn about balance on a bicycle, so will market losses let you learn more about yourself and the balance points of the markets.

Fractals and the Elliott wave are tools that reveal the underlying structure of the market. The Elliott wave provides a directory to the up-and-down moves of the market. The Profitunity approach to analyzing the Elliott wave takes out 90 percent of the ambiguity and gives alternative strategies for dealing with the other 10 percent.

Trading is much like the beginning of a new manufacturing endeavor. The first thing you want is to produce a quality product, or you will face returns from dissatisfied customers. The time to increase production is only after you have a quality product. In the markets, a quality product is being able to make profits consistently on a one-contract or small number of shares basis. If you are not doing this, you either do not have a quality approach to trading or you are not implementing the technique properly.

The advanced beginner has become a quality producer of profits. The next move is to the competent level, where you begin trading on a multiple-contract or larger number of shares basis, and the skills learned at Levels One and Two become automatic. A trader's focus at this point is on maximization of the ROI as opposed to profit per contract. Professionally, at this level, a trader is in the top 3 percent of the profession. We are talking *real* money.

LEVEL THREE: THE COMPETENT TRADER

At Level Three, a piano student can play *exactly* what is written on the sheet music. Passages that should be loud are played loud; up-tempo parts are played fast. Being competent means following the directions precisely as indicated on the sheet music. In trading, being competent means increasing your total ROI. You are reading the market script accurately. When the market says buy, you buy; when it says sell, you sell; and when it says stay out, you stay out. You are bringing home the bacon competently and consistently. You are not getting in the way of your profit-producing tools.

Level Three opens up another type of universe. In history, it is characterized by the Industrial Revolution, when new opportunities and benefits opened up because of new and different understandings about production and economics. In math, this level is characterized by algebra, which allows us to look for and solve problems with unknown quantities. It permits the finding of x, the unknown factor. It is the early beginnings of understanding chaos. Level Three begins to monitor what most people call "causes" rather than just effects.

The tools of the market at this level include Profitunity techniques, which allow maximum flexibility and profit from monitoring the underlying and unseen structure of the market. It allows one to get into the rhythm and to start dancing to the tune the market is currently playing. It also allows one to know whether an analysis is wrong or out of touch with the market. If wrong, the appropriate strategy is to stop and reverse. If out of touch, the best strategy is to get out.

The purpose of the Profitunity Trading is to squeeze the maximum amount of profits for the specified move, letting the market (rather than some arbitrary system) determine the most appropriate strategy. Profitunity Trading provides the most profit/least risk formula for asset allocation.

At this level, you no longer spend hours each day analyzing the market. Most traders spend so much time in analysis they miss most of the opportunities the market offers daily.

Once you reach Level Three, you are a self-sufficient professional trader. You are acquainted with the always underlying and usually unseen structure of the markets. You no longer need or desire outside opinions. You do not need to read the *Wall Street Journal*, listen to market-centered TV, subscribe to newsletters, or waste money on hotlines. However, this is only half the equation. The other half is the trader as a person.

There are thousands and maybe hundreds of thousands of musicians who are much more competent than Frank Sinatra, yet more of his records have been sold than anyone else's on earth. In live concerts, he was often flat, and his timing was his own doing. But the difference that sells records and made him profits is that he did *not* sing a song exactly the way it was written. He added and communicated *feeling*. The largest leap in the entire five-step progression from novice to expert is between Level Three and Level Four. At Level Four, you have an educated intuition or a gut feeling about the market that is usually very accurate. You are manipulating your own structure to correspond with the market's structure. At Level Four, winning becomes the path of least resistance.

LEVEL FOUR: THE PROFICIENT TRADER

At Level Four, a musician's prime objective is to able to communicate feelings through the language of music. Feelings are translated, through a pianist's fingers, to the piano keys, which make sound waves that move listeners' emotions. In trading, you are trading your belief systems (aligning your underlying structure with that of the market), and your enjoyment comes not only from making profits but also from the satisfaction of feeling your trading is in sync with the market.

Level Four is a quantum leap beyond the three lower levels. In history, it is the electronic revolution that allows us to bring in much more powerful data processors than ever before available to humans. Stability we formerly counted on changes at an ever-increasing rate. My computer for writing this book has more manipulating power than everything available in the entire world a century ago. Think about this: From this single keyboard, I have more computing power than the entire world had only one hundred years ago. To give you an idea of what is happening at an ever-increasing rate, think back to 1975. At that time, a Rolls Royce sedan cost $65,000. Computing power at that time was much more expensive than it is now. If Rolls Royce had reduced the ticket price of a sedan as much as the price of computing power that has been reduced, the same model Rolls purchased new today would cost 30 cents. We now have the power, at very little expense, to look at infinitely large masses of data and infinitely small particles and divisions. This ability puts power into the budget of every trader. The complexity of chaos, which has been anathema to progress, is now becoming available everywhere. In math, this level is calculus, which allows us to differentiate to microinfinity on the one hand and to integrate to macroinfinity on the other.

Traders also make a quantum leap to this level. They begin to see that they are a vital part of this whole process, and they bring to the equation all of their background, philosophy, and belief systems. At this level, traders make use of the fact that no one trades the markets, they trade their own individual belief systems. Just as the computer revolution has allowed us to see inside the masses of data and to make sense of them, the new science of chaos is allowing us to look into our behavior with a focus not available to the Aristotelian, Euclidean, Newtonian, and classical physics/psychology approaches.

At this level, we begin to understand and work with our own personal body type and our individual brain structure. The Profitunity Trading Group has developed this understanding to a new level of precision. Our objective is to align our own persona underlying structure with the underlying structure of the market. Let me restate that when that happens, winning becomes the path of least resistance.

LEVEL FIVE: THE EXPERT TRADER

Level Five is the beckoning point that invites us into realms of understanding we have only dreamed of until now. At Level Five, we see that basically everything is information, and our purpose in dealing with this information is to *find out who we are.* At this level, trading truly becomes a game in the largest and best sense of that word; everything is important and everything is a teacher. We understand ourselves and the market, and that understanding gives us more control over both.

At Level Five, we flow deeply into the realm of *chaos.* In sports, this realm is sometimes called the "zone." Chaos does not mean disorder; rather, it is a higher form of order that becomes all-inclusive. There is no randomness. What we call random at Levels One through Three is really a catchall for our lack of insight and understanding.

At Level Five, trading is a low-stress way of living. You feel as though you are floating down a river that is providing you with any desire you name. Your nice fantasy has become completely achievable by following the Profitunity approach.

 SUMMARY

In this chapter, we looked at the five steps that will take you from being a novice trader to being an expert, and at the parameters that indicate the level where you are currently trading. We have also listed the objectives and tools that are appropriate at each level. For quick reference, they are:

Level	Objective
1. Novice	To not lose money while gaining experience
2. Advanced Beginner	To make money consistently on a small account
3. Competent	To maximize the total ROI
4. Proficient	To trade your own belief systems
5. Expert	To trade your states of mind

Congratulations for hanging in. We waded through some very interesting and deep psychological principles that we believe are necessary for you to know to make a profitable career in trading and investing. Now you are ready to try this new philosophy in the actual markets. The question is just how can we translate this learning into the charts representing the market itself. Now the fun really begins, and we will walk you through exactly what has produced profits in our personal accounts. The market is guaranteed to provide you with the opportunities and all we have to do is to mark those opportunities and bring home the profits. Welcome to the best trading years of your life.

CHAPTER 8

The Mighty Alligator

Our Compass and Odds Maker

*In this early part of the twenty-first century,
we have a choice to either be a part
of the last generation of traders and investors
using linear (ineffective) techniques,
or the first generation using effective
nonlinear (chaotic) techniques.*

GOAL

To learn how to construct a compass to guide our market journey into profit territory.

UNDERSTANDING NEW INCOMING INFORMATION (CHAOS)

One of the keys to profitable trading is to understand that new incoming information is what moves the markets. If there is no *new incoming information* (other words for chaos), the market is dead and there would be no significant movement of price in either direction. The market would be a straight horizontal line. The problem is that no one can examine and evaluate all the new incoming information as pertains to its ability to move price up or down. Our trading group has completed more than 20 years of intensive research into applying the new science of chaos (along with quantum physics, holography, cybernetics, nonlinear dynamics, information theory, and Fractal geometry) to the world of stock and commodity trading.

After processing literally millions of iterations, our research resulted in a simple visual representation that we call "the Alligator." The Alligator serves as a compass to keep us trading in the appropriate direction regardless of which way the immediate price is moving.

The Alligator is a personification of this process and influences every signal in our trading arsenal. This book is the third that we have written on this subject as new and more profitable tools have come to the surface. Our first book, *Trading Chaos*, published in 1995 (Wiley) is still valid and profitable in the market. Our second book, *New Trading Dimensions* (Wiley, 1998), enlarged on the first book and included newly discovered concepts to increase the profitability of our techniques. Now we invite you to witness and use our latest, most efficient and profitable strategies. Everything written and used in the previous books is still profitable and now it becomes even easier to be a consistent winner in all the various markets.

The question arises, how can these techniques work in all markets and in all time frames. The answer is that our trading and investing techniques are based on human nature rather than economic data. The markets are quite different now than when our earlier books were published, but the earlier techniques still work because human nature changes extremely slowly, if at all.

We will demonstrate both the setup and how to use this valuable tool while trading. This chapter describes the Alligator, what it does, how to construct it, and how it influences our entries and exits.

A TRADER'S BIGGEST PROBLEM

Trading is likely the most exciting way to make a living or accumulate a fortune. You are your own boss and your own worst enemy. You alone must deal with the frustration of your own choices. If you lose, there is no one else to blame. You made the losing decision, even if that decision was to let someone else make your decisions or to follow someone else's approach. However, if you win, you do not have to say thank you to anyone. You are not obliged to anyone except yourself. There is no political agenda nor anyone to whom you must cater. The term *politically correct* does not need to be in your vocabulary.

But here is the problem. Most of the time, the market goes nowhere. Only 15 to 30 percent of the time does the market trend, and traders who are not on the floor make nearly all of their profits by being in a trending market. The Alligator is, without question, the best indicator of when a trend begins and how long it will endure.

The Alligator is:

- An integrated approach to monitoring the market's momentum
- A simple indicator to trade only with the current trend
- A protection device to not lose money during a nontrending market
- An advanced indicator to signal the end of a current trend.

Here is our problem: We do not want to spend our time and resources entering and exiting a market that is going nowhere. If the market is going nowhere, then opportunity is *no-where*. We want to change that statement to opportunity is "now-here." Our technique for moving that hyphen over one letter is the Alligator.

WHAT IS THE ALLIGATOR?

Basically, the Alligator is a combination of Balance Lines using Fractal geometry and nonlinear dynamics. (See Figure 8.1; because this book does not include color, you may want to visit to our Web site to see how it looks

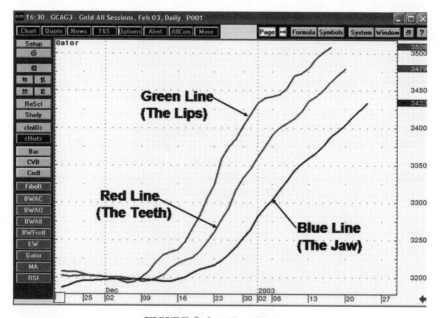

FIGURE 8.1 The Alligator.

in color.) The Blue Line that we call the Alligator's jaw on Figure 8.1 is the Balance Line for whatever time frame is on the chart. The (blue) Balance Line is where the market would be if there were no new incoming information (chaos). The distance between this line and the current price is an indication of how the traders interpret this new incoming information.

The Red Line is the Balance Line for one significant time frame lower. Significant in this case is approximately one-fifth of the time frame on the chart. So, roughly, if the time frame on the current chart is a daily and refers to the Blue Line, the Red Line would approximate an hourly chart. Remember that these lines are simulations that were discovered and created by a mainframe computer with a confidence level of more than 99.5 percent. This confidence level means that you may miss not more than 1 out of 200 trades that would be created by a mainframe using nonlinear feedback calculus.

The Green Line is the balance line for still another significant time frame lower. Again, it would be approximately one-fifth of the time frame of the Red Line. So if the chart we are examining is a daily, the Red Line would approximate the hourly chart and the Green Line would approximate a 5 to 10 minute chart.

Putting this another way, as seen on Figure 8.1, the Blue Line is where the market would be on the daily chart, the Red Line is where the market would be on an approximately a one hour chart, and the Green Line is where the market would be on an approximately 5- to 10-minute chart. Remember these time values are approximate and not connected to clock time. All lines are drawn using current price sequences. You do not need three different time charts.

New incoming information would first affect the Green Line, followed by the Red Line and finally by the Blue Line. To personify the Alligator a bit more, we refer to these lines as follows: The Blue Line represents the Alligator's jaw, the Red Line represents the Alligator's teeth, and the Green Line represents the Alligator's lips. As you become more familiar with this notation, the Alligator seems to take on a life of its own. The Alligator then becomes an excellent guide as to when to get into a market and when to wait for it to get hungry, which happens when it starts to open its mouth. Remember, the purposes of the Alligator are to

- Provide an integrated approach to monitoring the market's momentum on three different time frames in one chart.
- Provide a simple indicator to know when a trend starts and stops.
- Create a protection device so as to not lose money during a bracketed, range-bound market.
- Provide an advanced indicator to signal the end of a trend.

ALLIGATOR ANATOMY 101

Once more, the Blue Line is where the price would be (in the current time frame of the chart) if there were no new incoming information. When significant new information appears to the market participants, the price bars will move away from the Blue Line. As stated previously, the Green Line will move first, followed by the Red Line. Last, the Blue Line will move. It obviously takes more information to move the Blue Line than either the Red or Green Line.

At any given time, probably not more than 1 percent of all the outstanding shares in stocks and contracts in futures are actively trading. The other roughly 99 percent of share and contract holders are not out there buying and selling. Most shares and contracts are being held away from the trading action.

During these periods the market is stuck in a small trading range. The same small pool of shares and contracts are trading back and forth among the active short-term and or professional traders. It is just a tiny fraction of the outstanding shares and contracts flipping back and forth, often for tiny gains and losses. In this kind of market, the three balance lines will intertwine, indicating that you basically want to stay out, because there is no new incoming information that will significantly move the markets. The markets easily achieve balance with this kind of thin trading, and that is why we see moves squashed at the nearest support and resistance points.

It takes fresh information, or a bigger catalyst, to bring in shares held by those who trade less frequently. The information has to be new and ideally unexpected to get more people in the fray and to expand the number of shares or contracts traded. It is this fresh new information that brings in a bigger supply of shares and contracts that creates the streaky trend movements in the markets as either supply or demand takes control.

This information helps to explain why thin trading can be particularly tough. The markets can be buffeted around more easily by smaller events and news flow and can stop and reverse—or achieve balance—before most people realize what is happening. They therefore tend to miss out on the best and most profitable trends.

The mighty Alligator will take care of us in either of the foregoing scenarios. The Green Line will be the first indicator that significant amounts of shares or contracts are coming into the markets and are biased in one direction.

The gold chart (Figure 8.2, which is the same chart as Figure 8.1 with the prices added) illustrates these two different phases of the market where the new incoming information was positive and created an upward trend, indicated by the separating lines and noted as the Hungry Alligator. In the

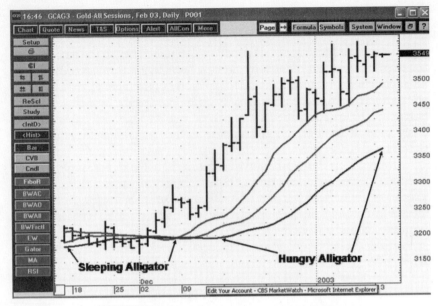

FIGURE 8.2   The Alligator on a gold chart.

lower left-hand corner, you can see the Sleeping Alligator, where most traders lose their money. So the big idea is to stay out of the market when the Alligator is sleeping and to be in the market when the Alligator is awake and hungry.

The Eurodollar chart shown in Figure 8.3 is another perfect example of a sleeping Alligator that "awakens" hungry and begins to "eat" prices. Notice during most of this up move, the prices stay above the Alligator's lips (Green Line), keeping you in this trend move for quite a ride up!

In the same vein, Figure 8.4 illustrates what happens when the new incoming information is bearish enough to move the market lower. The Alligator, by opening its mouth (separation of the Green, Red, and Blue Lines) to the downside, gives us the opportunity to sell short for a sizeable profit potential.

Notice in Figure 8.5 how the trading range illustrated by the sleeping Alligator is ended as the Alligator opens to the downside for this steep down move. Again in this example, the prices are away from the Alligator's lips, indicating a strong trend move downward.

Figure 8.6 shows an extended sleeping Alligator in a bracketed market. We never want to disturb the Alligator while it is sleeping, so we do not enter new positions until the Alligator wakes up hungry! If you try to trade this market while the Alligator is asleep, you will surely lose money due to the choppy market conditions.

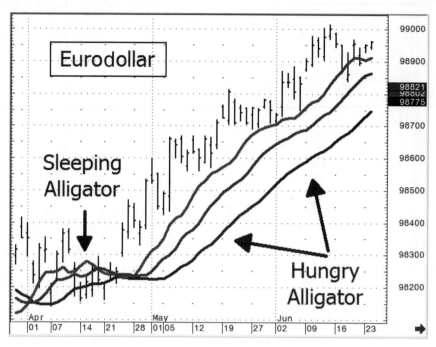

FIGURE 8.3   The Alligator on a Eurodollar chart.

FIGURE 8.4   The Alligator on an AOL Time Warner chart.

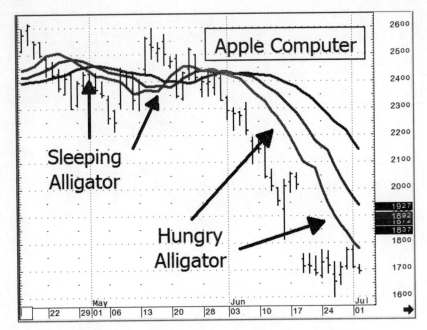

FIGURE 8.5   The Alligator on an Apple Computer chart.

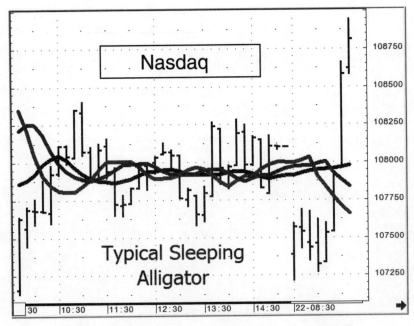

FIGURE 8.6   The sleeping Alligator on a Nasdaq chart.

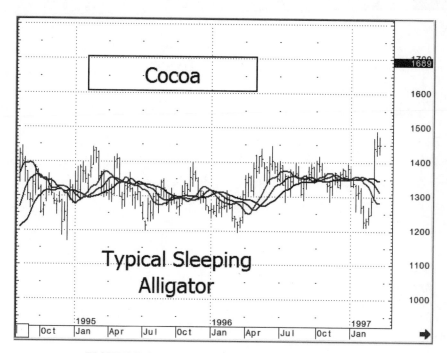

FIGURE 8.7   The sleeping Alligator on Cocoa chart.

Another example of markets to stay away from is shown in Figure 8.7. This weekly cocoa chart shows an Alligator that has been asleep for more than two years in this time frame. Our experience shows that the longer the Alligator sleeps, the hungrier it will be when it awakes!

As we watch the continuation of the previous cocoa chart in Figure 8.8, when the Alligator finally awakens after a long sleep, it is very hungry and a long, strong down move ensues for more than a year! Trading along with the Alligator keeps us on the right side of the trend and allows us to profit from most of the down move.

Remember,
The Blue Balance Line is where
the current price would be
if there were no
new incoming information,
also known as

chaos.

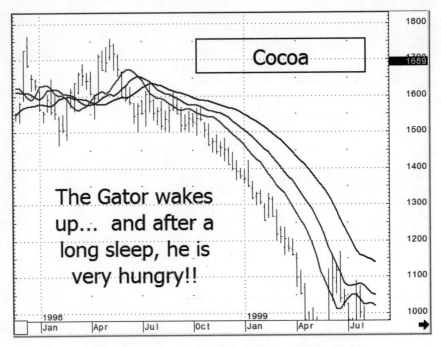

FIGURE 8.8   The hungry Alligator on cocoa chart.

CONSTRUCTION OF THE ALLIGATOR

The constructions of the Balance Lines are (Figure 8.1):

- Blue Line—a 13-bar smoothed moving average offset 8 bars into the future
- Red Line—an 8-bar smoothed moving average offset 5 bars into the future
- Green Line—a 5-bar smoothed moving average offset 3 bars into the future

These moving averages are available on most market charting programs and are also available on Investor's Dream, our proprietary software. You are welcome to download a free demo of this advanced charting software, which includes an abundance of historical data from our Web site at www.profitunity.com. Note that all three of these averages are displayed on the same chart overlaid on the price bars.

A smoothed moving average is often calculated and displayed differently by various charting programs. The smoothed moving average calculation that we use is the one included in Commodity Quote Graphics (CQG) (www.CQG.com). Custom programming is sometimes needed in other charting applications to accurately reproduce the smoothed moving average as used by CQG. Profitunity Trading Group does provide some preprogrammed versions of all our indicators to our students for other charting programs such as TradeStation and MetaStock.

LOOK TO THE FUTURE

After reviewing Figure 8.9, we understand that the Alligator is made up of lines that are offset into the future. Now consider another way that this information can help us. Look closely at Figure 8.10. Note that the Alligator seems to be going to sleep as indicated by the average lines coming together on the right side of the chart. But this chart does not tell the whole story. Because the Alligator is offset into the future, wouldn't it be great to see the rest of the Alligator that is offset to the right of the price bars? Maybe it could give us an indication of the future price movement?

After studying the current position of the Alligator in Figure 8.10, look at the same chart in Figure 8.11. Now we easily and clearly see that the Alligator is suggesting that the up move is going to continue! Look at the difference in what the Alligator is telling you when it is displayed into the future on a chart; that is certainly information you need to know. Several charting applications (including our own Investor's Dream, CQG, and TradeStation) allow displaying the Alligator into the future.

- Jaw Line (Blue): The Balance Line for the current time frame displayed on the chart. It is a 13-bar smoothed moving average offset 8 bars into the future.

- Teeth Line (Red): The Balance Line for one significantly shorter time frame. It is an 8-bar smoothed moving average offset 5 bars into the future.

- Lip Line (Green): The Balance Line for still one more significantly shorter time frame. It is a 5-bar smoothed moving average offset 3 bars into the future.

FIGURE 8.9   The Alligator setup.

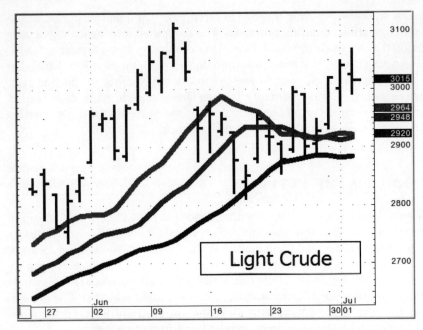

FIGURE 8.10   The Alligator on light crude chart.

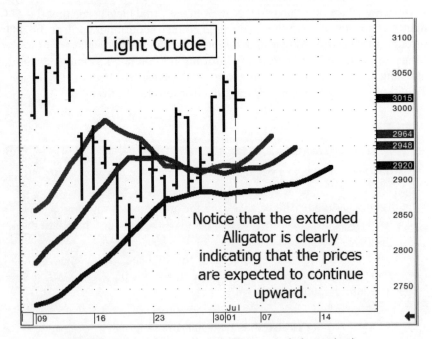

FIGURE 8.11   The extended Alligator on light crude chart.

THE ALLIGATOR ON THE PRICE CHART

Again, Figure 8.2 is the same chart as in Figure 8.1, except prices have been added. Notice that when the offset moving averages are intertwined (Figures 8.6 and Figure 8.7), the Alligator is asleep, and the longer he sleeps the hungrier he gets. When he awakes from a long sleep, he is very hungry and chases the price (Alligator food) much farther because it takes more prices to fill his stomach. This terminology is rather unusual for describing market movements, but it creates an accurate picture of what is happening.

Whenever the Alligator has had enough prices to eat, he starts to close his mouth and begins to lose interest in eating. (An open mouth indicates the Alligator is eating prices, and the closed or intertwining mouth indicates the Alligator has had enough for a while and is resting or sleeping.) At this time you want to start taking profits from the trend move. Then you simply sit back, let the Alligator take a nap, and get back into this market when the Alligator starts to awaken again.

The Alligator keeps us out of choppy markets and gets us into every significant move. It is the best trading tool for following the trend we have experienced—ever. In Chapter 9 we refine our early entries even closer to a trend change by going inside the chart and examining the individual price bars and correlate that with both the Alligator and the momentum oscillator.

Another simplification allowed by using these Balance Lines is that we can trade the Elliott waves without the necessity for accurate wave counting. If the current price bars are outside the Alligator's mouth, we are in an impulsive wave of one degree or another. If the price is meandering around the Balance Lines, we are in a reactive wave of one degree or another.

 SUMMARY

This chapter introduced the idea of using the Alligator to sharpen up entries and exits and cut down on whiplashes. What moves the markets are traders responding to new incoming information (chaos). The Blue Balance Line is where the price would be on this time frame if there were no new incoming information. In other words, the markets only move when chaos is present. If there were no chaos, the markets would be static. Our job is to ferret out the characteristics of this new incoming information and to use it to our advantage while trading.

These lines were first determined by mainframe computers using nonlinear feedback calculus to determine the appropriate dimensions and offsets that could be placed on personal computers. The lines have a level of confidence above 99.5 percent, which means that using these lines as opposed to a main-frame computer doing the actual calculations, you would miss no more than 1 out of 200 trades determined by the computer and extremely complicated mathematics.

In Chapter 9, we examine the first of our three wise men whose job it is to get us into a new trend very early by taking a countertrend trade. At this point, you should thoroughly understand the workings of the Alligator and the three different Balance Lines. You should also understand how to determine when the Alligator is sleeping and when it is eating.

The First Wise Man

Nature's way is simple and easy, but men prefer the intricate and artificial.

—Lao Tzu

GOAL

To understand how countertrend trades will increase your success and profits in trading.

Now that we understand the Alligator and realize how much that will aid in our understanding of what the market is telling us, we are ready to look for some entry points. In both of our earlier books we took our first position only after the Alligator had decided to go either up or down. Our first entry was a Fractal (explained in Chapter 11) outside the Alligator's mouth. For the past several years, the market behavior has been changing. No longer do we see the long and steady runs from a calmer period. The buy-and-hold strategies of the past do not produce the profits they once did. To be successful in today's markets requires more agility and more knowledge in reading the market's shorter-term desires. The long-term traders suffered greatly after the market topped out in early 2000. To be successful today one must be more agile and be ready to take whatever Mother Market is kind enough to give us.

This situation has led to a strategy that gets into a trend much earlier than before. We are no longer content to give up the profits from the exact point that the market reverses to its confirmation above or below the Alligator's mouth. Another aspect of more up-to-date profit taking is the willingness to go either long or short. In that context our new methodology is to get closer to the exact point of the trend change.

Our best tool by far is a bullish/bearish divergent bar.

THE BULLISH/BEARISH DIVERGENT BAR

In the past, bull markets ended when all the bulls had bought and there were no new buyers. Today, however, aggressive short sellers also attend the tops of trends and that fact changes many behavioral characteristics of modern markets. It also changes the market behavior at the end of significant trends. The bears giving way to the bulls in a downward market marks all reversals in a downward trend. So we need to look for the earliest indication of that turnaround. Our best shot is either a bullish divergent bar or a bearish divergent bar that has *moved away* from the Alligator.

A bullish divergent bar is a bar that has a lower low and closes in the top half of the bar. (See Figure 9.1.) A bearish divergent bar is just the opposite. It is a bar that has a higher high and closes in the lower half of that bar. (See Figure 9.2.)

The bullish divergent bar tells us that the bears were in charge in the beginning of the bar and then the bulls took charge and carried the price to the upper half of the bar on the close. The bearish divergent bar indicates

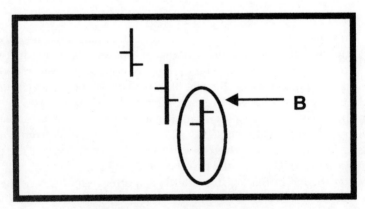

FIGURE 9.1   A bullish divergent bar.

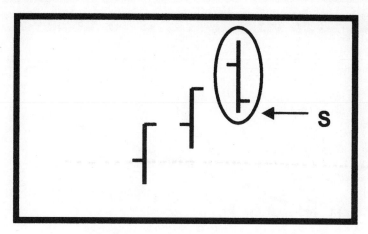

FIGURE 9.2   A bearish divergent bar.

that the bulls were in charge in the beginning of the time frame of the bar (taking the price to new highs). Then the bears took charge and the price closed in the lower half of the bar.

Both the bullish and bearish divergent bars are quite easy to distinguish on any chart including candlestick charts. Again, the key is that the market has taken the price beyond the recent price ranges and with enough enthusiasm to end up well outside the Alligator's mouth.

ANGULATION

We mentioned earlier that a bullish/bearish divergent bar must be moving away from the Alligator. We suggest that you pretend there is a rubber band around the Blue Line (the Alligator's jaw) and the current price. When the price is moving at a steeper angle than the Alligator, it is obvious that the imaginary rubber band will be stretched more and more, giving it more power when it decides to reverse the current price movement. We call this formation *angulation*, meaning that if you drew a line along the path of the alligator and another line along the path of the prices, you would get an opening angulation. This formation is illustrated in Figure 9.3, with the bonds on a bullish angulation producing a bearish divergent bar signal.

The APPX chart in Figure 9.4 shows another way of looking at angulation on a candlestick chart. Note that the prices are angling away from the Alligator as shown by the dotted triangle lines.

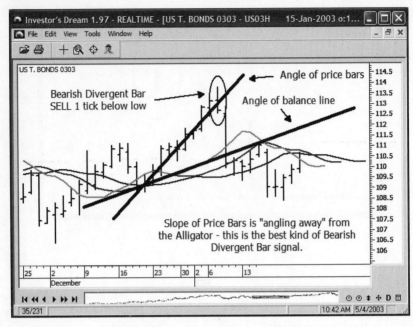

FIGURE 9.3   March bonds, daily chart.

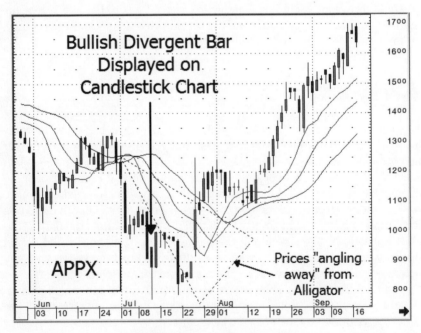

FIGURE 9.4   APPX chart daily.

Rules for Angulation

The question arises as to how to determine precisely whether angulation is present. With just a bit of practice this determination becomes instantly easy and obvious. Here are the four simple rules:

1. Begin where the price bars cross or go through the Alligator's mouth (jaw, teeth, and lips).
2. Draw or imagine a line that follows the Alligator's mouth. We usually pay attention to the jaw and teeth more than the lips.
3. Draw or imagine another line that basically follows the edges of the price bars. You would look at the bottom edge of the prices in an up move and the top edge of the prices on a down move.
4. If those two lines show clearly that they are moving away from each other, you have angulation. See Figure 9.3 and Figure 9.4.

Remember that the bullish/bearish divergent bar signals are invalid unless the angle described previously is increasing. *The bullish/bearish divergent signals are not taken unless this angulation is present. This requirement is extremely important, and making it a necessary component of your entry will save you many potential losses.* Consider the UOPX Apollo Group Stock daily chart in Figure 9.5. This UOPX daily chart shows the

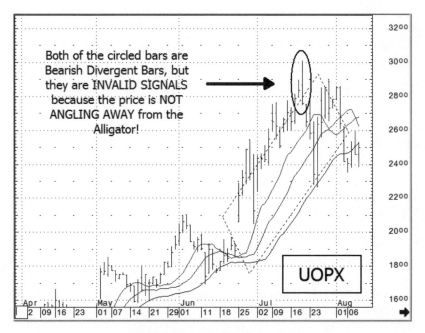

FIGURE 9.5　UOPX daily chart.

prices moving upward at a similar angle (and not angling away) from the Alligator. Therefore, the bearish divergent bar encircled would *not* be a valid signal.

ENTRANCE STRATEGY

Once the bullish/bearish bars have been created (again, this signal is only valid when the bar is well *outside* the Alligator's mouth; the farther away, the better the signal), we are ready to place our entry stops. On a bullish divergent bar, we place the buy stop just above the top of the bullish divergent bar (see B, Figure 9.1) and on the bearish divergent bar we place our sell stop just below the bottom of the bearish divergent bar (see S, Figure 9.2). Because all bullish divergent bars are created while the market is in a down move, we expect the AO (awesome oscillator; explained in Chapter 10) to be red (momentum moving down). In the same way when a bearish divergent bar is created while the market is in an up move, we expect the AO to be green (indicating that the momentum is moving up). The bullish/bearish divergent signal will always be a countertrend trade.

> Before every great trade—where you are really
> moving contrary to the crowd—
> there comes a point when
> people think you are crazy.

The Japanese yen chart (Figure 9.6) illustrates a good simple example of a bullish divergent bar (encircled), which is well below the Alligator's three lines and has good angulation. A buy stop would be placed one tick above the encircled bar. As you can see it was hit and turned out to be a very profitable trade.

MORE EXAMPLES

Now that we understand that we only take the bullish/bearish divergent signals when we have the proper angulation, we can examine some charts. Figure 9.7 shows a chart of the DIA or diamonds, which moves in sync with the Dow. The market came down and created a bullish divergent bar with angulation on December 31. It then changed directions and gave us another bearish divergent bar on January 13, resulting in two very profitable trades in a row.

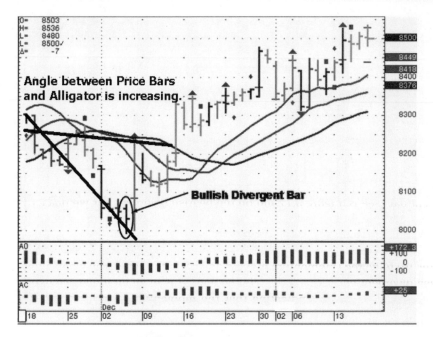

FIGURE 9.6   Japanese yen chart.

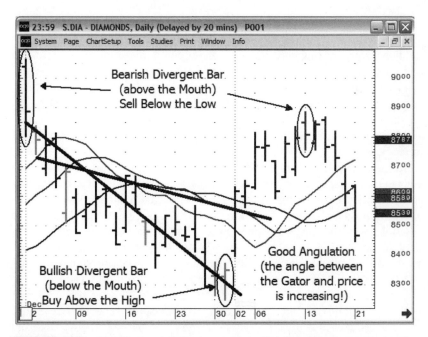

FIGURE 9.7   The diamond daily chart with bullish/bearish divergent signals.

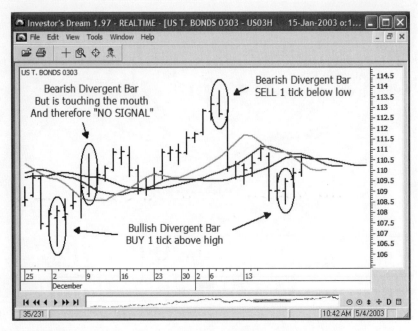

FIGURE 9.8   U.S. bonds showing valid and invalid divergent signals.

On December 3, on the left side of the bond chart (Figure 9.8) there was a bullish divergent bar with angulation, so you would buy one tick above the high. On December 10, there was a bearish divergent bar that is not valid because there is no angulation. However, on January 7 there was a valid bearish divergent bar that you would take because it does have angulation. In late January, another bullish divergent bar appeared with angulation. You would reverse to the upside, again, because there is a valid bullish divergent bar signal.

In the next chart, Figure 9.9, is a Forex (Foreign Exchange—cash market). On the left side, there is a bullish divergent bar circled but, as you can see, there is little or no angulation so it was not taken. Seven bars later is a bearish divergent bar that is entangled with the Alligator and therefore we would not take that sell signal either. Following onto the right side of the chart on about the 29th of the month is a valid bullish divergent bar because it does have angulation. Therefore we would take this signal and buy on the gap opening the next day, creating another profitable trade.

Let us look at still another example. Figure 9.10 shows a daily chart of the Nasdaq Composite Index. On the top left you see two bearish divergent bars that are valid because the angle of the price bars is steeper than the angle of the Alligator in the same time period.

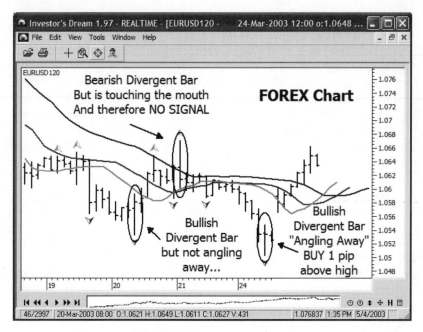

FIGURE 9.9   A Forex chart.

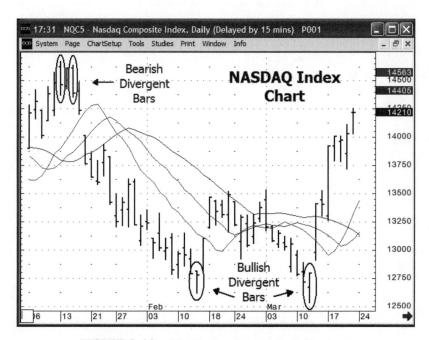

FIGURE 9.10   The Nasdaq Composite Index chart.

This chart illustrates the importance of angulation. Notice the Alligator and the prices on the left side of the chart are staying parallel to each other. This configuration almost always is an important signal for the continuation of the trend down. Then during the week of February 10 we had a bullish divergent bar (circled). However, the price line and the Alligator are still parallel, so we did not take this trade. The prices came back into the Alligator's mouth and then turned down once more. On this move down, though, the price line is at a steeper angle than the Alligator, thus creating angulation and a valid divergent bar signal, which was taken on the gap open up the next day. Another quick and very profitable signal.

Repeating for emphasis, it should be clear when and how we would take a bullish/bearish divergent signal—*only* when we have angulation. If you do not fully understand what we mean by angulation, please contact our office and we will stay with you until it is crystal clear.

The QLGC (Q Logic Corp.) daily chart in Figure 9.11 reminds us that not all bullish divergent bars are valid signals. The encircled bullish divergent bar has two problems: (1) The prices are not angling away from the alligator (see dashed lines on chart) and (2) the price bar penetrates the Al-

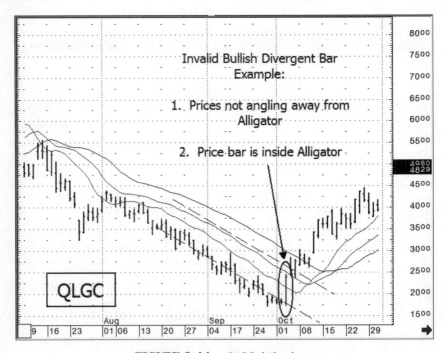

FIGURE 9.11   QLGC daily chart.

ligator. This signal is not valid despite the subsequent price reversal to the upside.

When we look again at a valid bullish divergent bar signal in the Eurodollar chart (Figure 9.12), we note that the first encircled bullish divergent bar clearly angled away from the Alligator and was our entry signal. A few days later, another bullish divergent bar appeared that would not have been valid because there is no angulation between it and the Alligator. No matter, we were already in this profitable trade. You might also note a bullish divergent bar around Nov 26th (about midway of the down move). This signal was also invalid and not indicated because there was no angulation between it and the Alligator.

It is important to realize that not every up or down move ends with a bearish or bullish divergent bar. Consider the Home Depot daily chart in Figure 9.13. None of the bars at the top of this price move were bearish divergent bars. If we were considering a short position, or a stop-and-reverse in this market, we would fall back on the other Profitunity signals and techniques, which we describe in our previous two books, *Trading Chaos* and *New Market Dimensions* and teach in the Profitunity Home Study Course.

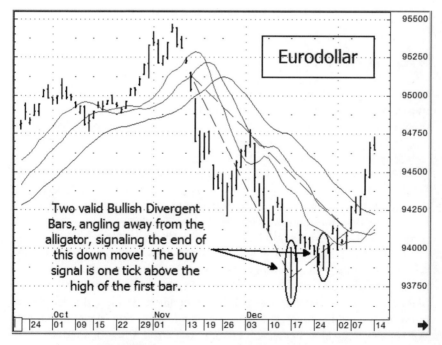

FIGURE 9.12   March Eurodollar, daily chart.

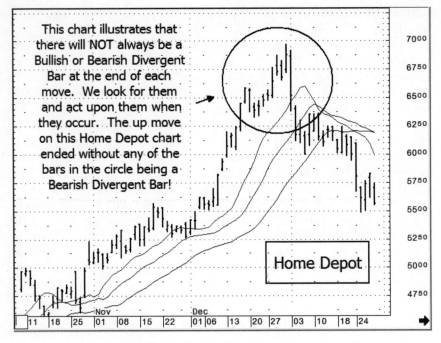

This chart illustrates that there will NOT always be a Bullish or Bearish Divergent Bar at the end of each move. We look for them and act upon them when they occur. The up move on this Home Depot chart ended without any of the bars in the circle being a Bearish Divergent Bar!

Home Depot

FIGURE 9.13   Home Depot, daily chart.

EXIT STRATEGY

Once our buy or sell stop is hit, we need a protective stop. The first protective stop would be placed just below the bullish divergent bar or just above the top of a bearish divergent bar. This position gives us a very close initial stop loss, which would be the length of the signal bar. We always place our first stop just past the other end of our signal bar.

With a bullish divergent bar, we expect the momentum as indicated by the AO to be red, indicating momentum is down. With a bearish divergent bar, we expect the momentum as indicated by the AO to be green, indicating that the base momentum is still up. Otherwise this would not be a countertrend trade. Again, the AO is explained in Chapter 10.

In the bond chart (Figure 9.3), notice the fifth bar from the left margin is clearly a bullish divergent bar. It is "away" from the mouth, thereby creating a valid buy signal. Once that signal is hit on the following bar, we place a protective sell stop just below the signal bar. Notice that the fourth bar after the bullish divergent signal bar is a bearish divergent bar but cannot act as a signal bar because it is not *outside* the Alligator's mouth.

The next signal is at the top of the chart and that is a bearish divergent bar that is well *outside* the Gator's mouth. Therefore it is a valid signal because, again, it also has good angulation. The key is that the angle the price bars are making is greater than the angle the Gator's mouth is making. Assuming that you were long in this trade, you would stop and reverse to go short just below the bottom of the bearish divergent bar. If you were long one contract when the bearish signal was created you would go short two contracts—one to get out of your long and one to be net short when the bearish signal is triggered.

Following the bars downward, notice that the third bar after the bearish signal is a bullish divergent bar but again is not valid because it is touching the Gator's mouth. The bullish divergent bar three bars from the right side of this chart is another valid signal because it has a lower low and closes in the top half of the bar, plus it too has good angulation. Repeating, for emphasis and because it is so important, good angulation here means that the path of the price bars is steeper than the angle of the Alligator. If you have trouble visualizing this angulation, simply look at the difference between the price line and the Blue Line of the Alligator. The buy stop or a stop and reverse to go long would be placed just above the top of the signal bar, which is the third bar from the right side. In this chart, which covers roughly 6 weeks of trading the bonds on a daily chart, you would first go long at 108.12. Then you would stop and reverse to go short at 113.25. On the next signal you would stop and reverse again back to the long side. Again, assuming you are trading only one contract per signal, you would have had a profit of $9,531.25 minus slippage and two commissions in a 6-week period of time.

If you traded all three wise man signals, your total profit would have jumped $4,843.75 by using the Wise Man 2 entries and exits and $2,656.25 by using Wise Man 3 for a grand total of $17,031.25 minus six commissions and slippage. This trade obviously was good and it happens every day the market is open. We are devoting a chapter to each of the other Wise Men trade signals. The bonus here is that very little monitoring effort is needed. To determine these entries and exits on daily charts would require no more than examining any chart about 2 seconds each day. This low time expenditure allows one to survey many different stocks or commodity charts and take only those trades that fit the wise man mold.

But Do I Really Want to Go Against the Trend?

The question then arises, why would one want to take a trade against the trend? The reason is simple: There is a very close stop and the profit potential, if the market does turn, gives us the world's best trade location.

I Am in a Countertrend Trade and Scared. Where Do I Put a Stop?

Again assuming that the market does in fact go our way, we want to turn our attention to the best closest stop. The very first stop would be at the bottom of the bullish divergent signal bar for a buy. The stop for a sell on a bearish divergent bar would be just above the top of the signal bar. If this formation forms a Fractal in the opposite direction, it would create a stop and reversal signal. See Figure 9.14 and Figure 9.15.

The exact opposite happens when you have a bearish divergent bar. The first protective stop would be just above the top of the bearish divergent bar. If the following two bars have highs that are lower than the bearish divergent bar, thereby creating an up Fractal, the initial stop then becomes a stop and reverse to go long.

More Examples

Another example is the diamond daily chart (Figure 9.7), which represents the Dow Jones Industrial Futures chart. This chart represents 6 weeks of the market where the market essentially ended up where it started. By using all three wise men, you would have taken out $11.96 profit trading on a per share basis. This amounts to 13.7 percent return over the 6 weeks trading only the dailies. Plus you are positioned for the down move now taking place.

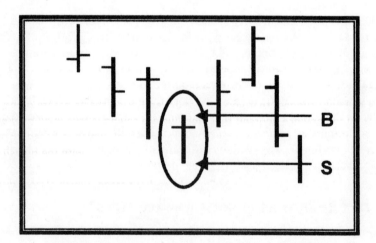

FIGURE 9.14   A bullish divergent bar plus two others form a Fractal sell.

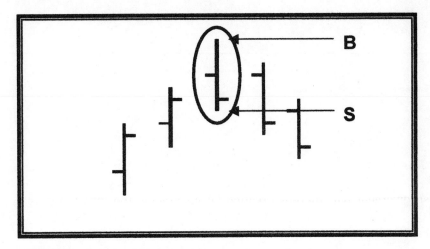

FIGURE 9. 15   Illustrating how a bearish divergent bar plus two lower highs create a Fractal buy signal.

 SUMMARY

As set forth in this chapter, proper use of the first wise man trading signal gives us the greatest trade location when the market does turn and the least possible loss potential. The limiting factor on using this signal is to make sure that the signal itself is well outside the Alligator's mouth (good angulation). We have found that basically all tradable trends will end in a bullish or bearish bar signal on one time frame or another. We use this signal whether we are trading weeklies, dailies, or a 5-minute chart. It works on all commodities, bonds, and stocks because it is a reflection of human nature, which does not change from market to market or various time frames.

We strongly suggest that you look at several price charts before going to Chapter 10 to convince yourself that what we are saying is true in all markets. In Chapter 10 we discuss our second wise man signal, which is based on the follow-through of the momentum, which originally changed with the bullish or bearish divergent bar signal.

Chapter 11 then discusses our Fractal breakout trade, which almost guarantees a good profitable follow-through on the trade.

The Second Wise Man

Adding On With Momentum

In the market:
honesty is power,
simplicity is energy
and innocence is ability.

GOAL

To understand how and when to add on after your first entry.

Assume that you have entered a trade at the direction of the first wise man, the bullish/bearish divergent bar, and the market is now moving in your direction. The next question should be, do I add on and if so where would be the most appropriate place? The market once again will manage our trade with only a bit of direction from us.

The second wise man signal is based on continuing momentum. The first wise man gets us in at the very best trade location but we still can never be certain that we are in at the right direction until the market itself follows through. Remember that the first wise man is really an anticipatory signal and if we are right we want to pile on aggressively.

The second entry signal is based on the awesome oscillator (AO). The AO is without a doubt the best momentum indicator available in the stock and commodity markets. It is like reading tomorrow's *Wall Street Journal.*

The Awesome Oscillator provides us with the
keys to the kingdom.

The AO measures the immediate momentum of the past 5 price bars,
compared to the momentum of the last 34 bars.

It is a 34-bar simple moving average of the bar's midpoints (H–L)/2
subtracted from a 5-bar simple moving average of the midpoints (H–L)/2,
plotted in a histogram form.

The AO tells us exactly what is happening with the current momentum.

FIGURE 10.1   What the awesome oscillator does and what it is.

It is as simple as it is elegant. Basically, it is a 34-bar simple moving average
that is subtracted from a 5-bar simple moving average (see Figure 10.1). It
is possible to be a profitable commodity and stock trader using only this oscillator, as we explain in the next section.

UNDERSTANDING THE AWESOME OSCILLATOR

The AO provides the keys to the kingdom when properly understood. The
AO can be used in trading both stock and commodity markets. It measures
the immediate momentum of the last 5 bars and compares this figure to the
momentum of the last 34 bars (Figure 10.2). It also is a measure of the continuing Market Facilitation Index (MFI) (see *Trading Chaos*, pp. 121–132).

We know that price is the very last thing to change in the markets.
What changes before price is momentum; what changes before momentum
is the *speed* of the current momentum; what changes before the speed of
the current momentum is the volume; and what changes before the volume
is all of us traders and investors making chaotic decisions about our activities in the markets.

When understood and used properly, the AO is the best and most accurate indicator we have found in almost 50 years of trading. If you really
know how to use this indicator, it should be worth at least seven figures to
you in the next few years.

Figure 10.2 shows how we display the AO on the bottom of the price
chart. For example, when the oscillator turns down, you could simply call
your broker and say, "Sell at the market." You stay short until it turns up,
and then call and say, "Buy at the market." Unbelievable? Try it on a couple
of charts and you will see. Please understand, we *do not* recommend this

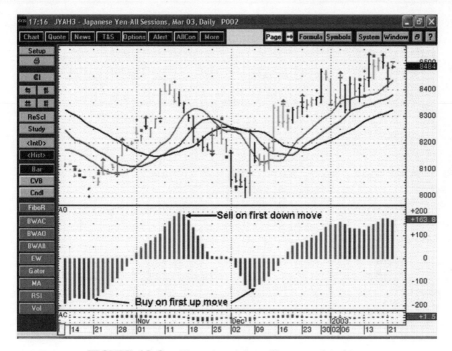

FIGURE 10.2   The awesome oscillator on the chart.

approach for trading because you can get much more precise with your trades. But think about other trader's reactions when you say that you can trade profitably without even looking at a price chart or even knowing the current price.

In the Profitunity's Investor's Dream advanced charting program, and in the indicators we have developed for other charting programs, we color green any histogram bar that is higher than the previous histogram bar, and we color red any histogram bar that is lower than the previous bar. This makes it very easy to see a change in momentum; all you do is look for a change in color.

The AO Buy/Sell Signal

The AO creates what is usually our second entry into an early developing trend. Assuming there was a bullish divergent bar that is clearly below the Alligator and we were stopped into a buy signal just above the bullish divergent bar, we are now long in this market and looking for a place to add on to our initial long entry. Remember that on the bullish divergent bar the AO should be red (again indicating that we are taking a countertrend trade)

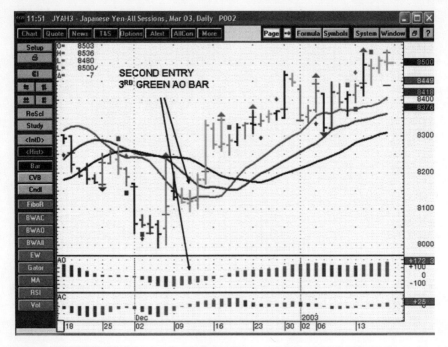

FIGURE 10.3   Three AO Green Bars create an AO add-on signal.

but when the momentum changes as indicated by the AO turning green (it normally will turn green within 2 to 4 bars after your entry) the market is setting up for an add-on position. We normally add on after three consecutive green bars. We place a buy stop just above the high of the price bar that corresponds with the third green bar on the AO.

The Japanese yen chart in Figure 10.3 illustrates the first and second wise men signals. At this point we have temporary confirmation that we have entered the trade wisely and have a very good trade location. We can find these setups easily with just a bit of practice.

Additional Examples

The BSTE daily chart illustrated in Figure 10.4 shows how bullish divergent bars can often stand out. This bullish divergent bar happened after a gap down and is clearly angling away from the Alligator. Notice that the AO is still decreasing. Remember, this is a countertrend trade setup. The AO continues to decrease for a few more days before creating a down peak on January 31. Three days later we have the third higher AO bar and the signal to add on to our long position one tick above the high of the price bar that day.

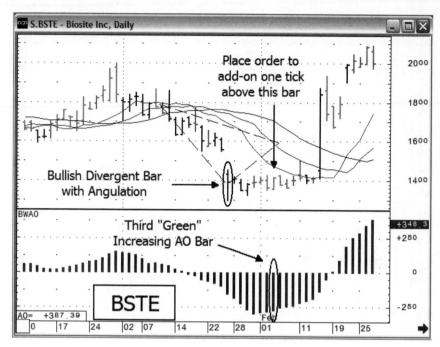

FIGURE 10.4 BSTE daily chart.

In this case, we would have been filled at the open on the following day, because BSTE opened above the previous high.

The Canadian dollar chart shown in Figure 10.5 reminds us to watch for both bullish *and* bearish divergent bars. In this example, the price is again angling away from the Alligator (as shown with the triangle on the chart) and we are going short while the AO continues up for a couple more bars. Note the AO sell signal (third lower AO bar) did not occur until six bars after the bearish divergent bar; do not expect it to happen immediately. When we enter on a bearish or bullish divergent bar setup, we expect the momentum is about to change, and often we end up waiting a few bars for that to happen.

The CMTL daily chart in Figure 10.6 is a nearly classic bullish divergent bar trade setup with an AO add-on trade. Looking at only the AO on this chart, you will see the long steady decline in momentum and note that the price changed direction a full four days before momentum changed direction. There is no way to be any earlier, or have any better trade position, than what this bullish divergent bar gives us. A few days after entering this trade, the momentum has changed direction and we have added on to our position as the third higher AO bar confirms our long entry.

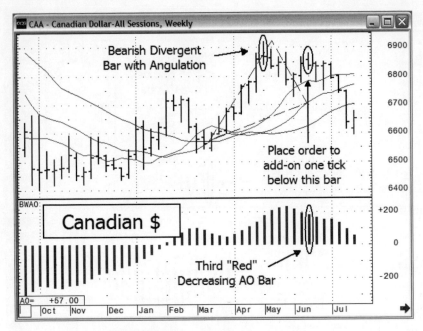

FIGURE 10.5   Canadian Dollar Chart.

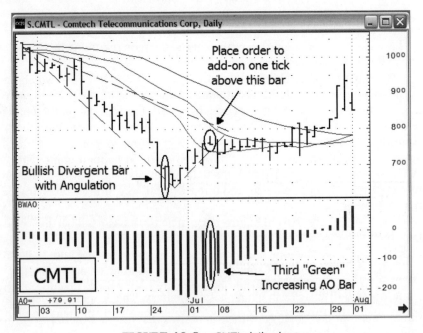

FIGURE 10.6   CMTL daily chart.

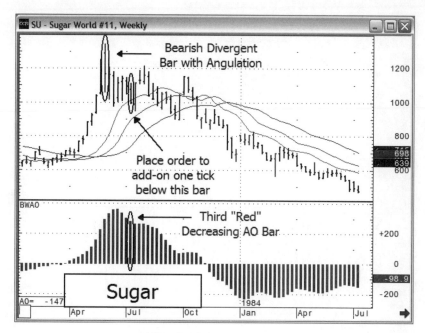

FIGURE 10.7   Sugar chart.

When we see price "breaking away" to the up or downside, like we do in the sugar chart shown in Figure 10.7, we should always be looking for a bullish or bearish divergent bar. Big, long divergent bars are strong reversal signals and often create their own angulation away from the Alligator simply by their sheer price range. Note the very large bearish divergent bar shown in this chart; this bar literally shouts, "I'm about to change direction and I hope you're watching!" The AO confirmation add-on is a few bars later, and the sugar market proceeds to decline steadily from there for the entire chart.

Now that we have considered several examples of bullish and bearish divergent bar entries and subsequent AO add-on trades, our next job is to protect our entry with either a stop or a stop and reverse strategy.

Figure 10.8 illustrates wise men numbers 1 and 2 on the dollar chart showing where you would go long in mid-November based on a bullish divergent bar (wise man 1) and added on based on the third green (up) bar on the AO chart. Then you would have taken profit and reversed to the down side based on the December 1 bearish divergent bar. You would have then added on the short side on December 5 and you would still be holding it at the end of this chart, which is late January. This is a good illustration how using the three wise men keeps you in tune with the market taking profit in both up and down markets. In Chapter 11, we illustrate how and

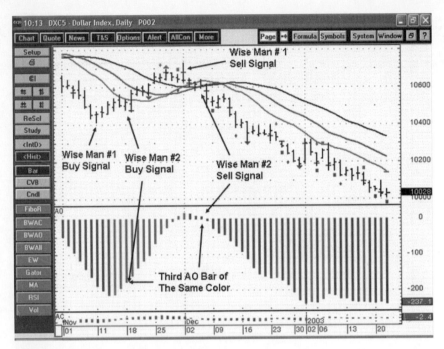

FIGURE 10.8 American dollar chart.

when you would add on to your position based on a Fractal breakout, which is our third wise man signal. If you wish more illustrations of these signals, go to our Web site at www.profitunity.com, where you will see these and other charts in color.

CONSTRUCTING A DERIVATIVE TO CREATE A SPEEDOMETER FOR MOMENTUM

So far, we have examined how we can use the science of chaos as it relates to trade/vesting in the stock and commodity markets. We explained how we use our primary decision and strategy maker—the Alligator—to filter out bad trades and now we are developing a strategy to add on to winning trades. We then looked at how to get started in an embryo trend using a bullish/bearish divergent bar. This gives us the best possible trade location that was demonstrated in Chapter 9.

Imagine rolling a bowling ball down a street. The weight and momentum of the bowling ball will cause it to continue on its path. If that path encounters an uphill portion of the street, the momentum will start slowing down. From a physics standpoint, the instant it starts to slow down it is really accelerating in the opposite direction. In other words, before the price can change direction (we traders call this a *trend change*), the momentum must come to a complete stop and turn in the opposite direction, either up or down. As pointed out earlier, trading the momentum is like reading tomorrow's *Wall Street Journal* and is the most sensitive measure of momentum we have ever witnessed.

PROTECTING OUR ENTRY

Now we are in this market and have added on with our second wise man signal. We need to protect our two entries and we have a choice of trailing our stop or placing a stop and reverse to go short strategy if we are wrong. As illustrated in Chapter 9, our first stop is just below the bottom of our entry price bar. Now that we have added on to our original long position, we perhaps may have created a Fractal sell signal. The Fractal signal is fully discussed in Chapter 11. At this point we simply want to point out that if you do have a Fractal sell signal, our strategy is to stop and reverse and go short. Generally, if this sell signal is hit, the market has proved us wrong in positioning ourselves on the buy side. Usually the new short position puts us back in line with the current momentum of the market. Most of the time, we will more than make up for any loss we might incur on the long side. In Chapter 11, after we have explained all three wise men entries, we discuss the best use of a trailing stop to maximize profits while minimizing losses.

 SUMMARY

In this chapter, we examined the second of the three wise men, which is designed to add on to our trade based on confirmation that we are in the market and aligned with the current momentum. In the countertrend entry, momentum was, by definition, against us, which creates a countertrend trade, and thus we are abiding by the "Buy low, sell high" rule of the market. In the next chapter we examine our breakout trade, which becomes the average good trader's first entry point. If we have chosen our first entry (bullish/bearish divergent bar) well outside the Alligator's mouth, we are far ahead of the game, having both better trade locations and closer (less expensive) stops.

Make sure that you understand both wise man numbers 1 and 2 entries before going to the next chapter. After wise man #3 you should begin to see how this entire strategy ties together in a profitable market following system. Following wise man #3 we discuss the best market-generated places to put your stops.

CHAPTER 11

The Third Wise Man

Trading the Fractal Breakaway Trade

"Come to the edge of the cliff," he said.
"We're afraid," they said.
"Come to the edge of the cliff," he said.
"We're afraid," they said.
"Come to the edge of the cliff," he said.
They came.
He pushed.
They flew.

GOAL

To understand and be able to recognize and trade initiating Fractals.

M any experienced traders say that making money trading the markets is easy; what is difficult is keeping it. The pattern of all markets is that they spend most of their time going nowhere and only a small amount of time (15 to 30 percent) in identifiable trends. Traders who are not on the floor and/or not specialists have a tough time while the market is not moving. Most traders have a tendency to place their stops too close to the market and consequently get whiplashed. Still, the greatest potential for profits occurs when the markets are trending.

Therefore, our first consideration is to *not be left out* of any significant trend move. Remember, the Fractal signal is usually the third entry point, although if an appropriate Fractal appears before the wise men 1 and 2, we would still place a trade on that Fractal.

FRACTAL BREAKOUT

Ideally, we have entered the market via wise man 1 (bullish/bearish divergent bar) and most likely have added on to our position with wise man 2 (three consecutive green [higher] or red [lower] bars on the AO). And now the market gives us a Fractal signal, which is a breakout of the market after the market has reversed direction as first indicated by the bullish/bearish bar. If this Fractal signal is our third entry, we should have built up some open equity in our first two entries. The Fractal breakout confirms that our identification of a change in trend is, up to this point, valid.

THE FRACTAL PATTERN

The Fractal pattern is a simple one. The market moves in one direction or the other. After a period of time, all the willing buyers have bought (in an up move) and the market falls back because of a lack of buyers and perhaps short sellers are also coming into the market. Then some new incoming information (chaos) begins to affect the traders. There is an influx of new buying, and the market, finding that place of equal disagreement on value and agreement on price, moves up. If the momentum and the buyer's strength are strong enough to exceed the immediately preceding up Fractal, we would place an order to buy just over the high of the Fractal. Let us examine some Fractal patterns.

In Figure 11.1, you see an idealized Fractal setup in Pattern A. The technical definition of a Fractal is a series of a minimum of five consecutive bars where the highest high is preceded by two lower highs and is followed by two lower highs. (The opposite configuration would be applicable for a sell Fractal.) One way to visualize this concept is to hold your hand outstretched in front of you with your fingers spread and your middle finger pointing up. Your fingers are your five consecutive bars, and your middle finger is the highest, creating a Fractal formation. In an up Fractal, we are interested only in the bars' high, and in a down Fractal, we are interested only in the bars' low. It is important to note the following restrictions.

Note that while Pattern A is a pristine Fractal, Pattern B fulfills all the requirements for both an up and a down Fractal. The two preceding and

Here are some common formations that you will see in the market.

(A) Is an example of a pristine Up Fractal.

(B) Is an example where the middle finger is an up and down Fractal.

(C) Fractals can share bars. The 3rd bar is the middle finger for the up Fractal and one of the two bars to the left of the middle finger for the down Fractal.

(D) Is an example of the Fractal needing 6 bars: the middle bar was equaled by a latter bar.

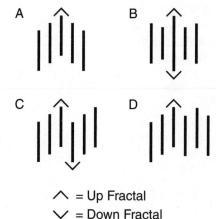

$\wedge$ = Up Fractal
$\vee$ = Down Fractal

FIGURE 11.1 The Fractal pattern.

the two following bars can have any high, so long as that high is not higher than the middle bar (finger). Pattern B then is both up an Fractal and a down Fractal because both preceding bars and both following bars are inside bars when compared to the middle bar of the Fractal.

Pattern C shows another formation that creates both an up Fractal and a down Fractal. As shown, these Fractals may share bars. Pattern D requires six bars to form an up Fractal because the fifth bar has a high equal to the previous highest high. The working definition is repeated here for emphasis: *A Fractal must have two preceding and two following bars with lower highs (higher lows in a down move). In a buy Fractal, we are interested only in the bars' high. In a sell Fractal, we are interested only in the bars' low.*

Figure 11.2 shows a variety of Fractal patterns. Fractal buys are in the upper section and Fractal sells are in the lower section. Fractals tell us a great deal about the phase space of the market's behavior, but we can improve our trading by knowing how a Fractal's behavioral functions change as the market moves from high to low and back again.

Looking at charts, Fractals are everywhere. Using charting programs like our Investor's Dream or other popular charting programs like TradeStation, MetaStock, or CQG, you can program indicators to alert you to both up and down Fractals. The Australian dollar chart in Figure 11.3 is an example of an Investor's Dream chart with only Fractal indicators displayed. You should practice recognizing Fractals on charts so that it becomes easy and intuitive for you. Once you can easily observe all Fractals on a chart, the next step is to understand which Fractals create buy and sell signals.

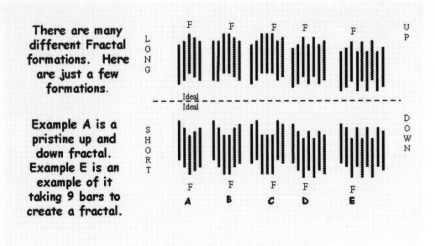

FIGURE 11.2   Various Fractal formations on the price chart.

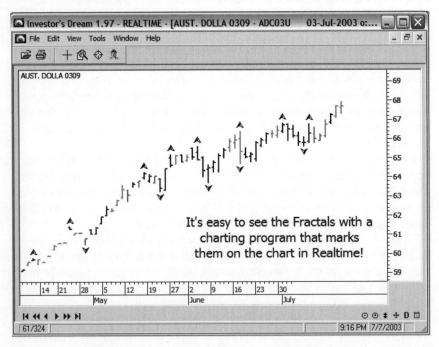

FIGURE 11.3   Fractals on an Australian dollar chart.

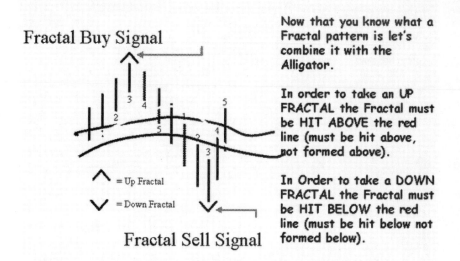

FIGURE 11.4   The initiating Fractal; the Fractal pattern with the Alligator.

Once a Fractal is formed, it will always be a Fractal, but the role it plays depends on its location in relation to the Alligator's mouth. Figure 11.4 shows both a buy and a sell Fractal. If the buy signal is above the Red Balance Line (the Alligator's teeth), we would place a buy stop one tick above the high of the up Fractal buy signal. If the sell signal is below the Red Balance Line, we would place a sell stop one tick below the low of the Fractal sell signal.

It is essential to understand that we would not take a Fractal buy signal if, *at the time it is hit,* the price is below the Red Balance Line. Likewise, we would not take a Fractal sell signal if, *at the time it is hit,* the price is above the Red Balance Line. This method is the best we have found to filter out nonprofitable Fractal trades.

Once a Fractal signal is formed and is valid in relation to its position outside the Alligator's mouth, it remains a signal until it is hit or until a more recent Fractal signal is formed. Remember that although a Fractal formation may be triggered, it has to be filtered through the Alligator. In other words, you would not take a buy if the Fractal were below the Alligator's teeth, and you would not take a sell if the Fractal were above the Alligator's teeth.

By definition, a break out signal should break out from somewhere and in this process it is breaking out from the Gator's mouth (the intertwining Red, Green, and Blue Lines discussed earlier). In Figure 11.4 you would go in whatever direction the price exceeds the Fractal breakout signal.

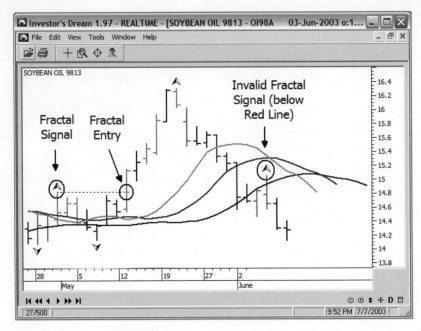

FIGURE 11.5   Fractal entry examples.

It is reasonably easy to identify valid Fractal signals! In the soybean oil chart shown in Figure 11.5, there is an example of a valid Fractal signal and subsequent Fractal entry, and another Fractal that is created inside the Alligator (below the Red Line) and would be invalid if hit at that point. The prices dropped further and the Fractal signal was not hit.

The daily McDonald's Corporation chart shown in Figure 11.6 shows two Fractal signal examples: the first down Fractal signal is invalid because it was hit above the Red Line; the second down Fractal signal was valid because it was hit below the Alligator. Remember, it is not where the Fractal signal is *formed*, but where it is *hit* that determines whether or not the signal is valid.

Figure 11.7 shows various Fractals, some of which would be taken and others that would not. For example, Fractals a, c, d, e, and f are all good signals in this initial up move. Fractal b was never hit and Fractals g, h, and j would not be taken because the market is obviously in a correction and is a bracketed market. For a full explanation of how to trade using the Elliott wave, see our earlier book *Trading Chaos* (Wiley, 1994, pp. 101–132).

The Boeing Co. daily chart in Figure 11.8 shows a series of consecutive valid down Fractal signals and hits during a down trend. Note that all Fractal signals and where each signal was hit were well below the Alligator.

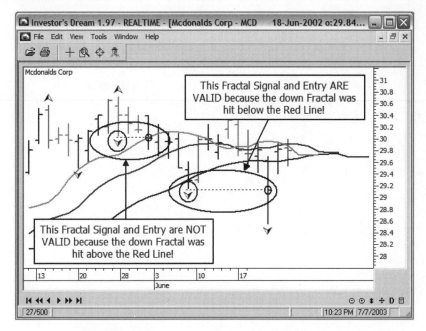

FIGURE 11.6   Valid and invalid Fractal examples.

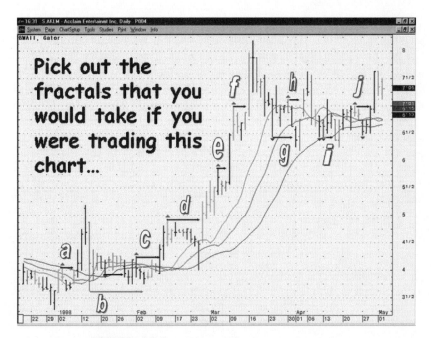

FIGURE 11.7   Taking different Fractal signals.

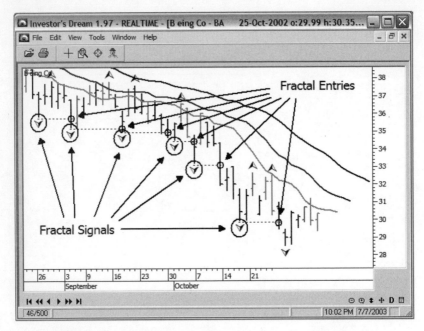

FIGURE 11.8   Boeing Co. daily chart showing Fractal signals.

Each of these Fractal signals was an opportunity to add on to your short position and increase your profitability from this trade substantially!

We know that the underlying structure of the market is the Elliott wave, and the underlying structure of the Elliott wave is the Fractal. Being able to locate Fractals properly allows a trader to be profitable trading the Elliott wave without having to know which wave the market is currently in. A Fractal is always a change in behavior caused by new incoming information (chaos).

- What happens between an up and a down Fractal is an Elliott wave of one degree or another.
- A Fractal is always a change in behavior. It is displayed as a five-bar sequence where the center bar (or group) has higher highs for up Fractals or lower lows for down Fractals.
- One way to trade the Fractal is whenever the market exceeds the outside extreme high on up Fractals and low on down Fractals, go with the outside direction/Fractal point.

FIGURE 11.9   A review of Fractal strategy.

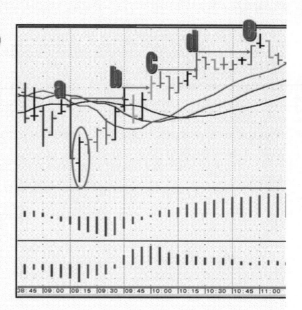

The Fractal guarantees us not to miss the trend. Fractal (a) was the first entry in the market. Most traders do no take that Fractal because it is in the mouth. At (b) many traders still do not take that trade. At (c) a lot of traders get on board now and at (d) everyone else gets on. Guess what - it's late and the traders who took (c and d) as their first entry are going to have a hard time making money. The key is to be conservative in the mouth but aggressive outside of the mouth.

By the time the Fractal (a) is hit the AC and AO are both positive. There was also a bullish divergent squat bar on the bottom bar, which would be the ideal first entry.

FIGURE 11.10   Combining the wise man signals.

Note that in Figure 11.10 our first entry would be a wise man 1 bullish divergent bar. This bar is encircled on the chart. The second entry would be the Fractal labeled a. There was also an AO buy between labels b and c. We would continue to add on at Fractals b, c, and d. Then at the topmost bar, we find a bearish divergent signal and would stop and reverse to go short just under this bar. Notice that this is a five-minute bar, and some heavy profit was generated in a short span of two hours.

 SUMMARY

In this chapter, we examined the phase space signal we label as a *Fractal*. A Fractal is a behavioral change and must be evaluated according to what is happening in the overall view of a market. The technical definition of a Fractal is: *A minimum of five consecutive bars where the highest high is higher than the previous two bars' highs and also higher than the following two bars' high.* The opposite is a sell Fractal. It is obviously better to get into a trend early and we generally take the first Fractal that is significantly out of the mouth of the

Alligator. Once a signal is hit, we continue to take other Fractal signals that are triggered in the same direction.

At this point you should be able to easily locate your first three buy/sell signals. Ideally the first signal would be a bullish/bearish divergent bar that is significantly outside the Alligator's mouth. The second signal (ideally) would be a bar that exceeds the high of the price bar corresponding to the third green AO bar. On the sell side, it would be the bar that exceeds the low of the price bar corresponding to the third red AO bar. Then, again ideally, the third entry would be the Fractal breakout signal. If the market continues to go our way, we continue to take each Fractal signal.

In Chapter 12, we examine what happens when the wise men get together.

What Happens When the Wise Men Get Together?

GOAL

To know the best strategies in all the various market formations.

Now that we understand all the three wise men, let us go a bit deeper and learn how to respond most profitably to various setups that the market gives us. First we examine the pristine setup, where we enter the market in the following order of market-generated signals.

1. Bullish/bearish divergent bar
2. Super AO—three consecutive bars of the same color
3. A Fractal signal

BUYING OR GOING LONG

In the gold chart (Figure 12.1), note that point 1 shows a bullish divergent bar with good angulation with the Alligator. Therefore we would buy or go long just above the top of the number 1 bar. This buy stop was hit on the very next bar as indicated by the notation 2. Notation 3 points to both the third green AO bar and also to the corresponding price bar. This signal was hit at notation 4 (AO bar entry). Notation 5 points to the top of a Fractal buy signal that was hit at 6, creating the first Fractal entry. Notation 7 shows the

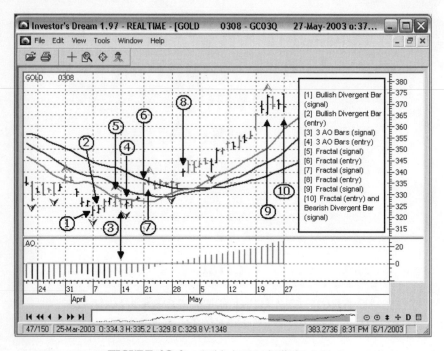

FIGURE 12.1   Gold chart in bullish move.

second Fractal formation and that signal was hit at notation 8. The market then continued up where a new Fractal signal was formed at 9. Notation 10 is the bar that was both the third Fractal entry and was also a bearish divergent bar. If the following bar goes below bar 10 we would reverse our entire position and go short. [*Note:* The very next bar did reverse our position to short, which is where we are as this is being written.]

How did all this turn out in the actual markets? Our entries with corresponding profits were:

Buy Signals	Profit/Contract	Profit-Reverse Pyramid
1. 324.9 Bullish divergent bar	$ 4,180	$ 4,180
2. 327.6 Three AO green bars	$ 3,910	$19,550
3. 330.1 Fractal	$ 3,660	$14,640
4. 337.6 Fractal	$ 2,910	$ 8,730
Total =	$14,660	$47,100

This list is a good example of what can happen in a single future or stock over a period of approximately 6 weeks. In a later section in this chapter we explain how we use reverse pyramiding to increase both our gross and percentage profits. Through the years we have often stated that once you become a profitable trader, we can show you how to at least double your profits using the exact same signals by simple asset allocation. In gold, we usually limit our investment to 15 contracts, which allows us to use reverse pyramiding. In this case, it increased our profits by a factor of 3.2 times, even though we did not get our fifth entry into the markets. Reverse pyramiding is explained later in this chapter.

To make sure there is no confusion, we review this strategy on the gold chart in more detail.

PROFITUNITY STRATEGY FOR GETTING IN AND OUT OF ANY MARKET

The ideal first presenting signal is a bullish/bearish divergent bar that has good angulations with the Alligator. The requirements for a pristine buy signal, assuming a downward moving market, would be:

1. A bullish divergent bar that has a lower low than the previous bars and the close is in the upper half of the bar (see Figure 12.1, circle 1).

2. The bullish divergent bar must be descending at a greater (steeper) angle than the Alligator, particularly the Blue Line of the Alligator. It is.

3. Place a buy stop either one or very few ticks above the high of the bullish divergent bar. If filled . . .

4. Place a protective stop just below the bottom of the bullish divergent bar (see Figure 12.1, circle 1).

5. If the market continues in an upward direction for two more bars and you have not been stopped out, the market most likely has created a sell Fractal whose reversal point is exactly where your protective stop has been placed. So simply call the broker and sell two contracts (or double the number of shares) for each one you are long. If that sell signal is hit, then you would be in a go-with market and following the immediate trend. (This did not happen in the gold chart Figure 12.1.)

6. If the market continues to move up and the AO bars are green, start counting the green price bars.

7. Assuming that the market is still going your way (moving up, in this case) and you have three consecutive green price bars, you want to add to your position by placing another buy stop one or a few ticks above the high of the price bar corresponding to the third green price bar (see circle 3 on Figure 12.1).

8. After the second buy signal has been hit, start looking for your third entry. The gold market continued in our direction and then fell back with at least two lower highs in the price bars. (See circle 4 on Figure 12.1.) At this point a Fractal buy signal has been formed, and we place our third entry just above the high of the Fractal formation (see circle 5 on Figure 12.1). If the market still continues up, trail a profit-protecting stop just under the lowest low of the last three to five price bars depending upon how much room you feel comfortable with. We have found this a good strategy in commodities, stocks, and bonds.

9. Continue to watch for any buy signals until you are fully committed. Notice on the gold chart that another Fractal buy was formed and hit (see circle 7 and circle 8). You would continue on those upward path until you were either stopped out or stopped and reversed to the down side, which is what happened as gold continued.

What Happens if the Fractal Is the First Signal Hit?

The question then arises as to what to do when the first buy/sell signal is not a bullish or a bearish divergent bar. What if the first presenting signal is a Fractal? If its peak is above the Red Line on the Alligator, take it. We place our stop either at a reversal Fractal sell signal or just below the lowest low of the past three to five price bars.

We would then add on to our long position on any other buy signals. If we think we have good trade location and feel the market will most likely continue upward, we would institute our reverse pyramid strategy, explained later in this chapter.

What if the SAO Signal Is the First Signal Hit?

What happens if our first signal after a market reversal is the Super AO—our second wise man? In this situation, we would enter just above the price bar that corresponds with the Super AO signal. We would then place our stop at the bottom of the trend change or more conservatively just below the bottom of the signal bar. Doing so will keep our losses at a minimum. Then institute a trailing stop just below the lowest low of the last three to five price bars and continue trailing this stop until stopped out.

Summarizing our entry process for going long, we basically have three possible alternatives:

1. The bottommost bar is a bullish divergent bar that is *away* from the Alligator's mouth and has good angulation from the Alligator's mouth. This sets up our best possible trade location with the least dollar risk.

2. The market creates a bullish Fractal buy signal and there is no bullish reversal bar at the bottom. Again, we buy just above the Fractal break-out and add on as the market gives us buy signals.

3. A Super AO buy signal is hit before there is either a bullish reversal bar or a Fractal buy signal. We buy just above the top of the price bar corresponding to the third green bar on the Super AO and protect our entry with the closest reasonable stop, which would be the lowest of the last three to five bars.

SELLING OR GOING SHORT

Selling or going short follows the exact same strategy as buying or going long. The first presenting signal is a bearish divergent bar—the circled fourth bar from the left margin. Note that it has good angulations with the Alligator. Again, good angulation means that the price bars are going up at a steeper angle than the Alligator and the Blue Line in particular. The requirements for a pristine signal assuming an upward moving market would be:

1. A bearish divergent bar that has a higher high than the previous bars and the close is in the lower half of the bar (see Figure 12.2, the encircled bar and notation at the top left of the chart).

2. The bearish divergent bar must be ascending at a greater (steeper) angle than the Alligator, particularly the Blue Line of the Alligator.

3. Place a sell stop either one or very few ticks below the low of the bearish divergent bar. It filled on the next bar.

4. Place a protective stop just above the top of the bearish divergent bar.

5. If the market continues downward for two more bars and you have not been stopped out, the market has created a buy Fractal whose initiation point is exactly where your protective stop has been placed. So simply call the broker and buy two contracts (or double the number shares you are short in the stock market) for each one you are short. If that buy signal is hit, then you would be in a go-with market and following the new upward trend.

6. If the market continues to move down and the AO bars are red, start counting the red price bars. (For more information on the AO, see our earlier book, check it out on our Web site, or contact our offices direct.) We normally lower our protective stop a tick or two above the bar that corresponds with the highest high of the three to five most recent price bars.

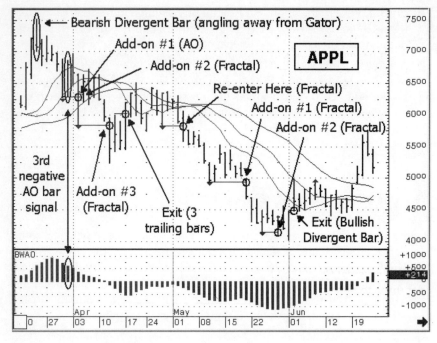

FIGURE 12.2   Selling Apple Computer stock.

7. Assuming that the market is still going your way (moving down in this
    case of Apple Computer) and you have three consecutive red price
    bars, you want to add to your short position by placing another sell
    stop one or a few ticks below the low of the price bar corresponding to
    the third red price bar (see the notation on Figure 12.2). When the sec-
    ond sell signal has been hit, then start looking for your third entry. The
    Apple Computer price continues down and then falls back with at least
    two higher lows in the price bars.

8. At this point a Fractal sell signal has been formed and you place your
    third entry just below the low of the Fractal formation [see the notation
    "Add-on #2 (Fractal)" on Figure 12.2]. If the market still continues
    down, you will trail a profit-protecting stop just above the highest high
    of the last three to five price bars. (Note that some traders prefer to
    give the market more room to roam by placing their protective stops
    using the last four or five bars. With just a bit of practice you will find
    what suits your temperament the best.)

9. After Fractal 2 was added, the market moved back up, stopping us out
    based on trailing an exit stop just over the high of the last three to five
    bars. In this case, we were using a three-bar stop.

10. After exiting this first shot at shorting Apple Computer, another sell Fractal was formed during the week of April 17 but that was followed by another higher Fractal signal being formed the following week of April 24. This Fractal was hit during the week of May 1 and was followed by three more Fractal sell signals that were taken.

11. During the week of June 1, we were reversed to the long side by the bullish divergent bar. At this point we would trade the upward move with the same three wise men signals. As you can see, this was a good, profitable campaign as Apple Computer lost nearly 50 percent of its value.

Not So Pristine but Still Quite Profitable Sell Signal

Just as in our example on the buy side, we would sell any Fractal signal that is below the Alligator's Red Line (teeth). We would then place our stop either at a reversal Fractal buy signal or the just above the highest high of the past three to five bars.

We would use the same strategy on the short side if the AO (second wise man) signal is hit first. We would then add on to our short position on any other sell signals. If we think we have good trade location and feel the market will most likely continue downward, we would institute our reverse pyramid strategy explained in an upcoming section of this chapter.

Summarizing our entry process for going short, we basically have three possible alternatives:

1. The topmost bar is a bearish divergent bar that is moving *away* from the Alligator's mouth and has good angulation from the Alligator's mouth. This configuration sets up our best possible trade location with the least dollar risk.

2. The market creates a bearish Fractal sell signal below the Red Line (Alligator's teeth) and there is no bearish reversal bar at the top. Again, we sell just below the Fractal breakout and add on as the market gives us more sell signals.

3. A Super AO sell signal is hit before there is either a bearish reversal bar or a Fractal sell signal. We sell just below the bottom of the price bar corresponding to the third red bar on the Super AO.

Practice Charts

Figure 12.3 through Figure 12.6 are practice charts. See if you understand and agree with the notations made on the charts for buy, sell, and exit signals

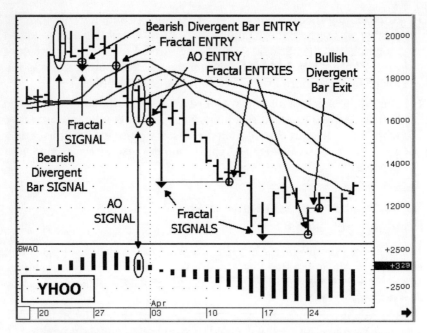

FIGURE 12.3   Yahoo stock chart showing buy, sell, and exit signals.

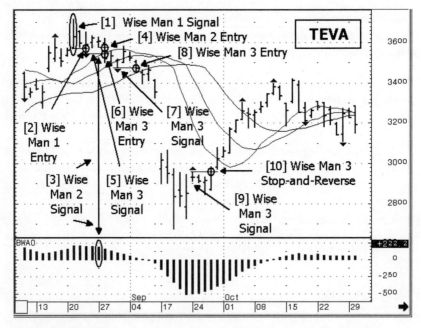

FIGURE 12.4   Teva stock chart showing buy, sell, and exit signals.

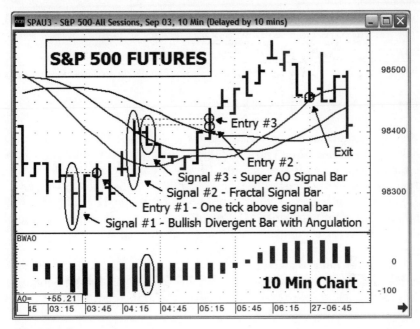

FIGURE 12.5 S&P 500 daytrading chart showing buy, sell, and exit signals.

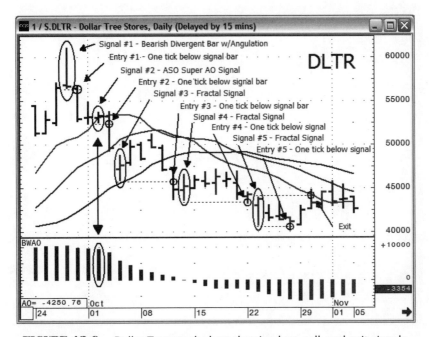

FIGURE 12.6 Dollar Tree stock chart showing buy, sell, and exit signals.

on those charts. Notice also in the S&P 500 daytrading chart (Figure 12.5) that the three wise men work well in all markets and timeframes, whether buying or selling, including intraday futures trading.

CHECK YOUR PROGRESS

Here is a chance to check your progress learning the three wise man signals and corresponding entries. Without looking at the solution printed after the chart, see if you can identify each circled item on the Costco Daily Stock Chart (Figure 12.7). First, identify whether the circled bar is a *signal* or an *entry*. Then identify the *type* of the signal or entry (bearish/ bullish divergent bar, Super AO, Fractal, exit). When you have completed this short exercise, compare your findings to the explanation printed after the chart.

How well did you do with the Costco Chart? Starting with the left-most circled price bar, we see first a bullish divergent signal bar on September 14, creating a long entry one tick above the top of that bar. The next circled

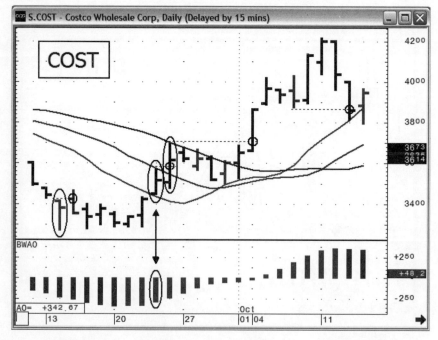

FIGURE 12.7   Costco stock chart showing buy, sell, and exit signals.

bar is the bullish divergent entry bar, where the signal from the previous day was hit and filled. We are now long from this point. The next circled price bar on September 23 is a super AO signal bar, creating a buy signal one tick above the high of this bar. The following bar on September 24 is both a super AO entry bar (from the signal the day before) *and* a Fractal signal bar. Notice there are price bars with two lower highs on each side of this bar creating a Fractal signal one tick above this bar. Then nothing happens for a few days, until the circled bar on October 4, which is a Fractal entry bar for the previously mentioned Fractal signal. The next circled bar on October 13 is an exit bar based on the price dropping below the lowest low of the five preceding bars.

To summarize this typical stock trade:

1. We entered long on September 15 a around $34.16
2. We added another position on September 24 at around $35.75
3. We added another position on October 4 at around $37.01
4. We exited all positions on October 13 at around $38.74

Our net combined profit for this one-month trade was $9.29 per share less commission and slippage on this $37.00 stock!

How did you do? If you had any difficulty with this chart, you should go back and study the charts in this chapter until you can easily recognize and identify each of these signals and entries.

ASSET ALLOCATION

One of the toughest jobs of any trade/vester is asset allocation—how many contracts or shares should I invest or trade? Many advisors suggest that you start with a minimum amount, for example, one contract. Then if that becomes profitable, take your profit and invest in more. If you started with one contract and you have enough profit to invest in two more contracts or shares, do it. We strongly disagree with this approach because your average price goes up geometrically, and if the market should retrace a few percentage points, you could and probably would be wiped out. We prefer what we call reverse pyramiding.

Reverse Pyramiding

We want our first entry to be minimal, because we are at greatest risk on this entry. It is like putting only your toe in the water to monitor the temperature.

Once that first entry becomes profitable and the second wise man comes into being, we want to get much more aggressive and put on a much larger position and follow that up with further decreasingly large entries.

For example, in the gold chart we felt comfortable trading a total of 15 contracts of gold. Our first entry was only one contract. Then on the second signal, we bought 5 contracts, then 4 contracts on the third signal, 3 contracts on the fourth signal and 2 contracts on the fifth market-generated signal. In stocks we trade the same multiples. If our total investment would be 15,000 shares, we would buy/sell 1,000 on the first signal; 5,000 on the second signal; 4,000 on the third signal; 3,000 on the fourth signal; and finally 2,000 on the fifth signal. At this point we have invested all we are comfortable with in this particular future or stock. Our average price is much lower and we simply trail a profit-protecting stop until the market says it has given us enough in this campaign.

In this gold trade we were able to extract 3.2 times more profit from the move by simply trading multiple contracts and varying the volume with each entry. This volume variation permits us to keep our average price very low while still managing to keep our stop losses to a minimum.

Once you become skilled at entering and exiting the markets, the best way to increase your percentage profit is by asset allocation. Over the past 20 years we have issued an ongoing challenge to anyone who can bring us a winning system on a one-contract basis. We can show them how to double the *percentage* profits without more capital. We have usually been able to more than *double* their overall profits without changing any entries or exits but simply by intelligent asset allocation. Reverse pyramiding is one of the best and simplest methods to accomplish this increase in profits.

EXITING A TRADE ONCE YOU ARE IN THE MARKET

Assume we are in the market on one or more buy signals—how do we protect our profits or prevent large losses? Assume we are long; the most common exit hit is the market going below the lowest low of the last three to five price bars. It is less common for a signal in the opposite direction to be created. Most of the time, we are already out of our long position before a short signal is created. The whole idea is simply to march in step with market behavior and the only equipment we need is our charts. We do not need information from any other source. In fact, we think it is a gross error to permit any analyst's prediction to influence our trading behavior. More traders are killed by outside recommendations than any behavior based on their individual thinking and strategy.

Get Out of All or Part?

Again, assume we are in a profitable long position and the market is about to hit our trailing stop—do we get out of our entire position or do we take only a portion out of the market. This obviously is a management decision based on too many individual factors to make a general rule. However, when we have a good entry and nice profits, we sometimes will take out half our profits and place a stop on the other half and just let the market run and see what happens. Sometimes we end up with fewer profits and sometimes we hit the grand slam home run. The decision to get out of all or part of your position is mostly a psychological call. If you are going to hang around talking about all the profits you could have made by getting out of your entire position, then do not use this strategy. It probably is more appropriate for experienced traders who trust their "feel" of the market.

 SUMMARY

In this chapter, we examined how to put our signals into the market with the most potentially profitable trade locations. In Chapter 13 we go back to the psychological part of trading with the very best exercise to get your mind into the right gear and increase not only your profits but even more than that, your enjoyment of life. As your trading improves you will experience a carryover into the other parts of your life. It is almost as simple as looking at yourself in the mirror each day and asking that question, "Who am I?"

However, this exercise is even more powerful and easier to do. Sharing these upcoming exercises is probably the most productive gift you could receive at this time in your life. So get ready to renovate your life for the better. Welcome to the upcoming new you.

CHAPTER 13

How to Get Out of a Hole Once You Are In

At this moment, what is there you lack?
—Zen Master Hakuin (1685–1768)

IT HAPPENS TO ALL OF US

No matter how much experience you have or how profitable you might be on average, every now and then you are going to get yourself in a hole. You will feel despondent and wonder how you might become more profitable or at least get back to your normal profitable trading. In this chapter we outline the very best method we have found for taking care of a trader who is experiencing this bottoming of optimism.

SHADOW TRADERS

One of our chief needs as trade/vestors is support. Unfortunately this support can be hard to find. One of our students was a full time trader with more than 20 years of full time trading in the markets. He came to us for advice about no support. His wife was a high-income professional who worked from 8 A.M. to 4 P.M. five days a week. He traded from home and almost never went out during market hours. When we asked him to explain his situation more fully, he told us,

"I trade all day long and my wife comes home around 4:30 P.M. She opens the door and this is how she starts the conversation *every day*. She always begins by asking 'How much of our money did you lose today?' "

159

He awaited our advice. We honestly told him that, assuming he wanted to continue trading profitably, there are only three alternatives: either (1) shoot her, (2) divorce her, probably a more reasonable alternative, or (3) send her to study with us. He was trying to trade profitably in a completely untenable situation.

Having support from your significant others is very important. But even more important is having support—from inside you.

Protecting the Trader Within

Remember your trader within is a child. Learning to let yourself trade profitably is like learning how to walk. You begin by crawling. Baby steps follow and then there will be falls.

Judging yourself by your early trade is abuse. Judging yourself by more successful experienced traders is also a big mistake. The fledgling trader behaves with well-practiced masochism. Masochism is an art form long ago mastered, perfected during the years of self-reproach. This habit is the self-hating bludgeon with which a shadow trader can beat himself right back into the shadows. What we are looking for in the beginning is progress, not perfection.

Trading is like marathon training. We want to log 10 slow miles for every 1 fast mile. This slow progress can go against the ego's grain. We want to be great—immediately great—but it does not work that way. There will be many times when we will not look good—to ourselves or anyone else We need to stop demanding that we do. It is impossible to get better and look good at the same time.

Remember to be a good trader, you must be willing to be a bad trader. Give yourself permission to make some mistakes and be willing to be a bad trader every now and then. You have a chance to be a good trader and over time maybe even a great trader.

Your Enemy Within—Core Negative Beliefs

Most of the time when we are blocked in any area of our life, it is because we feel safer that way. We may not be happy but at least we know what we are—unhappy. Much fear of our own success is fear of the unknown.

Here is a list of deeply held but rarely spoken, and sometimes unconscious negative beliefs that we have found with most traders.

I cannot be successful because
- Everyone will hate me.
- I will hurt my family and friends.

- I will go crazy.
- I will abandon my family and friends.
- I do not have good enough ideas.
- I do not understand this economy.
- My ideas do not coincide with what I see on TV about the markets.
- I will embarrass myself in front of my family and friends.
- I will never have a steady livable income.
- I will never have any "real" money.
- I will feel bad because I do not deserve to be successful.
- It is too late (I should have studied the markets much earlier).

None of the negative core beliefs are true. They come to us from our parents, our religion, our culture, and our fearful friends. Negative beliefs are exactly that: beliefs, not facts. The world was never flat, although everyone believed that it was. You are not dumb, crazy, egomaniacal, grandiose, or silly just because you falsely believe yourself to be.

What You Are Is Scared

Core negative beliefs keep you scared. Let's explore some logic-brain/trader learning tricks. These may strike you as hokey and unproductive. Again, that is resistance. If internalized negativity is the enemy within, what follows is very effective weaponry. Try it before discarding it out of hand.

Your Ally Within: Affirmative Weapons

Just pick an affirmation. For example "I (*your name*) am a brilliant and profitable trade/vestor." Write that out 10 times in a row. While you are busy doing that, something very interesting will happen. your censor will start to object. "Hey, wait a minute. You can't say all that positive stuff around me, it's just not really true." Objections will start to pop up like burnt toast. We call these *blurts*.

Listen to the objections. Look at those ugly, stumpy little blurts. "Brilliant and profitable . . . sure you are . . . since when? You're just kidding yourself . . . an idiot . . . grandiose . . . who are you kidding? Who do you think you are?" All these are blurts.

Where do your blurts come from? Mom? Dad? Teachers? Church? At least some of these will spring violently to mind. Instead substitute some positive affirmations, as exemplified in the following list, to replace those negative blurts.

ative Affirmations

..... a channel and my works come to good.

- My dreams come from the Tao and I have the power to accomplish them.
- As I create and listen, I will be guided in my trading.
- My creativity heals my losses and myself.
- I am allowed to nurture the trader within.
- My paraconscious always leads me to truth and love.
- My paraconscious leads me to forgiveness and self-forgiveness.
- As I listen, I am led.
- I am willing to win in the markets.
- I am willing to learn and let myself trade profitably.
- I am willing to be of service through my trading.
- I am willing to experience my creative energy.
- I am willing to use my creative talents.

Now look at your own list of blurts. They are very important to your profit sheet. Each of them has held you in bondage. Each of them must be dissolved. Use your affirmations and then go on to what we call "the morning pages." This idea and procedure comes directly from Julia Cameron and her book *The Artist's Way* (G. P. Putnam's Sons, 1992). It is without doubt the very best approach we have found for getting our mind into a winning paradigm. It is a procedure that allows you to get into the flow of the market.

This procedure is not a problem-solving technique but rather a method of blending, melding, and attaining oneness with the market and the world. It is the Aikido way of trading the market and influencing everything that we do. You do not trade the markets in a vacuum. You are in the market and a fellow creator of that same market.

HOW TO USE THE MORNING PAGES FOR CREATING PROFITS

Following Cameron's lead, we suggest a rather rigid weekly structure and we encourage you to try this approach whether you believe it makes sense or not at this time. Try this procedure for six weeks and you will find it makes a significant difference in both your trading and your life. These exercises are crucial and these morning pages are *absolutely essential*. Let me illustrate its importance with this fact. Over the past 20 years of teaching traders how to drastically increase their profitability, we obviously have experienced a very few cases that did not increase their profitability. When that happens, we really dig in to find out the cause of their failure. Without a single exception those few who failed were *not* doing these exercises. Does that mean that if you do these morning pages you will succeed? We cannot prove you will, however we do know that those at the top of the list of successful traders do indeed keep doing their morning pages. Your challenge here is to try it for six weeks and then make it a life habit. Here is the procedure.

In the morning immediately after getting out of bed, sit down and write your morning pages. The morning pages consist of three pages of stream of consciousness. Do not stop until you have completed the three pages. This commitment is so essential that if you are not willing to make this a serious commitment, even more important than that last 30 minutes of sleep in the morning, I strongly suggest that you quit right now. There is no compulsion for you to do this program. You well may choose to go on living your life and trading the way you have always traded. It is your life and you should make this choice. I hope you choose to join this program, otherwise you will never know what is on the other side nor what glorious possibilities lie deep down inside of you, wanting only to get out and enjoy the radiance of living a profitable and creative trading life.

The commitment is between 30 minutes and an hour a day plus 2 to 3 hours at one time sometime during the week. So we are talking about 5 to 7 hours per week. If you do not see that this time is beginning to pay off in spades within the first 2 weeks, quit! This procedure may not be for you at this time.

CREATING VERSUS PROBLEM SOLVING

When you solve a problem, that is all you have—a solution. We are interested in higher approaches. We are interested in the *creation* of what we want. In the case of the market, we are interested in creating profits. There are certain basic principles of creativity.

- Creating is the natural order of life. Life is energy that is pure creative thought.
- There is an underlying, creative force infusing all of life—including the market and ourselves.
- When we open ourselves to this creativity, we open ourselves into realms that we have never witnessed before and profits we have never dreamed of before.
- We ourselves are the product of creation. And we in turn are meant to continue this creation by being creative ourselves.
- The refusal to be creative is self-will and is counter to our true nature.

- As we open ourselves to these levels, many gentle but powerful changes are to be expected.
- It is safe to open ourselves to greater and greater creativity.
- Our creative dreams and yearnings come from a source deep within us. As we more toward our dreams, we move closer and closer to our real selves.

What to Expect

Most trade/vestors wish they could be more successful and enjoy that success more. You may know other more profitable traders who are not as smart, as educated, as dedicated as you. Plus they do not seem to even try as hard as you do. Why then do they profit more? During this procedure you will find the answer to that question.

With others who have gone through this procedure, we see a certain amount of giddiness in the first few weeks. This giddiness is sometimes followed by a strong urge to abandon the process and return to life as we knew it before. This is the bargaining period, called the creative U-turn. Recommitment to the process next triggers a free fall of a major ego surrender. Following this period, the final phase of the process is characterized by a new sense of self marked by increased autonomy, resilience, expectancy, excitement, as well as increased profitability and fun in trading and in life in general. So let us move to the next step—the basic tools.

THE BASIC TOOLS: THE MORNING PAGES OR THE MORNING PERSONAL NEWSPAPER

What are the morning pages? Again, the morning pages are simply three pages of writing, strictly steam of consciousness: "Oh God, another morning. I have nothing to write. I need to wash the car and call Bob. Must not forget to go by the post office before noon, yada yada yada." We could also call this process the Brain Drain or as one person suggested, "Draino for the Braino."

There is no wrong way to do the morning pages. They are not meant to be precise writing. Writing is simply one of the tools. Pages are meant to be simply a recording of the stream of consciousness, writing down whatever is happening in the head. Nothing is too petty, too silly, too stupid, or too weird to be included.

These pages are not supposed to sound smart—although they oftentimes will. And do not even read them for the first 8 weeks. Just write three pages and three more tomorrow before you do anything else except maybe go to the bathroom. All that angry, whiny, petty stuff that you write down in the morning is what stands between you and your profitability. Worrying about your results, the laundry, the funny knock in the car, the weird look in your lover's eye—this stuff usually stays with us and eddies through our subconscious and muddies our days. Get it on the page and do it early.

These morning pages are the primary tools of profit recovery. We are victims of our own internalized perfectionist, a nasty internal and eternal critic, the censor, who resides in our (left) brain and keeps up a constant stream of subversive remarks that are often disguised as the truth. The censor says wonderful things like: "You call that writing? What a joke. Why are you wasting your time like this? This won't help your trading—it might even make it worse," and on and on.

Make this rule: Always remember that your censor's negative opinions are not the truth. By spilling out of bed and straight onto the page every morning, you learn to evade the censor. Because there is no wrong way to write the morning pages, the Censor's opinion does not count. Let your Censor rattle on (and he will), you just keep writing.

Think of your censor as a cartoon serpent, slithering around your profitability Eden, hissing vile things to keep you off guard. If you do not like the idea of a serpent, use a shark as from *Jaws*. Just make the censor into the nasty, clever little character that it is as you begin to pry loose some of its power over you and your profitability.

Morning pages are not negotiable. Never skimp or skip on morning pages. Your mood does not matter. The rotten things that your censor says do not matter. Morning pages will teach you that your mood does not really matter. They will teach you to stop judging and just write, which will soon translate to stop worrying and just trade.

Your trader inside needs to be fed. Morning pages will feed this profitable trader. So write your morning pages. Three pages of whatever crosses your mind—that's all there is to it. If you cannot think of anything to write, then write "I can't think of anything to write." Do anything to fill the three pages. When people ask, "Why do you write the morning pages all these years?" I joke, "To get to the other side." Really it is to get to that smart part of me and get the censor on the road to somewhere. The morning pages teach the logic brain (the censor) to stand aside and let the other brain play.

The morning pages will allow you to detach from your negative censor. The censor always wants to be reasonable. Reasonable loses in the market. That is why you do not see rich professors (especially economists) who make money trading in the markets.

The morning pages become a type of meditation and through this activity we acquire and eventually acknowledge our connection to an inner power source that has the ability to transform our outer world. It is impossible to write the morning pages for any length of time without coming into contact with an unexpected inner power. The pages are a strong and clear sense of the self.

The morning pages map out our own interior. Without them, our dreams would remain terra incognito. It is very difficult to complain about the same situation morning after morning, month after month without being moved to constructive action. These pages lead us out of despair and into undreamed of solutions. Anyone who faithfully writes morning pages will be led to a connection with a source of wisdom within.

Pages are a way of meditating. Lawyers who use them swear that they make them better in court. Dancers claim their balance improves—and not just emotionally. Traders swear that their profits increase and their trading becomes enormously more fun. Loving the morning pages is a good sign.

Boredom is just "What's the use?" in disguise. And "What's the use" is fear, and fear means you are secretly in despair. Now to the second part of this care and feeding for successful trade/vestors.

THE TRADER'S DATE

The other tool in the move from failing to tremendous success may strike you as a diversion. It is a two-step, two-directional process: out and then in. During your morning pages you are sending—notifying yourself and the universe of your plans and dreams, dissatisfactions and hopes. During the trader's date you are receiving—opening yourself to insight, inspirations, and guidance.

A trader's date is a block of time, perhaps 2 hours weekly, especially set aside and committed to nurturing your creative consciousness, your inner trader, your creative child. If your first thought is you cannot possibly have the time, identify that reaction as resistance. Your inner child needs to be taken out, pampered, and listened to. Your inner trader is a child. Time with the parent (you) matters more than money spent.

In looking for a parallel, think of a child of divorce who gets to see a beloved parent only on weekends. What that child wants is attention, not expensive outings. Spending time in solitude with your inner child is essential to self-nurturing. A long walk, a solitary expedition to the beach for a sunrise or sunset, a sortie out to a strange church to hear gospel music, or even bowling.

Commit yourself to this weekly date and then watch your killjoy side try to wiggle out of it. Watch how it gets moved around and how a third party wants to join. Recognize this resistance as a fear of intimacy—self-intimacy.

The morning pages acquaint us with what we think and what we think we need. We identify problem areas and concerns. We complain, enumerate, identify, isolate, and fret. The morning pages constitute step one, analogous to prayer. In the course of the release engendered by our date with our inner trader, in step two we begin to hear solutions. Perhaps, equally important, we begin to fund the creative reserves we will draw on in fulfilling our destiny as successful trade/vestors.

Following the procedures in this chapter will absolutely change your life. However, most of us are willing to go to almost any extreme to remain losers. It keeps our cognitive dissonance down. Another word for this is secret doubt. Boiled down to its essentials, the doubt goes something like this: "Okay, so I started winning this week. So what. It's just a coincidence. Okay so I am beginning to notice that the more I let myself explore the possibility of there being some power for good, the more I notice lucky coincidences turning up in my life. So what? I can't really believe I am being led. That's just too weird . . . ."

The reason we think it is weird to imagine an unseen helping hand is that we still doubt that it is okay for us to be a winner. With this attitude firmly entrenched, we not only look all gift horses in the mouth but also swat them on the rump to get them out of our lives as fast as possible.

I like to think of the mind as a room. In that room, we keep all of our usual ideas about life and trading, God, what is possible, and what is not. The room has a door. The door is ever so slightly ajar, and outside we can see a great deal of dazzling light. Out there in the dazzling light are a lot of new ideas that we consider too far-out for us, and so we keep them out there. The ideas we are comfortable with are in the room with us. The other ideas are out, and we keep them out.

Morning pages and a weekend date with me? Ridiculous! (Slam the door).

Inner work triggering more profits? (Slam).

Something deep inside bothering to help my own trading? (Slam).

Synchronicity supporting my trading with serendipitous coincidences?

(Slam, slam, slam!)

Setting skepticism aside, even briefly, can make for very interesting explorations. In going from losing to winning, it is not necessary that we change any of our beliefs. It is necessary that we examine them. More than anything else, winning is an exercise in open-mindedness. Again, picture your mind as that room with the door slightly ajar. Nudging the door open a bit more is what makes for open-mindedness. Let the two exercises in this chapter be your door opener to greater profits and a better, more rewarding life.

SUMMARY

Every trader/investor will at one time or another have a down period. When that happens we need a strategy to get out of our slump. We need support from others and most of all from ourselves. In this chapter we have looked at ways to protect the good trader that is inside us. Our nemesis is our own negative belief about both trading and ourselves. Fear makes us afraid to make decisions, especially financial ones. We listed a number of affirmative weapons we can use that will make our bottom line much more profitable.

We also examined the crucial difference between creating versus problem solving. One of the best techniques for increasing our creative trading and investing is the use of the morning pages. In addition to the morning pages, we strongly suggest a solitary date with yourself at least once a week. Following these instructions will put you in the appropriate frame of mind to win consistently in any market.

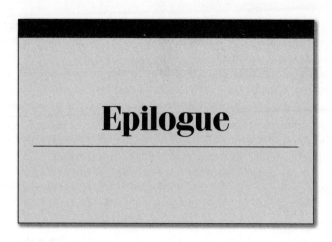

Epilogue

Thomas Jefferson caused a lot of problems when he said that we all have an inalienable right to "life, liberty, and the pursuit of happiness." Life certainly, liberty, no disagreement, but it is the last one, the pursuit of happiness that causes us so much concern. We go astray when we think that happiness is something out there to be pursued. But happiness is not a pursuit. It is not something out there, nor it is external to us. Happiness starts with the most personal commitment that any of us can make. And, like good trading, happiness is very simple.

First, we decide to be happy. Happiness begins the moment that we decide to be happy, no matter what the external circumstances may be. Put simply, the decision to be happy communicates itself to the world and all other things in the world, including especially the markets. When we make that decision, it communicates itself to the world and all of the other things that are already happy—people, places, activities, markets, and circumstances—begin to communicate back.

As we more forward into the 21st century the market becomes one of the last bastions of freedom and democracy. It is the ideal place to find out who you are and what you are capable of. The markets are the postdoctoral schools for human enrichment and understanding. None of the new microtechnology, new gizmos, new medicines or new trading ideas can make you happy without the decision first coming from deep inside your paraconscious mind. When that happens you experience a quantum leap.

And we are definitely in the era of quantum leaps. We want bigger things quicker and with less effort. The markets are the only place I can think of where you can increase your income with no increased effort. If you are an efficient profitable trader, all you do is increase your trading volume. It takes no more effort to buy 1,000 whatevers than to buy 10, only the decision that it is time to move up a notch. We all want that quantum leap in our trading prowess. The term *quantum leap*, like *breakthrough*, may sound tired, but it is nevertheless accurate.

The approaches to the markets contained in this book are a quantum leap forward. This Profitunity approach is designed for three purposes:

1. To eliminate from the trade/vestor's life all the stuff and messes that interfere with profits and create confusion.

2. To allow the trade/vestor to concentrate on inner changes that will allow an accurate view of the markets as they really are instead of what the newspapers, radio and TV say they are.

3. To make trading so efficient that it dramatically increases the amount of free time away from the markets, which can be devoted to personal relationships, increased health, more travel, and so on—all of those personal interests that make being a trade/vestor worthwhile.

We had three goals while preparing this material and sharing it with you. Our goals were:

1. To learn.
2. To have a good time.
3. To make a difference.

We hope that you had the same experience as we have while internalizing and using that material.

So please accept our deepest thanks for spending your valuable time on this book. We are humbled that you would trade the very substance of your life (time) to listen to what we have learned about trading the market profitably and having a great time doing it. In Appendix 1 we present two lists to go through to make sure that we are following the rules precisely and profitably. In Appendix 2 we address some of the most frequently asked questions from those who are trading these techniques. So if, after reading all this, you still are having problems reaching that easy, happy, and profitable plateau, feel free to contact us personally and we will be happy to support you.

Checklists for Trade/Vesting in the Markets

Inherent in every intention and desire is the mechanics for its fulfillment . . . intention and desire in the field of pure potentiality (markets) have infinite organizing power. And when we introduce an intention in the fertile ground of pure potentiality, we put this infinite organizing power to work for us.
—Deepak Chopra

In this appendix we share with you some forms that we and others have used to ensure that we are trading with the rules that have been established as profitable. Plus we share other miscellaneous concepts that contribute to a good bottom line.

One of the best things about the markets is that every day is a new day. Think of it as if you were playing a new video game. The market does not remember playing with you the day before or even the trade before, therefore each game must be played according to the market's behavior for that day or time frame. If we try to play the game as we played yesterday, we will almost always lose. The market does not remember if you won or lost yesterday, nor does it care. It is simply doing what it is supposed to do because that is its function. Think about the millions of iterations a video game has to run; it never plays the same game. It is always changing, therefore the challenge continues. The same holds true for the markets. If anyone really discovered how to win every time, the markets would no longer exist, and the game would be over. How much fun would that be?

What we can do each day as we begin our "game" is be ready for what the market has to offer instead of hanging on to our preconceived notions

171

of what it is supposed to give us. Trading is the most naked psychotherapy in the world. So make sure that you have all the tools in place to trade well and have fun at the same time.

You must do research to find an approach you are comfortable with and understand it thoroughly. Do not leave any questions unanswered. Trading is your future, and you need all the insight you can get to do your best.

Here are some things that are a "must do" before being ready to trade. Data sources are very important; you must have a reliable provider to ensure correct data. There are many to choose from and it is worth doing the research to get the right one for your needs. End-of-day data is much less costly than real-time quotes.

Before you put real money in the markets, we suggest that you paper trade for awhile; if you cannot make money on paper, you should not expect to make it in the real markets. It is much better to make mistakes on paper than with your starting capital. There are simulated trading accounts such as Auditrack where you can practice until you are completely comfortable with the signals and the approach. If you are a seasoned trader this exercise may not be necessary for you. If you need more assistance, contact our office.

You must set up a trading account. Once a client came to a tutorial with $10,000.00 in cash to trade, unaware that was not how it goes. There are many brokers to choose from. There are full-service brokers, discount brokers, and even on-line brokers. If you are a novice trader, you may choose to start out with a full-service broker to assist you with placing your trades and make sure that you are not making clerical-type mistakes. If you are an experienced trader, you simply need someone to execute your orders. You will pay according to the service you require.

It is important to see what features the different brokers offer. Some will give free data quotes with an account; some even pay interest on the money in your account. It is important to make sure you have a reputable firm and receive the services you need. Look at its record. Does it have satisfied customers? If you choose an on-line broker, make sure that you have an alternative way (telephone number) to reach them if your Internet service goes down. This is very important if you are an intraday trader. In most cases, you can negotiate better commissions depending on your account size and the number of trades you execute each month. Just remember your broker works for you. He should not influence your trades or decisions. Make sure that you understand the language of the markets when placing trades. Do you understand a stop limit order? Do you know what a contingency order is? If not find out! This information should come from your broker.

One day you will say, "Sell" instead of "Buy." This is a simple mistake, much different from not knowing what your order means. If you are trading commodities, there are a few more things you must know, such as contract month expiration. In the stock market, contract month expiration does not exist. Commodities have different contract months. They change and expire so it is important to know when to exit a contract month and roll over to the following contract month. You do not want 5,000 pounds of pork bellies delivered to your house.

Know your margin requirements. Margin is the amount of money required to trade each contract. This money must be in your account before you can enter the market. Tick size and price movements are also different in commodities. Each commodity may have a different point value and may move in different increments. For example, the Swiss franc moves 1 point at a time and each point is worth $12.50. Soybeans move or trade in quarters and each one-quarter is worth $12.50 or $50.00. All these small details are what make the difference in you being a prepared or an "impaired" trader. You would not want to fly a plane if you did not know how to read the instruments. Why would you want to risk your money without having the knowledge available to you?

Many traders begin with a limited amount of equity, therefore it is imperative that they do not overtrade or have unrealistic goals. The smaller the account size, the longer it will take to build up equity, but small consistent profits eventually can equal large profits. In the beginning, most traders will have a drop in equity before it takes off. This drop is common, almost a safety feature. We have found that traders who make large amounts of money quickly because they were luckily in the right place at the right time normally end up losing it all. They think they know how the market behaves. They were just lucky. It is important that you trade markets appropriate for your account size, trading style, and experience.

For example, some traders come to us with the idea of only trading the S&P 500, even though they have never traded before. The end result or goal is unrealistic. They do not understand that it is better to make mistakes in less volatile markets while fine-tuning their trading skills before jumping in with the big dogs. If you were just learning how to drive, would you want to go directly to the freeway with experienced drivers going 80 mph? No, you would want to practice on the back roads and empty streets until you were comfortable with all the aspects of driving. Same is true with the markets. We want to be ready for those drivers doing 80 mph, not scared of them.

Once you learn all the details, trading becomes "automagic." Remember how awkward everything was when you first learned to drive? There were so many things to coordinate all at the same time. Remembering to put your foot on the brake to go into reverse, looking in the rearview mirror, trying to judge distances—it all seemed so difficult. Now think of how easy or automagic it is when you drive compared to then. Most of us are talking on our cell phones, looking around, or having conversations with our children. We are not thinking about each individual step it takes to drive; we just do it. That is how we want our trading to be—automagic.

Once you have all the technical tools in place, such as your account, a broker, and a trading approach, you must make sure the most important part of your trading system is ready, *you*!

Here are some checklists to help you get ready for each trade.

Chart Checklist for Daily Trading

Elliott wave: Impulse wave _____ Corrective _____
▶ Overall trend—the trend is your friend!: Up _____ Down _____
▶ Alligator: Opening _____ Closing _____ Sleeping _____
▶ AO: Above zero _____ Below zero _____
▶ Direction of the AO: Up _____ Down _____ Level _____
▶ Does it agree with your side of entry to the market? _____
▶ Bullish divergent bar entry \$_____ Bearish divergent bar entry \$_____
▶ Super AO Entry: Buy \$_____ Sell \$_____
▶ Fractal entry: Buy \$_____ Sell \$_____ Bracketed entry _____
▶ Initial risk in trade: \$_____
▶ Margin required: \$_____ or price per share \$_____
▶ Stops: Green Line _____ Red Line _____ Trailing _____ Extreme Squat _____
▶ Risk per contract/share: \$_____
▶ What other reasons are there for entering this trade beside the signals?
▶ Positive reasons: _____
_____
_____
▶ Negative reasons: _____
_____
_____

Head Checklist for Trading

▶ How am I today? _____
_____

▶ Are my morning pages done? _____ Do not look at the markets until they are done.

▶ Why am I trading today? _____
_____

▶ What do I want from the markets today? _____
_____

▶ What do I expect from the markets today? _____
_____

▶ Do they owe me? _____

▶ Am I trading my last loss or for my next win? _____

▶ Am I trading for the right reasons? If not, why? _____
_____

▶ Am I trading in the now? If not, how can I?_____
_____

▶ Do I want what the market wants or what I want? _____

▶ Do I care which way the market goes? _____

▶ Am I in tune with the market? _____

▶ Who is in charge, my ego or my instincts? _____

▶ What animal does the market represent to me today? _____

▶ What have I learned from this trade and this experience? _____
_____
_____

▶ What ideas do I have to improve my experiences and profits in trade/vesting? _____
_____
_____
_____
_____

Frequently Asked Questions

So happy to see you,
I have nothing to say!
—Zen Master Hakuin (1685–1768)

This appendix contains questions that have been asked of us most frequently and their answers. We thought you might benefit by reading them.

Q: I have never traded before, will this method work for me?

A: Yes it can. We have individually trained more than 2,000 traders over the past 15 years who are now independent successful speculators. Sometimes it is better to have a clean slate. That way you do not have to unlearn anything or have predetermined ideas about the markets.

Q: I have read all of your book—the material was fantastic. What can I do to learn more about your trading methods?

A: If you like our books and want to learn the complete methodology behind our trading you can sign up for our home study course. It contains manuals, videos, audio relaxation tapes, interactive CD Rom, and our end of day software. We also offer a 2-day private tutorial in our office, which is an intensive, hands-on *live trading* experience.

Q: What do I need to get started trading?

A: You will need an account with a broker, a trading strategy, software, a data source, a phone, and a computer! That is all you need to trade.

That is one of the greatest things about trading, you can be in your hotel room on vacation and still trade!

Q: If I have questions after I have taken the home study course, do I have access to help? Is there a charge for this, or a time limit?

A: Absolutely. There is no time limit or fee for trading or technical help. We believe that one of the reasons our traders do well is their ability to ask questions and receive feedback about their trading. I still answer questions from clients who took our course more than 10 years ago. We also know that the markets are constantly changing. We need to adjust our strategy if and when the market behavior changes, so keeping in touch with us is the best way to keep up with our newest work.

Q: Do I need a broker or do I trade through you? If I need a broker, can you recommend one?

A: We do not trade for you, so you will need to open an account with a reputable broker. There are so many to choose from, it can be confusing. We are happy to recommend our broker to you for commodity trading. If you are trading stocks, there are numerous brokers to choose from on the Internet. Make sure you research the company and have a phone backup number in case the Internet goes down. We have been trading with the same broker for 15 years; Bill was their first client!

Q: How much money do I need to get started trading? Is there a minimum account size?

A: We recommend a minimum of $10,000 for a commodity account and $25,000 for a stock account. Keep in mind that you have about 50 to 1 leverage in commodities compared to being fully vested in stock trading. The smaller the account, the longer it will take you to build up your equity.

Q: Is risk management included in your methods? Can it vary from person to person or is it standard for every account size?

A: We do discuss risk management in our courses but we prefer to work with each client one-on-one based on many variables such as account size, trading background and experience, types of markets you are trading, what your belief systems are, and the risk-reward ratio that you will need to feel successful and comfortable trading. Each trader is different; we all come to the table with different expectations, fear/greed processes as well as experiences, so these factors help us know how to direct you in learning how you trade best without losing your money.

As you gain experience in trading you will know when to trade 10 contracts instead of 2, you will feel comfortable with more than one or two positions in multiple markets, or you may be happy with 2 contracts that bring small consistent profits.

Q: I have a full time job. Will I be able to trade the Profitunity methods successfully part-time?

A: Yes, many of our traders have full-time jobs and trade as well. With our methods it should not take you longer than 30 to 45 minutes to evaluate all markets, and it could take only 10 to 15 if you can really focus on the markets instead of your opinions about the markets. Our opinions tend to be our biggest enemy! Our goal is that our traders have the abilities and skills to trade full time if they choose, once they have become comfortable with our methods as well as successful.

Q: Is there a certain amount of time I must spend every day to trade?

A: No, there is not. It varies from day to day depending on the number of positions you are in, or the number of markets that you analyze each day. It really should not take more than 30 minutes a day. If you are spending your evenings in front of the computer, then you are doing it wrong!

Q: Do I need more than one computer to trade?

A: No, you only need one that has your software program and data. You will need an Internet connection to be able to download your data each day.

Q: Do I have to watch the screen all day to trade successfully?

A: Absolutely not! All you need to trade on a position basis is a few minutes at the end of the market day to place your orders for the next day. As a position trader, you are not paying attention to what is happening intraday, you have your stops in and let the market do what it is supposed to do.

Q: What are the minimum requirements necessary to run Investor's Dream software? Can I have it on my home computer and laptop?

A: We recommend that you use Windows XP as your operating system. You can have Investor's Dream on two computers.

Q: Is there a better time frame to trade? I have heard that intraday trading is the most profitable.

A: What time frame you trade will depend on your personality and what markets you like to trade. I prefer to trade the daily charts. They tend to produce more profits long-term because you are able to increase the size of the investment with the trend. I also trade intraday if the daily time frame does not produce signals. If I trade intraday, I tend to look at the 10-minute time frame for volatile markets like the indices. All other markets like the currencies or the grains I trade the 30-minute charts. You can trade any time frame you like or are comfortable with; we have found these to be the best for us and our traders over time.

Q: How do I get data into my charting package? Do you supply that?

A: First of all, check out our Appendix 4 in this book. You will find instructions for how to import various data formats into your computer. If you have difficulty importing data, contact first your data provider. If they cannot solve your problem, contact our tech support department at techsupport@profitunity.com

Q: Is market data expensive?

A: Not really. You can even get some data free on the Internet. However, to get good, fast, and reputable data, you may have to pay a nominal amount. Good error-free data should be an investment not an expense.

Q: Do you provide technical support for your software included with your course?

A: Yes, we do supply free technical support for our software, and we have programmed indicators for MetaStock, TC2000, E-Signal, and TradeStation software. CQG takes care of our technical support if you are using their software and data package.

Q: What is the success rate of your students?

A: Success has a different meaning to everyone. We believe that trading should be a holistic approach to the markets, therefore our clients have more success than most. I would say our success rate both financially and emotionally is in the 75 percent to 85 percent range. I attribute this high rate of success to the ongoing support our clients receive.

Q: What is the average time it takes a student new to the markets to be able to trade profitably? Are there steps to take or do you just jump in once you have finished the home study course?

A: We like to see you paper trade first after completing the home study course to make sure you understand the mechanics of trading, then start trading on a one-contract basis (or a relatively small number of stock shares). This trial trading should not take long. The average client is trading successfully immediately to a few months. Some go faster than others. It depends upon the depth of your understanding of this approach and your own personality type. If you are an experienced trader, you will mostly likely be immediately more successful. If you are totally new to the markets, you may expect a learning curve of one to a few months. It may take that long for you to experience the different moves and personalities of the various markets.

Q: I only want to day trade the S&P 500 on a 1-minute chart. Will your method work?

A: Yes it can, but we recommend that you do not trade on less than a 5-minute chart. We also like to recommend diversification. If the S&P is not trending, there will be others that are. We like to look at all the opportunities that the market gives us.

Q: What is the average return I can expect on my investment monthly?

A: Our goal is 10 percent per month ROI. That is more than 300 percent per year. Obviously 10 percent a year is more than most traders earn. However, we know it is there and many of our students do, and have done, that well or better in the current markets.

Q: I have had some terrible experiences in the past with different systems. What makes yours better?

A: Our system has been thoroughly tested over almost half a century of successful trading and investing. Obviously we are not acquainted with all the details of other approaches but we are willing to put our techniques up against any other for success and profitability. At this point, our approach has been so well proven and documented that we feel quite secure in our statements.

Q: If this works so well, why do you share your knowledge and not just trade?

A: First, we do trade—every day. And we strongly suggest that you not follow anyone who is not willing to trade in front of you. We were either the first, or certainly one of the first, to openly trade in front of large groups of people. We have openly demonstrated the profitability of this approach *real-time* in 16 different countries. One thing that we know about the markets is that there is enough money there for most to do well. We know from experience that if you share and give what you have learned it will come back to you in more than monetary ways. My father has always been a teacher and enjoys helping others change their lives for the better. To be able to teach others take control over their lives and their time is the best reward of all for us. By sharing this knowledge we continue to learn and grow, which are the most important things we can do as humans.

Q: What will I learn at the private tutorial? Will we get to trade? Will you trade?

A: During your 2 days in our office, we cover all the nuances of the markets that we cannot put in a book or the home study course. We do personal and psychological exercises to determine what your underlying structure is and what is motivating you currently—how we can be more in tune with the markets, what new signals are being used, and hands-on trading. The tutorial is a great way for us to get to know you better, which allows us to help you more in an ongoing situation after the tutorial. Once we learn your underlying structure and belief systems, we can guide you better to what will work for you as a trader to bring personal and financial wealth.

Q: What can the home study course teach me that I cannot learn from your books?

A: The three books that we have written give you a great insight into how we trade and what we trade but most people feel that they cannot learn to trade just from a book. There are so many aspects of the markets and conditions that are best taught in several formats, such as audio, visual, personal interaction as well as written. Not to mention the technical help that is given. Being able to have feedback from someone experienced in the methods you are trying to learn is invaluable to a trader, especially a new trader. Plus it is often just plain inspiring to talk with someone who is currently making large profits while trading this approach. We also include our software with the course and interactive charts with questions to make sure you understand the material before you move to the next section. We are available to help you place your first trades, decide where to place stops, and even what markets to trade. The more help you are able to get in the beginning to build your foundation, the better. This is your future and your money! No one will take care your money the way you will.

Q: I have only traded stocks in the past. How hard is it to trade commodities?

A: Once you learn the language, it is easy! There are a few differences in trading commodities versus equities, but I prefer the leverage in commodities. You have about a 50 to 1 ratio, which is pretty nice because it also allows you to make more money with less money. Many people feel that commodities are more risky than stocks. We do not think so.

Q: Are there more opportunities in the commodities markets than in equities?

A: There can be. With the leverage and the constant movement based on true momentum, there are endless possibilities. What we find in commodities is that it is a more equal playing field. What I mean is that it takes true market volume to move a market. The stock market has less potential due to the leverage advantage in the commodity markets. Knowing that you can make money with less money makes the commodity markets more appealing to some traders.

Q: How long have you been trading?

A: Bill has been actively trading on a daily basis for 45+ years; he has been investing for more than 50. I (Justine) have been actively trading for almost a decade.

Q: Should I rely on my broker to keep track of my trades?

A: No, that is not their responsibility. You must keep track of your trades and positions. You should check your broker's information to make sure you are getting accurate fills. Brokers make mistakes too. Your broker will only let you know if you have a margin call. There are many different types of brokers; you can pay more for a full-service broker if you require the help. After absorbing the material in this book, you should not need to pay for full-service brokerage. You should shop around for the best price per round turn or per share that will give you excellent service on filling your orders. As you trade more, you will be able to negotiate lower commissions.

Q: What is the average win-loss ratio of Profitunity traders?

A: That varies from trader to trader and from trade to trade. What is important is that we have a consistently profitable equity curve. Sometimes we may have more losing trades than winners but our winners are so much larger that the profits continue to accrue. It is important to cut your losses quickly and let your winners run in order to keep an increasing equity curve in your account.

Q: Do you have a formula for percentage of risk per trade? Does that even apply to your type of trading?

A: No, we do not. Our rule of thumb is never margin over half of your account at any time. That will ensure that if everything goes against us, we would still have half of our account left to trade. We have never had that happen but it is a safety precaution. We prefer to work with each client individually based on account size and goals for that person. If you place your protection based on a percentage loss you are *not* trading the market, you are trading your wallet or your bank account, which has absolutely no relation to the markets or what is happening inside the markets.

Q: Will I need to attend the private tutorial after completing the home study course? How many days is the class?

A: It is a great complement to the course to attend our private tutorial, as being able to see us trade and have hands-on experience is invaluable in this business. We are also able to go over things that can only be done in front of a chart together. If you are looking for Elliott wave help for example, hands-on is the way to go.

Q: How often do your teach the private tutorials? How many students attend?

A: We teach once a month and there are four students in a class. This allows us 2 to 1 intensive instruction for the 2 days.

Q: If I feel I would benefit from one-on-one training rather than a classroom situation is that possible?

A: Yes, many of our clients prefer one-on-one, and we will accommodate them either in our office or theirs. Some prefer to be in their office where they have their own computers and comfort level. We will do whatever will help our traders become successful.

Q: In your experience, what qualities make a good and successful trader?

A: Patience, consistency, motivation, dedication, and, most of all, to be balanced within and happy. These qualities help make the best traders. However, the very most important attribute you could develop is the ability to see reality as it "really is," rather than what you wish it were. The ability to get off your position is a necessary prerequisite for long-term success.

Q: When a new trader that has had substantial losses previously comes to you, can you help him or her get over the fear and trade again?

A: We can and we have, but it can be difficult. A person must be able to let the losses go and move forward before he can be successful again. Our psychological facilitation is the key to this success. The other important factor is building confidence again. We prefer to take small steps to re-enter the trading world. We want to take incremental steps with each success in the rebuilding phase. Remember the old saying about getting right back on the horse after falling off.

Q: In your opinion what is the biggest reason traders fail?

A: That is easy—*ego* and *opinions*! Our egos are our biggest enemy in the markets. Having to be right instead of being in tune will produce a loser every time.

Q: If you could give every trader one piece of advice what would it be?

A: Obviously, read this book again and pay particular attention to the Sacred Cow Terminators in Chapter 1 of this book. Realize that the markets are not what the TV and newspapers say they are. Markets are emotional energy exchanges and energy takes the final form of money (profit/loss). The next step obviously is to learn what the markets really are all about and then *go for it*! Life is to be lived, not talked about or feared.

How to Control Your Mind While Trading

Autogenic Training for Trade/Vestors

[*Note:* This portion of this book was written by Ellen Williams, a psychotherapist who has spent decades working with and counseling traders and investors. She has worked with some of the most experienced traders in the world and also with those just starting out. In this appendix she shares what has become a very effective technique in solving traders' and investors' tension management.]

Life today is portrayed as highly stressful. When we watch television or read magazines and newspapers, we are informed that we work too many hours, juggle too many responsibilities, and that many people suffer from stress-induced illnesses. These same sources tell us to exercise, take a vacation, try a pill, do yoga, play a sport, or sit down and clear our minds through meditation.

Most traders are Type A personalities, which means they attack the stress issues the same way they take on a new project: They schedule the sport or relaxing activity and expect to learn how to manage their tension in an hour. The stress often increases and the time available to relax decreases. Guess what effect this has on already tired-out individuals? They push and push but other things happen, such as sleep problems and overeating.

As these scenarios played out, it became clear that a simple, easily learned technique designed for traders would be useful to Profitunity clients and all trade/vestors. Your greatest asset, your brain, is the most underutilized organ of your body. That 3-pound universe is central control. This organ enables us to learn, love, laugh, sing, plan, create order in our lives, and experience the heights and depths of emotions. Yet, encased in a cage of bone, we take this fragile assembly of neurons, cells, blood, and brain matter, for granted. We have the ability to live one hundred years or more with the central control system composed of delicate skin, fragile bone, pulsing blood, and alive nerves in fine tune with our heart and lungs. This nervous system is more elaborate than that of any other mammal. We alone seem to know that we are finite.

Our minds are able to conceive and develop the most elaborate plans for industry, art, and commerce, yet how much time do we give to our own personal well-being? In between our job, marriage, family, and social obligations, we seek the time to exercise, relax, and somehow, have a good time. But all too often, our nervous system is too overloaded to let us find peace.

In Europe, Dr. Johannes H. Schulz developed a method of deep relaxation called *Autogenic Training* (AT). Used in clinics, hospitals, and doctors' offices throughout Europe, thousands have found relief from headaches, digestive disturbances, hypertension, insomnia, and many other physical problems. Some have found it a remarkable help with stopping smoking and drinking to excess.

It was also discovered that AT was of great benefit to healthy people. Since AT is a natural relaxation technique, learning to use AT is a simple pathway to feeling peaceful. This method has been developed and refined over years of sound medical research. Millions of stressed-out individuals have tried yoga and countless other meditation techniques and still search for a simple, sound way to health and happiness. Autogenic training offers traders a fast, efficient and above all, effective way to maintain a peaceful attitude while trading in a fast-paced environment.

When we think about all of the material that floods our minds, we frequently feel overwhelmed. What should we do? Take a class, join a health club, get a massage, or learn to meditate? Isn't that something monks do after years of practice in a serene controlled environment? And don't they sit for hours, all day? How can we take the time to realize our dreams, tap into our highest potential when we are wrestling with earning a living, our relationship, our children's needs, and last of all, regrettably, our own needs?

What if you knew that 10 minutes, twice a day could lead to a wealth of self-knowledge, a reduction of anxiety and stress—would you be willing to give it a chance for 6 weeks? When traders begin seeking answers to their stress-related situations, they often try a few different ways to compensate. Most Profitunity clients have tried to master their stress and are interested in a new approach.

Marty K., a new client, was making a big life change. Marty knew how to trade the bonds; after all, he had been in the bond pit in Chicago for 9 years. Nine years was a long time to spend in a pressure cooker.

When his father died, Marty came into a substantial amount of money.

Enough money to pay off his house, his and his wife's cars, and leave the bond pit for a trading office in his home. Marty's wife, Carol, kept her job. The children were in high school so Marty had an ideal setup; no noise and all the comforts of home.

Except, Marty could not sleep. He was tired when he went to bed, or so he thought, but as soon as his head hit the pillow, his mind began churning. Carol called it the hamster wheel brain exercise. Around and around, slow down a little, no, there it goes again. Marty reviewed every trade he placed and any bad decision he might have made in relation to the trades. Any loss sent him off. Was the stop too close? Was there an announcement? What was he thinking when he sold at 88; all he had to do was hang in through another half-hour when he would have made a healthy profit.

Marty needed sleep and he craved a break. He tried more exercise, a warm bath before bed, no television after 9 P.M., an over-the-counter sleep aid. Then he saw his doctor and got a prescription for sleeping pills. No good—the sleeping pills made him so hungover he questioned his judgment the following day. Next, he began getting massages. They helped his shoulders and back but still Marty was lucky to sleep 3 hours a night.

When Marty called my office, he sounded desperate. We talked about his trading and how worried he was about some recent losses and the small amount of sleep that he was getting. He was nervous about trading when he was so sleep deprived but trading was what he did. Trading defined him, his self-worth, his manhood; trading had been his working life for years.

Barbara's story was different but also involved the financial markets. She worked for an international bank and analyzed foreign currency markets. Barbara could sleep; she loved her deep sleep but what made her hands sweat and her breathing turn into a storm in her chest was the presentation of a daily report to her supervisor. Her suggestion that she make her report via e-mail was a big mistake. Then she developed a nervous cough. Barbara knew that if she did not overcome her problem, her future with her company was going to change. She had the skills, the education, and she knew she was up for a promotion that would involve more public speaking.

Both Barbara and Marty made it clear that they did not want to go into therapy nor were they willing to take any medications. Marty believed that the sleeping pills had interfered with his trading analysis. Barbara did not like to take even an aspirin. Both needed a way to calm their nervous system, to reduce nervous tension, and to increase their self-confidence.

Both started on a simple exercise to be repeated twice a day. Autogenic training is a form of hypnosis induced by the AT student himself. It is important to understand the effect of hypnosis on the autonomic nervous system. The nervous system is divided into two parts, the central nervous system, which is under the control of the will, and the autonomic nervous system (ANS), which is not under the control of the will. The central nervous system influences the contraction and tone of the voluntary muscles. The ANS is divided into two more systems, the sympathetic and the parasympathetic. When we experience danger or fear, the sympathetic system causes us to have reactions such as a fast heartbeat that pumps oxygen and sugar to the muscles. We may tremble as vision and hearing become acute and our breathing quickens to send more oxygen to the blood.

Primitive man alternated between the danger reaction and the security reaction so that he could hunt and do battle and once in a safe place, could sleep, eat, and relax. The ANS is important in relation to the hypnotic state. Once the AT technique is mastered, one can switch to that mode of peace, calm, and relaxation. The AT student easily learns how to change his perception from the material surroundings to his subjective experience and a degree of control over the autonomic functions.

The goal of an AT session is a hypnotic state of light trance. This state leads to a relaxation of the skeletal muscles and an increased blood flow to the legs, hands, and feet. By the blood being more evenly distributed through the body, there is a feeling of pleasant warmth.

The practice is done twice daily: 10 minutes in the early morning and again at any time available in the late afternoon or evening. Most people use a timer or wristwatch alarm to be sure to practice for 10 minutes only. Initially, students go through a routine of turning off the telephone, putting up a Do Not Disturb sign, and letting others around them know that this time is their 10-minute practice period. The following preparations are vital to a good practice. If people find it hard to assure themselves of 10 minutes, twice a day to practice, it is a wake-up call to see that they really need this practice.

Getting Ready to Practice AT

1. Put out a Do Not Disturb sign.
2. Turn off phone.
3. Get a light blanket or pillow (if needed).
4. Remember your return.
5. Set timer.
6. Remember the phrase "I am at peace."

The AT practice can be done lying on a firm surface or sitting in a chair. After making sure that they will not be interrupted, they lie down, make the statement "I am at peace" and begin their practice. They learn to do what is called *the return*, which ensures that they are alert following such deep relaxation. To practice the return, lie on the floor or bed or sit in a chair and make tight fists, raise arms above the head, rotate the wrists, then vigorously shake out the arms. If lying down, protect your lower back and turn onto one side and easily push to an upright position. If AT students forget the return, they may find themselves feeling sleepy and tired after the 10-minute practice. We say, "Remember the return," just before beginning the practice to be sure that we remember to do it at the end of the practice. This return is performed two or three times.

The first lesson consists of a phrase, "My right arm is heavy," repeated silently three times. Left-handed people change this to "My left arm is heavy." This phrase works to promote the relaxation of the striated muscles. When the mind wanders to thinking and planning as everyone's does, simply repeat the phrases again and again. The muscles relax, the joints loosen, and a deep sense of heaviness is felt. Then, remind yourself to do the return to ensure feeling refreshed after a deep relaxation experience.

Barbara called after her first few days of practice to report a feeling of floating and wondered if this was the desired result. Floating means that you have let go of muscle tension and that you have entered a light self-induced trance.

Marty had a different reaction. For the first 2 days, he was unable to lie still for 10 minutes. He called me to discuss the tension he was experiencing in his legs. " I get tense and then there's no position that feels right for my knees." Marty said. He added a rolled up pillow under his knees and found that he could stay still throughout the 10 minutes. On the fourth day, he called to say that he was certain that he had fallen asleep.

Both Barbara and Marty met their goal of feeling heaviness from head to toe by the end of the first week. Each experienced a different sense of heaviness; one felt as if she were floating, the other seemed to fall asleep. Often, people experience heaviness in the legs only, or in the arms, but persistence with the phrase results in a generalized heaviness.

Heaviness is a subjective experience and many students report feeling very light and think that they are missing the desired experience. With the progressive relaxation produced by AT, muscle tone decreases, causing a loosening of the joints, and the sensory organs register a sort of yielding or sinking onto the respective surface. However, lightness means that tension has begun to fade, so the student may feel light and be on target with his or her practice. Frequently, the first feeling of heaviness may be in the opposite arm, the trunk of the body, or a leg.

The next phrase, "My right hand is warm," is added to the first phrase of heaviness during the second week of practice. With warmth added to the heaviness, some traders report feeling as though their hands are swollen. Since warmth sensors are much closer together in the hand than in other parts of the body, warmth is usually felt first in the hand. The experience of warmth leads to better peripheral circulation, producing a feeling of comfort and actual improved physical well-being.

Each formula is expected to be mastered in one week. Some may go faster and some much slower. For those who are quick to experience heaviness and warmth, they should still stay with one formula per week until all six are learned. For those who need more time, do not worry, a week or two will only serve to firmly embed the practice in the memory.

Just as the first lesson deals with the musculature of the body, the second phrase about warmth is beneficial to the circulatory system. Each practice begins and ends in the same way. These two simple statements produce deep results. They teach the student how to reduce stress and they show how our ability to relax our muscles and increase the circulation leads to better mental and physical health.

Marty was still having some sleep problems so I suggested that he use the statement for heaviness at bedtime or if he wakened during the night without setting a timer or doing a return. It is important to do two practices per day, using the return in order to experience a deep, relaxed state, knowing that the return will bring the student back to an alert state of mind. For those with sleep problems, the phrase for heaviness is an excellent sleep aid. If using AT to go to sleep, do *not* remember the return. In cool climates, students use heaviness and warmth for the sleep induction. If it is a warm night, just use "My right arm is heavy."

Barbara was dreading giving her regular report. She entered the room with her hands sweating and tried my suggestion of saying to herself "I am at peace," then letting her tense shoulders and neck experience a sense of heaviness. By the time she began to speak, she was able to control her voice and speak with less tension coming from her throat. Her voice lowered and although she still had sweating palms, she was able to finish without feeling she might faint before she got through her charts and figures.

Marty is sleeping better and is doing more planning of his trade entries, exits, and stops the night before trading. This routine helps him to go to sleep using the heaviness formula and helps him in that he knows his big trading decisions are already made for the next day's trading. When he becomes stressed during the day, he likes to lie down and take a 10-minute stress break.

These simple techniques that require very little actual time, provide the trader/investor with hours of peace and tranquility. Both Barbara and Marty went on to learn the next four formulas, which deal with the central nervous system, giving them more control over their breathing and pulse rate. They then move on to the other four phrases. "My breathing is calm and regular." The last two phrases help with decision making. They are, "My solar plexus is glowing warm," and lastly, "My forehead is cool."

Consider these last two phrases and what they can do for you. These exercises in maintaining a warm center and a cool head lead to handling any stressful situation by calmly saying, "cool head, warm center," and experiencing the calm attitude that can be called up when needed. In Aikido and other Eastern disciplines, the area of the solar plexus often called the *Hara* is the point sought as a center of balance and mastery. By learning to control emotions through AT, traders have a real edge in planning their trades.

Jeff M. was a good trader; he made money, did not worry about the market much and played competitive tennis. He began AT practice after a shoulder injury; he wanted to do whatever he could to help the healing. Jeff went to physical therapy three times a week and practiced AT four times daily. Within a short time, his therapist saw an improvement in Jeff's ability to regain full range of motion At the end of the 6-week AT training, Jeff told me that he had not realized how much tension he was storing in his shoulders and back. During the learning period, Jeff had some problems with getting his left elbow and wrist in a comfortable position. He used a small rolled washcloth under his wrist on the left side that allowed the arm to rest without strain.

Occasionally, those with lower back pain require a pillow under the knees. If a pillow does not help, doing AT sitting in a chair is the best solution. In nursing homes, we teach AT sitting upright. For those who have weak bones and neck muscles, a pillow may be propped behind the head.

People of all ages with all sorts of emotional problems and many physical conditions have used AT successfully. My observation is that AT is simple, and as humans, we tend to over complicate nearly everything we do. Children love AT; they do not have barriers to trying it.

Some of the problems that people call about are interesting. The most common is that people report falling asleep but say they got up in 10 minutes so how could they have been asleep? They were in a light trance, a feeling so relaxing that people associate it with sleep. Also, while repeating the phrase "my right arm is heavy" or any of the six phrases, their minds become quieter. Focusing on a phrase, then feeling the heaviness, quiets that busy monkey mind.

Monkey mind, as some Zen masters like to call it, does not need any explanation to those who lie awake, longing for sleep. Monkey mind steps in and takes over for those who have a problem, or have suffered a setback in life or a bad trade. Monkey mind is when the mind stays stuck in a groove and all attempts to control one's thoughts or to think of a new thing or best yet, to stop thinking at all, become futile.

In such frustrating times, AT can be a way out of these obsessive thinking patterns. We practice AT twice daily every day so that when we really need a boost, a method that gives us rest, we can call on all of the phrases or just one that applies to the current situation. Autogenic training is far more effective than counting sheep.

Jeff said that AT gave him the kind of break from worrying and planning that allowed him to return to tennis and win his first doubles match since his injury. Jeff used AT every morning and after 6 months of practice asked me to help him develop a formula or phrase to be used for his tennis game.

Advanced AT is designed to allow more and more creative thinking as well as show the way to individual phrases. A note of caution is needed here. It takes a minimum of 3 months' practice to begin working with a special formula because we want you to have such a good grasp of each phrase that you can be in that place at will. My preference is that people practice 6 months before moving to advanced AT but in some instances, there is a real need for a special phrase. This advanced practice involves seeing colors, floating objects seen with the mind's eye, feeling a desired emotional state, visualization, and seeking answers to questions.

Jeff wanted to see himself in a perfect tennis game. A whole game would be difficult to imagine in this manner so we focused on Jeff's arm and range of motion for his shoulder. After reaching his relaxed state, Jeff added the perception of color to his practice. Jeff pictured himself at peace in a large color field, then added his new phrase, "My shoulder is free and powerful," which brought up images of hitting the tennis ball and watching it fly across the court.

Continued practice has shown Jeff how much AT has helped his game. His tension levels have dropped and he is still winning important matches. Barbara is still working with her fear of speaking but the difference after AT is that she can do her job without the sweating palms and other signs of nervousness. She has moved up in the company and continues to use AT. Marty is sleeping well, making money, and spends more time with his family. He is planning to start an on-line market newsletter now that he has more time.

Traders regularly report that AT has benefited their trading and greatly improved their self-knowledge, which is so important to trading success. The addition of AT, morning pages and the date with the inner trader give the novice or experienced trader a variety of tools to help achieve their lifetime goals. Profitunity clients receive the AT cassette tapes and can contact Profitunity for help with learning AT. If you are having difficulty with AT, feel free to contact me at ellen@profitunity.com.

Setting Up Investor's Dream for Profitunity Signals

Investor's Dream is our own proprietary advanced charting program, which is available in both end-of-day and real-time versions to our students and clients. A fully featured demo version of Investor's Dream is always available for download from our Web site: www.profitunity.com.

As configured after installation, Investor's Dream has many indicators and features not covered in this book. To make only the Alligator and AO appear for the three wise men, we need to dumb down Investor's Dream a bit. (See Figure A4.1.)

We start by hiding some of the multiple subgraphs in InnerWindows. To do this, simply right-click within the subgraph you wish to hide, and then select "Minimize This InnerWindow" from the pop-up menu displayed. (See Figure A4.2.)

After you have minimized all of the InnerWindows *except* the AO, your chart window should look something like Figure A4.3.

Now you are ready to start applying the three wise men from this book with the Alligator and AO all ready for you. In addition, you will note that Investor's Dream also displays Fractal signals above Fractal signal bars for your convenience. Keep in mind that many of the features in Investor's Dream are not discussed in this book, but are presented in our previous books and are taught thoroughly in our home study course and subsequent optional private tutorials.

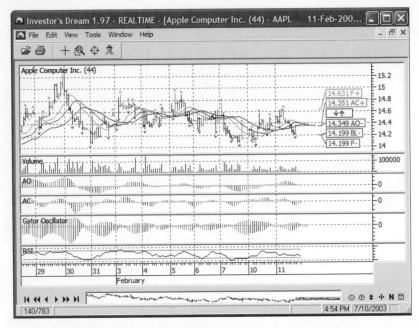

FIGURE A4.1   Investor's Dream default chart window.

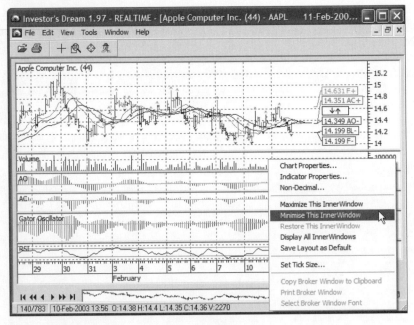

FIGURE A4.2   Minimizing InnerWindows in Investor's Dream.

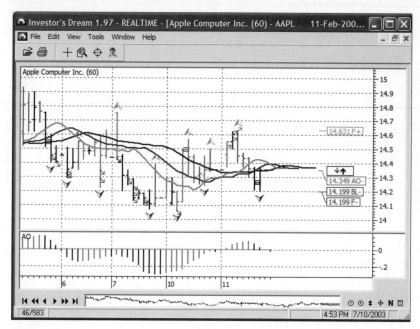

FIGURE A4.3   Investor's Dream configured for three wise men trading.

Setting Up CQG

CQG has been our preferred data and charting service for many years. All of the Profitunity trading techniques and methods were developed and tested using CQG products. Many of our students who trade for a living prefer CQG over other market data and charting services. You can find out more at the CQG Web site: www.cqg.com or call our office for a referral to our contact within CQG who works with the Profitunity trading techniques.

A set of our basic indicators for CQG is furnished without charge to our home study course. A much more complete set of indicators and additional features is available as the "Bill Williams indicators" available for an additional monthly fee from CQG. If you subscribe to the Bill Williams indicators from CQG, their legendary technical support will help you set them up if help is needed.

To get started, just display a regular price chart within CQG as illustrated in Figure A5.1. Now, right-click on the chart background, and then select Add Study from the pop-up menu displayed. See Figure A5.2 for an illustration. From the list of available studies shown, select the BW AO study and click the Add button in the dialog window as shown in Figure A5.3. Your chart window should now look similar to that shown in Figure A5.4.

In the same manner and fashion, add the BW Alligator study as before from the pop-up menu shown in Figure A5.5. Now your CQG window should look clean and simple like that in Figure A5.6, with the prices and Alligator occupying approximately three-quarters of the upper window area, and the AO occupying approximately one-quarter of the lower window area.

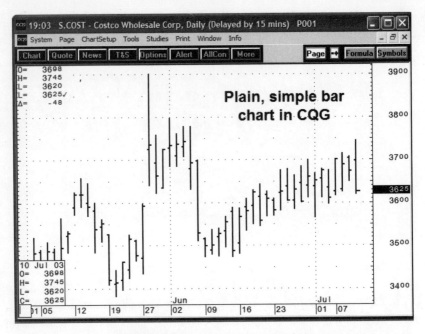

FIGURE A5.1   CQG plain price chart.

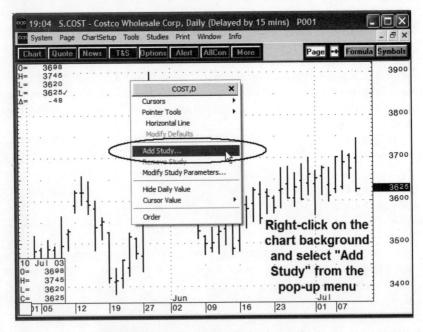

FIGURE A5.2   CQG Add Study window.

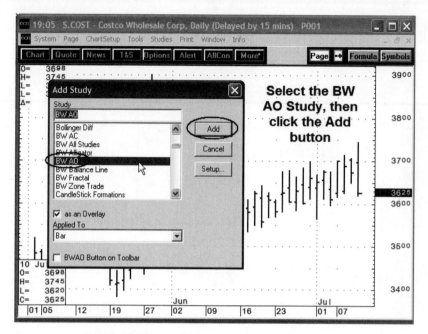

FIGURE A5.3   CQG Add Study selection window.

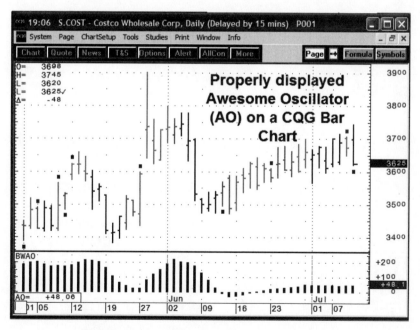

FIGURE A5.4   CQG AO subgraph window correct.

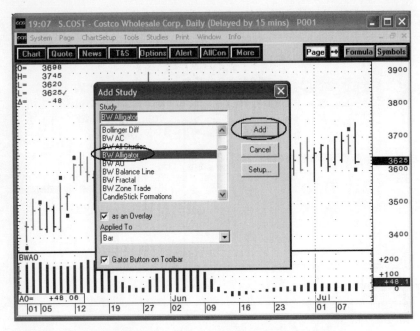

FIGURE A5.5   CQG Add Study selection window.

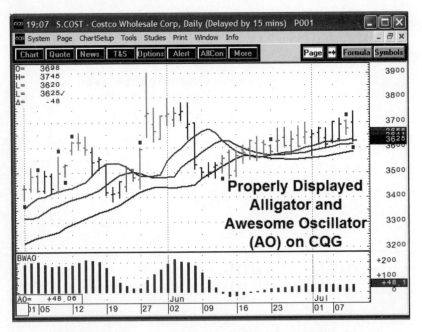

FIGURE A5.6   Properly displayed Alligator and AO on CQG.

APPENDIX 6

Setting Up MetaStock Professional 8.0

The full suite of the Profitunity indicators have been included in Meta-Stock products since version 7.0, so setting up MetaStock for the three wise men is a straightforward task. To get started, just display a regular price chart within MetaStock as illustrated in Figure A6.1. Now,

FIGURE A6.1   MetaStock simple price chart.

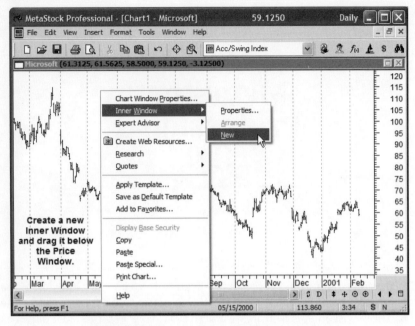

FIGURE A6.2 MetaStock add Inner Window.

right-click on the chart background, and then select Inner Window → New from the pop-up menu displayed. See Figure A6.2 for an illustration. The new inner window may be displayed above the price bar window. If such is the case on your computer, simply drag the title bar of the new inner window below the price graph window. See Figure A6.3 for proper positioning of the windows. We want to remove the title bar for the new inner window we just added, so right-click anywhere in the background of the new inner window and select Inner Window → properties from the pop-up menu as shown in Figure A6.4. Now we want to uncheck (clear) anything in the "Show title bar" checkbox and then click the Apply button as shown in Figure A6.5 before closing this window.

It's time to add the (built-in) Awesome Oscillator indicators to the new (lower) inner window. First, click on the indicator pull-down menu in the main tool bar, then left-click and drag each of the Profitunity—PTG AO Green and Profitunity—PTG AO Red indicators from the drop-down menu list to the lower inner window. See Figure A6.6 for an illustration of MetaStock's drop-down indicator menu. After you drop each AO indicator in the lower window, right-click on it to display the pop-up menu, and select Properties as shown in Figure A6.7. In the Indicator Properties dialog window, we simply want to make sure that the indicator is configured to display the

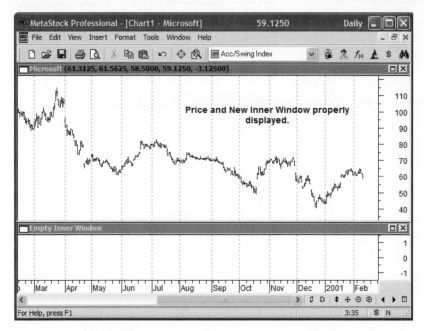

FIGURE A6.3 MetaStock proper window positions.

FIGURE A6.4 MetaStock Inner Window properties menu.

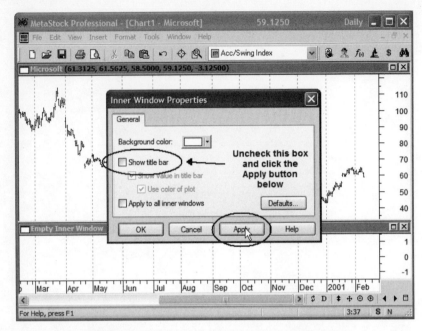

FIGURE A6.5   MetaStock inner window properties.

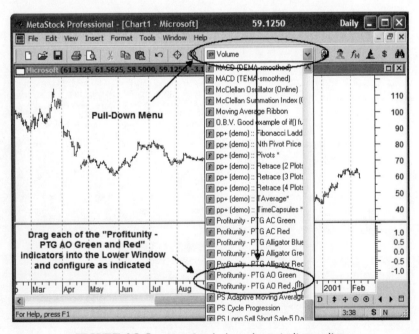

FIGURE A6.6   MetaStock drop-down indicator list.

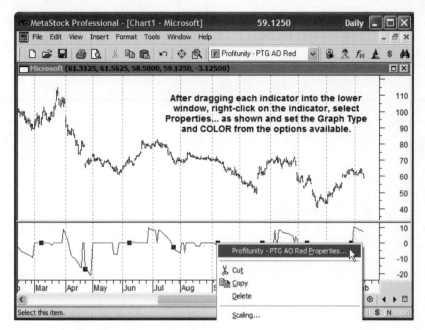

FIGURE A6.7 MetaStock indicator properties menu.

correct color (red or green, depending on which AO indicator you are configuring), and that it is displayed as a histogram before clicking on the Apply button and closing the window. See Figure A6.8 for an example of this window. Figure A6.9 shows a correctly configured AO indicator in the lower inner window:

In a similar manner, we are going to click-and-drag each of the three Alligator lines from MetaStock's drop-down indicator menu as shown in Figure A6.10. Note that we are dragging each line over the prices bars, because the Alligator is displayed over the price bars.

After dragging and dropping each Alligator line on the price bars, remember to right-click on each line and configure it for the appropriate color (blue, red, or green) in the Indicator Properties dialog window (like we did with the AO indicators). After dragging the first Alligator line onto the price bars, your chart window should look like that shown in Figure A6.11.

When you have added all of the Alligator lines to the price bars and configured the colors correctly, you have the finished chart you will need to trade using the three wise men as illustrated in Figure A6.12.

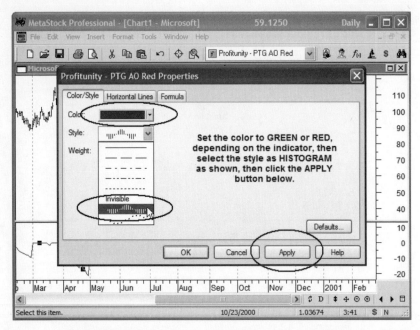

FIGURE A6.8   MetaStock indicator properties dialog.

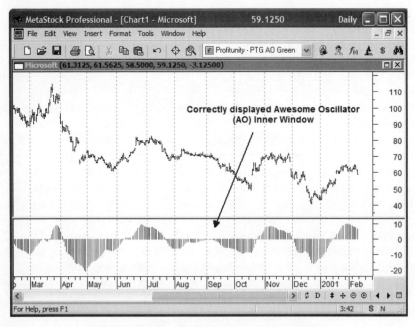

FIGURE A6.9   MetaStock correct AO display.

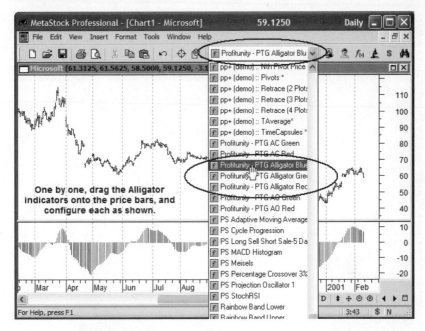

FIGURE A6.10   MetaStock adding the Alligator lines.

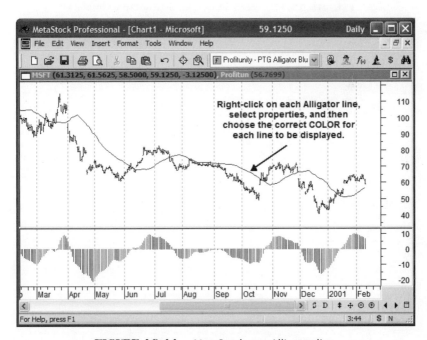

FIGURE A6.11   MetaStock one Alligator line.

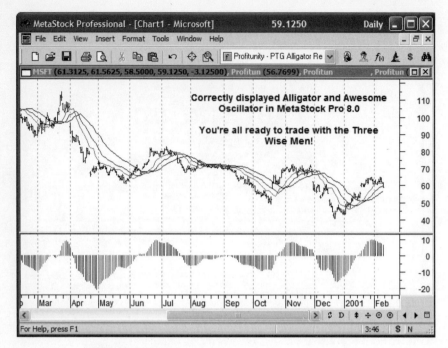

FIGURE A6.12 MetaStock complete setup example.

Setting Up TradeStation 2000i

W e have provided the entire suite of Profitunity indicators (including custom indicators for trading spreads) for TradeStation products since 1997. The Alligator and AO indicators described here will work without modification in all versions of TradeStation 2000, TradeStation 6 and 7, and will also work with older versions of TradeStation and SuperCharts with some minor modifications.

While creating ad installing indicators in TradeStation is well beyond the scope of these instructions, we will provide the EasyLanguage code for both the Alligator and awesome oscillator at the end of these instructions. We provide the complete suite of Profitunity indicators for TradeStation products to our home study course students and clients at no charge upon request.

These instructions assume TradeStation version 2000i; if you have an older or newer version, please adapt these instructions to your particular version. To get started, just display a regular price chart within TradeStation as illustrated in Figure A7.1.

First, we need to set some general chart window properties to allow our indicators to display correctly. Begin by right-clicking anywhere on the chart window background and select Format Window from the pop-up menu as shown in Figure A7.2. Click on the rightmost tab labeled Properties and confirm that the Bars to Right setting is set to 8 and that the Use as Default box is checked. Then click the OK button to close this dialog. See Figure A7.3 for an example. Now, right-click on the chart background, and then select Insert Analysis Technique from the pop-up menu displayed. See Figure A7.4 for an illustration.

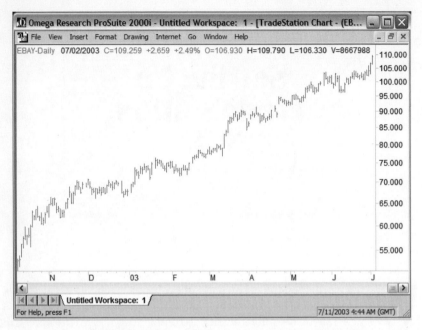

FIGURE A7.1   Simple TradeStation price chart.

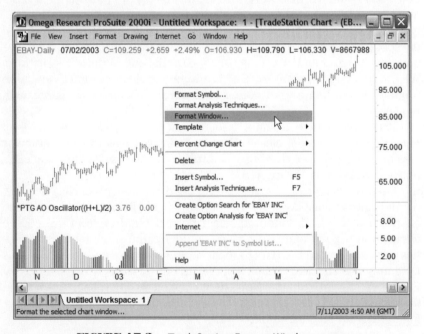

FIGURE A7.2   TradeStation Format Window menu.

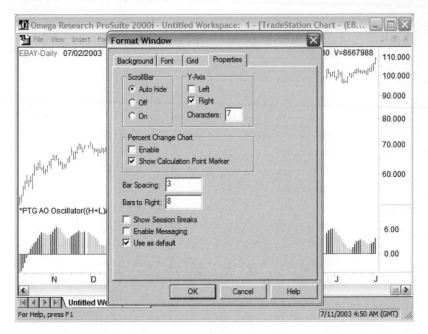

FIGURE A7.3   TradeStation Format Window dialog.

FIGURE A7.4   TradeStation Insert Analysis Techniques menu.

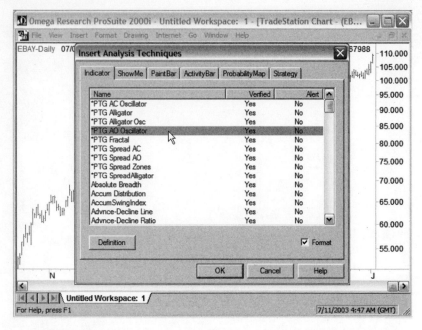

FIGURE A7.5   TradeStation Insert Analysis Technique dialog.

From the list of available Analysis Techniques shown, select the *PTG AO Oscillator technique and click the OK button in the dialog window as shown in Figure A7.5. *Note:* You may have named the AO differently from the suggested *PTG AO Oscillator." If so, please select whatever name you used for the AO. When the Format Indicator dialog window appears, check the rightmost Properties tab to confirm that the subgraph is set for "Two" before clicking the OK button to close the dialog. See Figure A7.6 for an illustration.

In the same manner, add the *PTG Alligator indicator as before from the pop-up menu shown in Figure A7.5. When the Alligator indicator's Format Indicator dialog window appears, again check the Properties tab to confirm that the subgraph is set to "One" before clicking the OK button. See Figure A7.7. Now your TradeStation window should look clean and simple like that in Figure A7.8, with the prices and Alligator occupying approximately three-quarters of the upper window area, and the AO occupying approximately one-quarter of the lower window area.

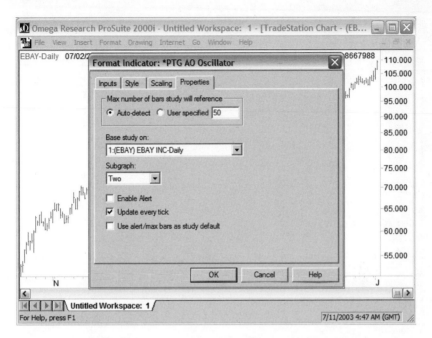

FIGURE A7.6   TradeStation Format AO Indicator dialog.

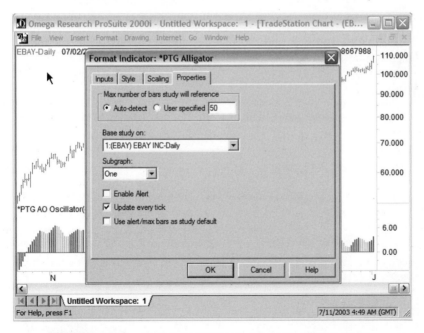

FIGURE A7.7   TradeStation Format Alligator Indicator dialog.

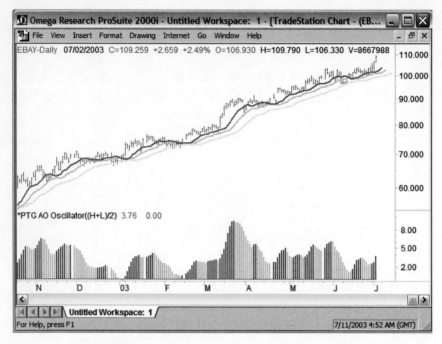

FIGURE A7.8 TradeStation correctly configured chart.

Following you will find the EasyLanguage code needed to create the Alligator and AO in newer versions of TradeStation products.

Alligator

===== EasyLanguage Alligator Code Begins Below This Line =====

```
{ --------------------------------------------------------------------
  --   Alligator Indicators                                         --
  --                                                                --
  --   Developed by Bill Williams, Ph.D., C.T.A.                    --
  --   Easy Language Programing by: Doug Forman 24Apr97             --
  --   Updated for TS2000i by Doug Forman on 29Mar99                --
  --                                                                --
  --   Copyright 1997 by Bill Williams - Profitunity Trading Group  --
  --------------------------------------------------------------------
     These are moving average plots, smoothed and displaced x bars   }
Inputs:      Length1   (13), Offset1 (8),
                 Length2   (8), Offset2   (5),
                 Length3   (5), Offset3   (3);
```

```
if Length1 > 0 then begin
      if @CurrentBar = 1 then
            begin
                  Value1 = @Average ( ( (HIGH + LOW) / 2 ) , Length1 );
                  Value2 = @Average ( ( (HIGH + LOW) / 2 ) , Length2 );
                  Value3 = @Average ( ( (HIGH + LOW) / 2 ) , Length3 );
            end
      else
            begin
                  Value1 = (   (Value1 * ( Length1 -1) ) + ( (HIGH+LOW) /2) )
                        {Current Bar Value} / Length1;
                  Value2 = (   (Value2 * ( Length2 -1) ) + ( (HIGH+LOW) /2) )
                        {Current Bar Value} / Length2;
                  Value3 = (   (Value3 * ( Length3 -1) ) + ( (HIGH+LOW) /2) )
                        {Current Bar Value} / Length3;
            end;
end;
{ next line modified 05Aug97 to prevent plotting Alligator on insufficient data}
if (Value1[offset1]  > 0 and Value2[offset2] > 0 and Value3[offset3] > 0) then
      begin
            Plot1        (Value1[Offset1], "Blue 13/8");
            Plot1[-1]    (Value1[Offset1-1], "Blue 13/8");
            Plot1[-2]    (Value1[Offset1-2], "Blue 13/8");
            Plot1[-3]    (Value1[Offset1-3], "Blue 13/8");
            Plot1[-4]    (Value1[Offset1-4], "Blue 13/8");
            Plot1[-5]    (Value1[Offset1-5], "Blue 13/8");
            Plot1[-6]    (Value1[Offset1-6], "Blue 13/8");
            Plot1[-7]    (Value1[Offset1-7], "Blue 13/8");
            Plot1[-8]    (Value1[Offset1-8], "Blue 13/8");

            Plot2        (Value2[Offset2], "Red 8/5");
            Plot2[-1]    (Value2[Offset2-1], "Red 8/5");
            Plot2[-2]    (Value2[Offset2-2], "Red 8/5");
            Plot2[-3]    (Value2[Offset2-3], "Red 8/5");
            Plot2[-4]    (Value2[Offset2-4], "Red 8/5");
            Plot2[-5]    (Value2[Offset2-5], "Red 8/5");

            Plot3        (Value3[Offset3], "Green 5/3");
            Plot3[-1]    (Value3[Offset3-1], "Green 5/3");
            Plot3[-2]    (Value3[Offset3-2], "Green 5/3");
            Plot3[-3]    (Value3[Offset3-3], "Green 5/3");
      end;
```

===== EasyLanguage Alligator Code Ends Above This Line =====

Awesome Oscillator

===== EasyLanguage AO Code Begins Below This Line =====

```
Profitunity Awesome Oscillator
Copyright @ Bill M. Williams, Jan. 1997
INPUTS:
PRICE((H+L)/2);

VARS:
AO(0),

VALUE1 = AVERAGE( PRICE, 5);
VALUE2 = AVERAGE( PRICE, 34);
AO = VALUE1 - VALUE2;

IF AO > AO[1] THEN PLOT1(AO,"AO Up");
IF AO < AO[1] THEN PLOT2(AO,"AO Down");

PLOT3(0,"ZERO"); {ZERO LINE}
```

===== EasyLanguage AO Code Ends Above This Line =====

Bibliography

Abraham, R. H., and C. D. Shaw. *Dynamics: The Geometry of Behavior. Part One—Periodic Behavior; Part Two-Global Behavior*. Santa Cruz, CA: Aerial Press, 1982.

Anderson, P. W., K. J. Arrow, and D. Pines. *The Economy as a Complex Evolving System*. Reading, MA: Addison-Wesley, 1989.

Babcock, B. *Trading Systems*. Homewood, IL: Dow Jones Irwin, 1989.

Bai Lin, H. *Chaos*. Singapore: World Scientific, 1984.

Bak, P., and K. Chen. "Self-Organized Critically," *Scientific American*, vol. 264, pp. 34, 35 (January 1999).

Balan, R. *Elliott Wave Principle Applied to the Foreign Exchange Markets*. London: BBS Publications, Ltd., 1989.

Barnsley, M. *Fractals Everywhere*, San Diego, CA: Academic Press, 1998.

Beardon, A. F. *Iteration of Rational Functions: Complex Analytic Dynamical Systems*, New York: Springer-Verlag, 1991.

Bernstein, J. *Timing Signals in the Futures Market*. Chicago: Probus Publication Co., 1992.

Bernstein, P. *Capital Ideas: The Improbable Origins of Modern Wall Street*. New York: Free Press, 1992.

Black, F., and M. Scholes. "The Pricing of Options and Corporate Liabilities," *Journal of Political Economy* (May–June 1993).

Briggs, J., and F. D. Peat. *Turbulent Mirror*. New York: Harper & Row, 1989.

Brock, W., D. Hsieh, and B. LeBaron. *Nonlinear Dynamics, Chaos and Instability: Statistical Theory and Economic Evidence*. Cambridge, MA: MIT Press, 1991.

Callen, E., M. Sculley, and D. Shapero. "Imitation Theory—The Study of Cooperative Social Phenomena," in *Collective Phenomena and the Application of Physics to Other Fields of Science*, ed. N. Chigier and E. Stern. Fayetteville, NY: Brain Research Publication, 1985.

Cameron, Julia. *The Artist's Way, A Spiritual Path to Higher Creativity*. New York: G. P. Putnam's Sons, 1992.

Casadagli, M. "Chaos and Deterministic versus Stochastic Non-Linear Modeling," *Journal of the Royal Statistical Society*, vol. 54 (1991).

Chen, B., and H. Tong. "On Consistent Non-parametric Order Determination and Chaos," *Journal of the Royal Statistical Society*, vol. 54 (1992).

Chorafas, D. N. *Chaos Theory in the Financial Markets*. Chicago, IL: Probus Publishing Co., 1994.

Colby, R. W., and T. A. Meyers. *The Encyclopedia of Technical Market Indicators*. Homewood, IL: Business One Irwin, 1998.

Cootner, P., ed. *The Random Character of Stock Market Prices*. Cambridge, MA: MIT Press, 1984.

Dalton, J. F., E. T. Jones, and R. B. Dalton. *Mind Over Markets*. Chicago, IL: Probus Publishing Co., 1990.

Davies, P. *The Cosmic Blueprint: New Discoveries in the Nature's Creative Ability to Order the Universe*. New York: Cambridge University Press, 1997.

Davis, L. *Handbook of Genetic Algorithms*. New York: Van Nostrand Reinhold, 1991.

Day, R. H. "The Emergence of Chaos from Classical Economic Growth," *Quarterly Journal of Economics*, vol. 98 (1983).

Deboeck, G. J. *Trading on the Edge*. New York: Wiley, 1994.

Degooijer, J. G. "Testing Non-Linearities in World Stock Market Prices," *Economics Letters*, vol. 31 (1989).

DeMark, R. R. *The New Science of Technical Analysis*. New York: Wiley, 1994.

DeVaney, R. L. *An Introduction to Chaotic Dynamical Systems*. Menlo Park, CA: Addison-Wesley, 1989.

Douglas, M. *The Disciplined Trader: Developing Winning Attitudes*. New York: Institute of Finance, 1990.

Dreyfuss, H. L., and S. E. Dreyfuss. *Mind Over Machine*. New York: Free Press, 1986.

Eckman, J. P., and D. Rjuelle. *Review of Modern Physics*, vol. 57, no. 3 (1985).

Edmondson, A. C. *A Fuller Explanation*. New York: Springer-Verlag, 1986.

Edwards, R. D., and J. McGee. *Technical Analysis of Stock Trends* rev. 5th ed. New York: John McGee, Inc., 1982.

Ewing, J. H. and G. Schober. *The Area of the Mandelbrot Set*. Numer. Math. 61 (1992).

Falconer, K. J. *The Geometry of Fractal Sets*. New York: Cambridge University Press, 1995.

Farmer, J. D. "Chaotic Attractors of an Infinite-Dimensional Dynamic System," *Physica*, vol. 4D, 336–393. pp. (1982).

Farmer, J. D., and J. J. Sidorowich. "Exploiting Chaos to Predict the Future and Reduce Noise," in *Evolution, Learning and Cognition*, ed. Y. C. Lee. London: World Scientific Press, 1988.

Feder, J. *Fractals*. New York: Plenum Press, 1988.

Fischer, K. L. *The Wall Street Waltz*. Chicago: Contemporary Books, 1987.

Flandarin, P. "On the Spectrum of Fractional Brownian Motions," *IEEE Transactions on Information Theory*, vol. 35, pp. 39–47. (1989).

Fritz, R. *The Path of Least Resistance*. New York: Ballantine Books, 1989.

Frost, A. J., and R. Prechter. *Elliott Wave Principle*. Gainesville, GA: New Classics Library, 1978.

Gallacher, W. *Winner Takes All*. Chicago: Midway Publications, 1993.

Gallway, T. *The Inner Game of Tennis*. New York: Random, 1981.

Gardner, M. "White and Brown Music, Fractal Curves and 1/f Fluctuations," *Scientific American*, vol. 238 (1978).

Garfield, C. *Peak Performers*. New York: Avon Books, 1986.

Glass, L., and M. C. Mackey. *From Clocks to Chaos*. Princeton, NJ: Princeton University Press, 1998.

Gleick, J. *Chaos: The Making of a New Science*. New York: Viking Press, 1987.

Graham, B., and D. L. Dodd. *Security Analysis*. New York: McGraw Hill, 1934.

Henon, M. "A Two-dimensional Mapping with a Strange Attractor," *Communications in Mathematical Physics*, vol. 50, pp. 106–114. (1976).

Hofstadter, D. R. "Mathematical Chaos and Strange Attractors," in *Managerial Themas*. New York: Bantam Books, pp. 214–239. (1985).

Jensen, R. V., and R. Urban. "Chaotic Price Behavior in a Non-Linear Cobweb Model," *Economics Letters*, vol. 15 (1984).

Jung, C. G. *Cenenary Brochure*. Zurich: Curatorum of C. G. Jung Institute, 1975.

Kasko, B. *Neural Networks and Fuzzy Systems*. Englewood Cliffs, NJ: Prentice-Hall, 1992.

Kaufman, P. J. *The New Commodity Trading Systems and Methods*. New York: Wiley, 1987.

Kelsey, D. "The Economics of Chaos and the Chaos of Economics," *Oxford Economic Papers*, vol. 40 (1988).

Kilpatrick, A. *Warren Buffett, The Good Guy of Wall Street*. New York: Donald I. Fine, Inc. 1992.

Kindelberger, C. P. *Manias, Panics and Crashes*. New York: Basic Books, 1988.

Korsan, R. J. "Fractals and Time Series Analysis," *Mathematics Journal*, vol. 3, pp. 74–93. (1993).

Koza, J. *Genetic Programming*. Cambridge, MA: MIT Press, 1993.

Laing, R. "Efficient Chaos Or Things They Never Taught in Business School," *Barron's*, July 21, p. 12. (1991).

Larrainn, M. "Empirical Tests of Chaotic Behavior in a Nonlinear Interest Rate Model," *The Financial Analyst Journal*, vol. 47, p. 78. (Sept./Oct. 1991).

LeBaron, B. "Empirical Evidence for Nonlinearities and Chaos in Economic Time Series: A Summary of Recent Results," University of Wisconsin, Social Systems Research Institute, 9117, 1991.

Lebon, G. *The Crowd*. Wilmington, Delaware: Cherokee Publishing, 1982.

Lei, T. "Similarity Between the Mandelbrot Set and Julia Set," *Communications in Mathematical Physics*, vol. 134, pp. 587–617. (1990).

Lewin, R. *Complexity, Life at the Edge of Chaos*. New York: Macmillan, 1992.

Lorenz, H. *Nonlinear Dynamical Economics and Chaotic Motion*. Berlin: Springer-Verlag, 1989.

McTaggart, Lynne, *The Field—The Quest for the Secret Force in the Universe*. New York: HarperCollins, 2002.

Mackay, C. *Extraordinary Popular Delusions and the Madness of Crowds*. New York: Crown, 1980.

Makridakis, S. S., J. J. Wheelwright, and B. E. McGee. *Forecasting: Methods and Applications*. New York: Wiley, 1983.

Malkiel, B. A. *Random Walk Down Wall Street*, 4th ed. New York: W. W. Norton, 1985.

Mandelbrot, B. "Forecasts of Future Prices, Unbiased Markets, and Martingale Models," *Journal of Business*, vol. 39 (1966).

Mandelbrot, B. "The Variation of Certain Speculative Prices," *Journal of Business*, vol. 36 (1963).

Mandelbrot, B. "The Pareto-Levy Law and the Distribution of Income," *International Economic Review*, vol. 1 (1960).

Mandelbrot, B. "The Variation of Some Other Speculative Prices," *Journal of Business*, vol. 39 (1966).

Mandelbrot, B. "When Can Price Be Arbitraged Efficiently? A Limit to the Validity of the Random Walk and Martingale Models," *Review of Economic Statistics*, vol. 53 (1971).

Miller, M. H. *Financial Innovations and Market Volatility*. Cambridge, England: Blackwell, 1998.

Von Mises, Ludwig. *The Theory of Money and Credit*. Indianapolis: Liberty Classics, 1980.

Moon, F. C. *Chaotic and Fractal Dynamics*. New York: Wiley, 1992.

Moon, F. C. *Chaotic Vibrations: An Introduction for Applied Scientists and Engineers*. New York: Wiley, 1992.

Moon F. C., and G. X. Li. "The Fractal Dimension of the Two-Well Potential Strange Attractor," *Physica*, vol. 17D, pp. 99–108. (1985).

Murphy, J. J. *Technical Analysis of the Futures Market, A Comprehensive Guide to Trading Methods and Applications*. New York: New York Institute of Finance, 1986.

Naisbitt, J. *Megatrends*. New York: Warner Books, 1982.

Naisbitt, J., and P. Aburndene. *Megatrends 2000*. New York: Avon Books, 1999.

Neil, H. *The Art of Contrary Thinking*. Caldwell, ID: Claxton Printers, 1990.

Pacelli, A. P. *The Speculator's Edge*. New York: Wiley, 1989.

Palgrave, F. T. *The Golden Treasury of the Best Poems.* New York: New American Library, 1961.

Pardo, R. *Design, Testing and Optimization of Trading Systems.* New York: Wiley, 1992.

Parket, T. S. and L. O. Chua. *Practical Numerical Algorithm for Chaotic Systems,* Berlin: Springer Verlag, 1989.

Peters, E. *Chaos and Order in the Capital Markets: A New View of Cycles, Prices and Market Volatility.* New York: Wiley, 1991a.

Peters, E. "A Chaotic Attractor for the S&P 500," *Financial Analysis Journal* (March/April 1991b).

Peters, E. *Fractal Market Analysis.* New York: Wiley, 1994.

Peters, E. "Fractal Structures and the Capital Markets," *Financial Analyst Journal* (July/August, 1989).

Plummer, T. *Forecasting Financial Markets: Technical Analysis and the Dynamics of Price.* New York: Wiley, 1991.

Priestly, M. B. *Nonlinear and Nonstationary Time Series Analysis.* New York: Academic Press, 1988.

Prigogine, I., and G. Nicolis. *Exploring Complexity.* New York: W. H. Freeman and Co., 1989.

Prigogine, I., and I. Stengers. *Order Out of Chaos.* New York: Bantam Books, 1984.

Rosser, J. B., Jr. *From Catastrophe to Chaos: A General Theory of Economic Discontinuities.* Boston: Kluwer Academic Publishers, 1991.

Ruelle, D. *Chaotic Evolution and Strange Attractors.* Cambridge, England: Cambridge University Press, 1991.

Scheinkman, J. A., and B. LeBron. "Nonlinear Dynamics and Stock Returns," *Journal of Business,* vol. 62 (1989).

Schroeder, M. *Fractals, Chaos, Power Laws.* New York: W. H. Freeman, 1991.

Schwager, J. A. *Complete Guide to the Futures Markets.* New York: Wiley, 1984.

Schwager, J. D. *Market Wizards.* New York: New York Institute of Finance, 1989.

Shannon, C. E., and W. Weaver. *The Mathematical Theory of Communication.* Urbana: University of Illinois, 1963.

Shaw, R. *The Dripping Faucet as a Model Chaotic System.* Santa Cruz, CA: Aerial Press, 1984.

Shiller, R. J. *Market Volatility.* Cambridge, MA: MIT Press, 1989.

Smith, A. *Powers of the Mind.* New York: Random House, 1975.

Steidlmayer, P. J., and K. Koy. *Markets and Market Logic.* Chicago: Porcupine Press, 1986.

Stetson, H. T. *Sunspots and Their Effects.* New York: McGraw-Hill, 1937.

Stewart, I. *Does God Play Dice? The Mathematics of Chaos.* Cambridge, MA: Blackwell, 1989.

Thompson, J. M. T., and H. B. Steward. *Nonlinear Dynamics and Chaos.* New York: Wiley, 1986.

Thurlow, B. *Rediscovering the Wheel: Contrary Thinking and Investment Strategy.* Burlington, VT: Fraser Publishing Co., 1981.

Tobias, A. *The Only Investment Guide You'll Ever Need* rev. ed. Toronto: Bantam Books, 1986.

Tong, H. *Nonlinear Time Series: A Dynamical Systems Approach.* New York: Oxford Science Publications, 1990.

Vaga, T. "The Coherent Market Hypothesis." *Financial Analysts Journal* (Nov./ Dec. 1990).

Vaga, T. *Profiting From Chaos.* New York: McGraw-Hill, 1994.

Waldrop, M. M. *Complexity, The Emerging Science at the Edge of Order and Chaos.* New York: Simon & Schuster, 1992.

Wallach, P. "Wavelet Theory." *Scientific American* (January 1991).

Weiner, N. *Collected Works,* vol. 1, ed. P. Masani. Cambridge, MA: MIT Press, 1976.

Wiggins, S. *Introduction to Applied Nonlinear Dynamical Systems and Chaos.* New York: Springer-Verlag, 1990.

William, F. E. *Technical Analysis of Stocks, Options & Futures: Advanced Trading Systems and Techniques.* Chicago: Probus Publishing Co., 1988.

Williams, B. M. *Trading Chaos: Applying Expert Techniques to Maximize Your Profits.* New York: Wiley, 1994.

Williams, B. M. *New Trading Dimensions: How to Profit from Chaos in Stocks, Bonds, and Commodities.* New York: Wiley, 1998.

Zeidenberg, M. *Neural Network Models in Artificial Intelligence.* New York: Ellis Horwood, 1990.

Zipf, G. K. *Human Behavior and the Principle of Least Effort.* Reading, MA: Addison-Wesley, 1949.

Zweig, M. *Winning on Wall Street.* New York: Warner Books, 1995.

Index